The

Cool

Crazy

Committed

World

of the

Sixties

Pierre Berton

The
Cool
Crazy
Committed
World
of the
Sixties

MCCLELLAND AND STEWART LIMITED / TORONTO / MONTREAL

The author wishes to thank Screen Gems
(Canada) Limited, producers of
The Pierre Berton Show, for permission
to use material from the program.

◯

◯

The Canadian Publishers

McClelland and Stewart Limited
25 Hollinger Road, Toronto 16

Printed and bound in Canada by
UNIVERSAL PRINTERS
WINNIPEG

CONTENTS

Introduction   ix   THE MOOD AND THE MEDIUM

Ray Bradbury   1   CASSANDRA ON A BICYCLE
*"All of yesterday's blasphemy
will be tomorrow's dicta."*

Maureen Murphy   11   CIVIL RIGHTS WORKER
*"Most of us look very young
but we mature very fast.
We have, obviously, no choice."*

Malcolm X   19   THE BLACK VIGILANTE
*"The black community has yet to form
a vigilante committee. This is why
we aren't respected as human beings."*

Malcolm Boyd   29   THE ESPRESSO PRIEST
*"Everybody's tired of
professional moralizing and
the old type of preaching."*

v

Lord Soper 43   THE SOAPBOX PARSON
"There are too many Bible study groups and not nearly enough socialist groups."

Dr. Anne Biezanek 55   THE CHURCH AND THE PILL
*"I thought:
'Is this God being very tactful?'"*

Gordon Sinclair 65   THE UNINHIBITED ATHEIST
*"I'm prepared to accept
the existence of* ANY *God."*

Lois Pearson 75   A WITCH IN SUBURBIA
*"I can assure you it's nothing
like the Women's Institute."*

Lenny Bruce 87   A CHILD BEFORE HIS TIME
*"In freedom of speech,
the accent is on freedom,
not on speech."*

Fred Paul 97   THE GATE CRASHER
*"If you want anything bad enough,
you'll get it."*

Murray the K 109   I WAS A TEEN-AGE ADULT
*"I would think the kids today
wouldn't get broken-hearted
very readily."*

Phil Spector 117   THE TEENAGERS' TYCOON
*"You just can't relate
or communicate with somebody
who doesn't understand."*

Michael Caine 127   PORTRAIT OF AN ANTI-HERO
*"If you start out broke
and a nobody what can
anybody ever do to you?"*

Jean Shrimpton 137   THE FACE ON THE COVER
*"I think it's rather good
that the public loses interest . . .
I think that's healthy."*

Mrs. Ian Fleming 147   WIDOW TO A LEGEND
"I thought I was marrying the foreign editor of the Sunday Times.*"*

Dixie Dean Trainer 157   THE QUEEN OF THE FAN MAGAZINES
"A lot of stars lead pretty dull, placid lives and you've got to give them glamour."

Robert Macaulay 167   THE YOUNG TURK AND THE OLD GUARD
"The public likes to see a nice, stable, quiet man . . ."

Jane Freeman 177   THE UNLOVED MOTHER
"I've never really had anything that I could call my own."

Jean Templeton 187   EPILEPTIC
"Dandruff can cause you a lot more trouble."

Matthew Saunders 197   MEMBER OF A MURDER JURY
"It's a bit like a high level charade . . ."

Marguerite Oswald 207   MOM AND APPLE PIE
"Lee didn't have a formal education, but he had the know-how."

INTRODUCTION

THE MOOD AND THE MEDIUM

What is it about the Sixties that makes them so different from the preceding decades? They are not Roaring like the Twenties, and they are certainly not Hungry like the Thirties. But neither have they the smugness of the post-war years about them.

It seems to me, looking back, that we could hardly wait for this new decade to arrive, so eager were we to get out of the Fifties. Remember all those slogans, back in 1960, about the Soaring Sixties, the Sizzling Sixties, and the Spectacular Sixties? They sound a bit corny today, but what other span of years has been given a set of themes *before* it began? That was the year, remember, when *Lady Chatterley's Lover* was in the news. How old hat that censorship battle seems today! It was also the year Khrushchov clobbered Susskind on TV; and it was the year of the U-2 and the Bomarc-B, not to mention payola, stereo, and that itsy-bitsy, teeny-weeny, yellow polka-dot Bikini. It was also the first of the Kennedy years – the beginning of a new decade, and the beginning of a new mood.

The Fifties were boom years, but it does not seem to me, looking back upon them, that they were terribly exciting. Self-satisfaction hung like a pall over the land. The bitter taste of McCarthy clung to our palates. The college kids all wanted to be organization men. It was a mind-your-own-business-as-usual decade.

Then, some time towards the end of the Fifties, the music began to change, and the spectacular shift of mood began. People sensed new undercurrents in politics, in morals, and in attitudes. The Sixties became the decade of The New Left and The New Morality, The New Frankness, and The New Concern. In these Go-Go years, we have heard the drums of revolution sound in almost every area, from the Anglican Church to Tin Pan Alley.

What we are watching is what Barbara Tuchman, dealing with the century's first decade, has called "the transfer of power." Half the people living on this continent cannot remember a world war or a depression, and they are a little impatient with those who can. The young men who began running things during World War Two, and who have been running things ever since, have become old men. And because life, like a jet plane, moves so much faster in the Sixties, the new generation is pressing harder than it ever has in history.

Its pivot is Kennedy and the Kennedy myth. He was Youth; he was Style; he was Action; he was Intellect; and we scarcely realized it before he was gone. Now every institution seeks its Kennedy. Here, in Canada, we yearn desperately, if vainly, for one of his kind. Hence our frustration with the Old Guard.

It seems to me that this impatience with the old, together with the tensions created by the transfer of power and the ferment generated by the New Concern, are at the root of three unprecedented headline stories that hit the country in a triple shockwave in the spring of 1966.

The Munsinger scandal was a product of pure frustration – the direct result of two old elephants locked tusk to tusk, while the young stood impotently by. Before it was over, the country was ready with that bitter phrase, coined for another Old Guard at another place and in another time: *"For God's sake, go!"*

The Truscott case was a *cause célèbre* which reflected a new kind of commitment on the part of great masses of people who had suddenly begun to care. I doubt that Isabel LeBourdais' book would have caused such a stir fifteen years ago, before the era of television and The New Concern.

The Seven Days wrangle was a classic case of the old versus

the new. An ex-announcer, an ex-naval man, and an ex-engineer, all reared in the age of radio, were pitted against a group of young intellectuals (a university professor, an M.A., and two Niemann Fellows from Harvard), struggling, not always wisely, to create a form of television journalism to fit the age.

The youth revolution, the Negro revolution, the sexual revolution, the religious revolution, the pop-culture revolution – these form the threads of our time, and all are intertwined. We are being pushed and pushed hard by a unique generation: the first generation raised with television, the first generation raised in a secular age, the first generation raised with the Bomb. If it is a mixed-up generation – "cool" and at the same time committed; hedonistic and at the same time idealistic – it is also remarkably self-possessed, able to accept with apparent aplomb a wide spectrum of hazards, from illegitimacy to epilepsy, from instant success to instant lynching.

It is for this generation that so many of the symbols of the decade exist: pop art, discotheques, sit-ins and teach-ins, spy movies, medicare, abolition petitions, new-wave films, *Candy*, birth-control pills, "happenings," espresso nights, miniskirts, folk songs, Beatle haircuts, Lenny Bruce monologues, freedom rides, pot.

Of course, the decade does not belong to them alone. It belongs also to men as old as Gordon Sinclair or Lord Soper, non-conformists who, in the words of the singing commercial, are among those who think young. It belongs to Robert Macaulay, the swinging politician, as much as it does to Jane Freeman, the unmarried mother. It belongs to the doomed as well as to the damned: the Marguerite Oswalds, the Malcolm X's, and the Ron Turpins. It belongs to Dixie Dean Harris who can invent a fan-magazine article in a morning, and to Lois Pearson who spends her Hallowe'en midnights in a sacred grove among a coven of her kind. The Soaring Sixties can also be the Sad Sixties, the Sick Sixties, and the Silly Sixties.

It may be that these years will look quite different to a succeeding generation. We cannot know since we are still engulfed in them. For that reason, the text that follows – selective but in no sense definitive – must be considered merely as an interim report on an exciting and turbulent era that has not yet run its course.

When the Sixties began, most people had been exposed to the television medium for ten years. Indeed, there are among us hundreds of thousands of young men and women of voting age who cannot remember the non-television era. This is one reason, I am convinced, why the mood of this new generation of the Sixties is *involvement*. Television involves its audience as no other medium (except, perhaps, the limited medium of the live theatre) has been able to do. At the movies, you sit detached from the distant screen, secure in the company of the lonely crowd. Radio is a disembodied voice drifting in from afar. But the TV set is a few feet away, and it is directed at *you*. Seasoned television performers do not talk to a vast, unseen audience; they talk to one person. That is why the firing of a TV star can become a national issue overnight; and that is why a cry for justice can become nationwide; in just three days, Mrs. LeBourdais' earnest face, discussing the Steven Truscott trial, was familiar to every television viewer in the country.

It has become commonplace to attack television's banality. Certainly much of its subject matter is trite and superficial. But the medium's detractors have failed to grasp the real significance of this new force: it brings the world into our living rooms, and thus frees us from our provincialisms. The streets of every major city have become our vicarious playgrounds. Never mind those eloquent documentaries, earnest political discussions, and award-winning dramas. Ilya Kuryakin travels to Brazil, and every ten-year-old catches a glimpse of the steaming jungle. Danger Man turns up in Spain, and every high-school drop-out sees what a sidewalk cafe and a flamenco dancer look like. Robin Hood has his weekly go at the Sheriff of Nottingham and, long before they toddle off to kindergarten, all the round-eyed moppets are given some idea of how people lived, dressed, warred, and wenched in Twelfth-Century England. Television has become the jet travel of the multitudes and, as everyone knows, travel is broadening. If, in the Sixties, films and books go relatively uncensored, unorthodoxies are indulged more readily, and personal intimacies discussed with greater candour and tolerance, it is, at least in part, due to the leavening influence of the TV environment. If television is responsible for The New Concern, I am also convinced it has a lot to do with The New Frankness.

It is the most intimate of all the media. By some curious alchemy, the people who appear on it are encouraged to open up to near-strangers – or at least that has been my discovery. I have tried to puzzle out why. Why is it, for instance, that a nineteen-year-old girl, entering the darkling cavern of the studio, surrounded by a thicket of lights and cameras, ringed in by shadowy technicians whose names she does not know, will, on cue, begin to talk to a man she has only just met about her illegitimate child? One reason may be that the man to whom she is unburdening herself is not a stranger at all, but one whom she has met nightly on her home set. But this is only part of the answer. The real truth, I suspect, is that TV has provided an environment which has become cosily familiar to her. She has been raised in an electronic climate, in which, year after year, people have stared out of the tube talking intimately about themselves and their backgrounds, their hopes and their fears, telling anecdotes, cracking jokes, expressing opinions. She is used to it; she knows what to expect; she knows what is expected of her. She is a child of her era, and her era is the era of instant communication.

All the words that appear in this book, except for my own prefacing remarks, were uttered originally on television. In the course of a nightly program, I have, over the past four winter seasons, spent 410 hours before the cameras, talking to more than one thousand people. This book is made up of the edited transcripts of twenty-one programs that I thought particularly significant and interesting. All of them are taken from the 1964-65 season and the 1965-66 season.

Not all television talk makes good reading, of course. On television, a pause can be as important as a paragraph. A facial expression or a blank look can be worth a thousand words. One of the best programs I took part in was recorded in Hollywood in January, 1966, with Lucille Ball. On paper, however, it has little interest because Miss Ball is essentially a mime. When she told me, for example, how she made herself look like a lightbulb, she did it all with her face. And when I asked her, later in the program, how she and her husband were able to act out the part of a happily married couple, when their own marriage was falling to pieces, the long pause that followed and the fleeting emotions that showed on her features told the viewers more than words could convey. One of the important lessons a television interviewer must learn – and it's not an easy one – is to *wait*. The radio medium is terrified of dead air. But there is no dead air on television. The picture is always there to tell the story.

Although these electronic encounters were generally seen in

Canada around the midnight hour, they were usually recorded on videotape at an afternoon session, sometimes several weeks before they were shown. As a rule, I do five interviews at one session, each interview lasting exactly one-half hour, with a fifteen-minute pause between shows. Sometimes I do as many as seven interviews at a time, and always a minimum of five. This, of course, requires me to change mental gears and moods from program to program, but as long as one is well prepared in advance this isn't as difficult as it seems. It can be exhausting, of course, but it can also be stimulating. After the first couple of programs, I find myself getting into the swing of things, so that quite often the best interviews are those done at the end of the day.

The programs are not rehearsed. I try to find out in advance as much as I can about my guests. I try to work out, again in advance, the most interesting questions in a logical and dramatic arrangement. As soon as I meet my guests and indulge in a few moments of small talk, I like to get on with it. The program isn't edited. Everything that is said eventually gets on the air. In that sense it's a "live" program, or "live-on-tape," to use the industry's phrase.

Of course, there are certain disadvantages in not being able to edit a program; but there are also great advantages. A good many programs of this nature suffer from over-editing. How often have we seen, on our home screens, one of those choppy, six-minute encounters, which seems to hop nervously from point to point – statements cut off in the middle, words actually hacked in half, questions ending so abruptly that one would think the interviewer was suddenly gagged? Sure, it often makes for a meatier six minutes, journalistically; but it doesn't necessarily make for better, more dramatic, or more honest television. Guests, who have something important to say, hate it. One of the ways my producer was able to persuade many hard-to-get celebrities to appear with me was by promising to give each of them a full half-hour, with no strings or taboos and no fooling around with the tape.

The "live" television interview also puts the interviewer and his guest on their mettle. There is a time limit and they both know it, and this knowledge can't help but force a pace. The deadline encourages us both to plunge into a subject without pleasantries or irrelevancies. The guest is persuaded to stick to the point, the interviewer to prod him ever onward. This curious kind of tension, when it works, communicates itself to the audience. If time runs out and the viewers are left wanting more – well, isn't that as it should be?

In editing the transcripts of these selected programs for the print medium, I have tried to tamper with them as little as possible. If some run longer than others, it isn't because great chunks have been excised: it's just that some people are more eloquent than others – or that they speak faster, say more, pause less, or don't bother to repeat themselves. Essentially, these programs are uncut. The one exception is the talk with Malcolm Boyd, which occupied two half-hour programs and from which I have removed one passage in the interests of space.

What I have done is to try to make them easy to read and easy to follow. Spoken and written communication require different techniques. People can speak in non-sequiturs; they can leave sentences and even thoughts dangling, half-finished, completing them with a shrug or a roll of the eye or the gesture of a hand. The average man doesn't talk in punctuated sentences: he runs on and on, stringing his thoughts together with a fistful of "ands" and "buts," "ers" and "ums." Repetitive phrases and words like "ya know" and "see," which give to speech an easy flow and an acceptable informality, become irritating in print. I've used them sparingly.

There is something else. Repetition for emphasis is a necessary technique in spoken exposition. Often when a guest says something, which I consider worth pausing over, I repeat it myself, and then often enough *he* repeats it, so the audience can digest it. Here is a minor example from the Jane Freeman transcript before it was edited:

PIERRE: Then he did want to marry you at this time?

JANE FREEMAN: Yes, he did want to marry me, but I don't.

PIERRE: You *don't* want to marry him?

JANE FREEMAN: No.

PIERRE: So, although you *could* get married to the father of your child, now . . . . (PAUSE)

JANE FREEMAN: Uh, huh.

PIERRE: . . . and, as some people would say, "make the marriage respectable". . . . (PAUSE)

JANE FREEMAN: Yes.

PIERRE: You are intent not to do that? You want to do something more than that? Would you explain . . . etc., etc.

☐

This technique is necessary because the audience can't stop and go back over the material as the reader of a printed page can. A reader chooses his own pace; television dictates the same pace for all. Thus, at certain points in a television conversation, it is necessary to pause and make sure the audience hasn't missed something essential. In this book, these unnecessary repetitive passages have been edited out, as the reader will discover if he compares the above transcript with the version on page 179.

I've also tended to cut down my own lines in the dialogues that follow, and for much the same reason. It is the task of the interviewer to goad, encourage, wheedle, reassure, and probe. Techniques vary from subject to subject. Sometimes a little small talk is required; sometimes a question has to be stated and then restated in several ways. Sometimes the interviewer must butt in and finish a sentence for a groping guest. Sometimes he must slow a guest down, with a phrase or two. But none of this is necessary to what follows. This book is not so much concerned with challenge as it is with response.

A good many people were responsible for this book, in addition to those whose names appear on the Contents page. The key figure, perhaps, is my producer for the past two years, Elsa Franklin, whose job it is to arrange, shape, and criticize the programs that I do. It was Mrs. Franklin, more than anybody else I think, who understood so thoroughly that a program of this type, while it cannot achieve day-to-day topicality, must be in tune with its times.

The Pierre Berton Show was originally conceived by Herb Sussan, then an executive of Screen Gems (Canada) Limited, the firm which still produces it. Without Herb Sussan's enthusiasm and support, I probably wouldn't have attempted it. The first producer was Ross McLean, one of the giants of Canadian television, who taught me so much of what I know about the medium, and with whom I have enjoyed a continuing association which spans more than a decade.

The chief of the research staff has been Mary Baillie Rutherford, an indefatigable young woman through whose eyes I have first met most of the people who appear in the book. She has been assisted, from time to time, by Marilyn Douglas in Toronto; Valerie Jennings in New York; Rosemary Davies, Ene Riisna, and Rae Knight in London; and Diana Hammond in Hollywood. Kaye Lorne, our unit manager for the past four seasons, transcribed most of the tapes and typed the bulk of the manuscript with speed and efficiency. Finally, I owe a special debt of gratitude to Screen Gems of Canada for its continuing support and enthusiasm, for keeping the program on the air for a fifth season and, most of all, for staying out of my hair.

CASSANDRA

ON A BICYCLE

"All of yesterday's blasphemy
will be tomorrow's dicta."

Anyone who has read The Martian Chronicles *knows that Ray Bradbury is in a class with Jules Verne and H. G. Wells. The best – as well as the best-known – of the modern science-fiction writers, he is one of the five most popular American writers in the Soviet Union. (The others: Hemingway, Faulkner, Steinbeck, Spillane.) Aldous Huxley called him "one of the most visionary men now writing in any field."*

I'm not sure what I expected when I met Ray Bradbury in Los Angeles. He had been a literary hero of mine for some time, but I had no real image of him. Certainly I was not prepared for the refreshingly wholesome man in the tweed jacket whose minor interests and enthusiasms were so uncannily close to my own. There was no stopping us when we began comparing notes about Dracula, Tarzan, Blackstone the Magician, Disneyland, old movies, and vintage comic strips; for we were both born in the summer of 1920 and raised in the era of silent films, early talkies, radio, and pulp magazines. About these things and about more

1

serious matters, Bradbury talks with immense enthusiasm, tremendous vitality, and great good humour. His eyes twinkle constantly behind his horn-rims, even when he is serious or angry. He has managed to achieve, as one of my researchers remarked, an almost impossible personal combination of contemporary sophistication coupled with a devotion to the old-fashioned virtues. For Bradbury is a modern moralist who clothes much of what he has to say in the protective garb of science-fiction.

He is as prolific as an adult as he was precocious as a boy. At fifteen, he determined to appear in The Best American Short Stories, *an ambition he achieved a decade later. His first sale, at the age of twenty, was made to* Super Science Stories, *and for the next several years his byline was a familiar one in most science-fiction magazines.* The Martian Chronicles, *published in 1950, gave him new stature; all in all, he has produced some fifteen books. A screen writer* (Moby Dick), *playwright* (The World of Ray Bradbury), *and novelist* (Fahrenheit 451), *he is also an occasional poet and* TV *script writer.*

Bradbury's fiction, often dark and macabre, deals with machines and speed, two aspects of the Sixties that he personally detests. Though his tales are often studded with space ships that hurtle through the void at close to the speed of light, Bradbury himself, living in the world's most car-conscious city, has stubbornly refused to learn to drive. How does he get about? On a bicycle! *Naturally, I began our conversation by asking him why.*

☐

RAY BRADBURY: Well, it is a little late in the day to change my image. I'm sort of a romantic myth now, you see, so I'm locked into this thing. Even if I *wanted* to learn to drive tomorrow, I wouldn't dare; it would spoil everything. But, basically and honestly, I grew up during the Depression when nobody could afford to buy a car. I think we had an old ten-dollar Buick. I think my Dad paid about ten dollars for it. We came West to Los Angeles in '34, and on the way, coming and going several times from Arizona to Illinois and L.A., I saw enough foolishness on the highway and enough destruction that by the time I was old enough to drive I didn't even think about it. And I haven't thought about it since. I rarely stop and think to myself: "Why don't you drive?" I took a bus here today.

2

PIERRE: Isn't it very hard to get a bus in Los Angeles?

RAY BRADBURY: No, I had good luck today. I went to a corner and there was a bus. I almost fell over! It was unbelievable! If I don't take the bus, I take my bicycle and I grab cabs. And then I'm picked up by strangers, which is a lot of fun. Several days ago I was outside the gymnasium in Beverly Hills waiting for a bus, and a Mercedes-Benz pulled up with a woman in mink, and she said: "Would you like a ride?" I said, "Yes," even though I was rather amazed, and I got in and she drove me several miles to where I wanted to go, and I said: "Why did you pick me up?" And she said: "You looked very English and very safe."

PIERRE: I don't know whether that is flattering or not.

RAY BRADBURY: I know; I don't *want* to look safe.

PIERRE: I would have thought in this enormous, sprawling city it would almost be impossible to get around if you didn't own an automobile. You don't find it awkward?

RAY BRADBURY: No, I've learned how to take a book with me and relax. When you're waiting for a bus you can get a lot of reading done.

PIERRE: Does the sort of thing you're doing represent a revolt against machines?

RAY BRADBURY: No, but a revolt against the way we are building our city. I would like to see it replanned and done over, and the automobile eliminated as much as possible. Most of the major cities of this continent and all over the world are going to outlaw the automobile in the next forty years. They're going to have to. We can't make do with this thing. It's just destroying our cities. The time will come when we will go along and put a bullet in the carburetor of every second car, which will just be a great day for all of us. We'll all be free again.

PIERRE: Suppose masked riders go out at night to kill machines?

RAY BRADBURY: Yes, absolutely. I'd like to do a story on that. It would be great fun.

PIERRE: Do you hate freeways too?

RAY BRADBURY: Yes, I hate them for several reasons. They ruin conversation. Have you ever tried to hold a conversation on a freeway? You're braking the car! If you're not driving, you're steering for the guy who is steering. You're going eighty miles an hour, which is an outrageous speed, or ninety. Most people go ninety in forty-mile-an-hour zones. You can't converse and you can't see what you're passing. One of the reasons we had the Watts Area problem here last year – the riots – I believe, is the

3

fact that nobody ever *saw* Watts. They were always passing it at eighty miles an hour. So if you're constantly passing an area and never seeing it, you don't even know it's there. It used to be that you had to go through Watts to where you wanted to go. Maybe you might have found out that it wasn't a very nice area to live in if you had actually driven through it. It is actually a twenty-five-mile-an-hour zone.

PIERRE: Funny to hear you say that eighty or ninety miles an hour is a terrible speed when you write about people who go much faster in rocket ships.

RAY BRADBURY: Well, actually, all of my people travel very slowly. They may be on a rocket, but they are innate philosophers and blabbermouths. They like to talk about going slower in spite of all their speed. I use many of the machines of the present and the future, but you find that the heart of the machine is the man who is travelling very slow and looking around and saying: "This isn't good enough. We've got to do better." So it only appears that I'm travelling fast.

PIERRE: You know, we've learned that science-fiction writers are the prophets of our time because so many of them have been right. Everything from the atomic bomb to satellites have been predicted in science-fiction magazines like *Astounding* and *Amazing Stories* for thirty years. As a science-fiction writer in 1966, what kind of a future do you prophesy?

RAY BRADBURY: Oh, I prophesy a Golden Age as the result of the hydrogen bomb, in which this one science-fictional device will enable us to get along beautifully without war. We've been so busy being terrified by the Bomb, we haven't realized what a godsend it is. I predict there will be no more gigantic wars. The war we are carrying on now in Vietnam, which we don't call a war, is a very small exercise, which will soon be ended regardless of our rather stupid President Johnson, and the stupid people around him. The war will end. It will be no hydrogen-war explosion. We'll go on having these guerilla excursions, here and there in the world. But we've stopped a lot of wars in the last twenty years because of this science-fictional device. People are always saying: "What do you predict?" I see the growth of the United Nations and the growth of understanding among nations – the result of all such science-fictional devices, including this one we are working with here, television. These are all empathy devices whereby these robots help us find out about one another. The more we can use them in these areas, the better world I think we're going to have.

PIERRE: I wonder if the next war – I use the word loosely – won't be a psychological war between man and the machine to see who gets dominance.

RAY BRADBURY: I doubt it. Let me use this example: I've been taken through the computer complexes out at the air force base in UCLA. And as we go through these computers, quite often a scientist will turn to me and say: "Isn't it wonderful?" And I always reply, "No! No! It isn't wonderful – *you're* wonderful. Let's put the emphasis where it belongs: *you* invented it; *you* built it; *you* put the information in; *you* take the information out. You're great and the machine is really of no importance, whatsoever." So, the battle will not occur between men and machines, but between men and men to build better machines. Because they are immoral. We have to look at an automobile, for instance, and say: "It's a lousy design!" All the automobiles in America right now are lousily built, lousily designed and proceed to destroy hundreds of thousands of us every five years. We're killing off about three hundred thousand people every five years. That's a huge war, isn't it? So we've got to look at that machine and redesign it. And finally the government is going to have to step in and make General Motors and all the other people behave and put a bumper on a car. We have no bumpers on our cars anymore! You touch them and they flake off! You touch any part of a car – you can reach up and rip off the lights, you can break the steering wheel very easily with one hand, a baby can go in and slam the door and it will fall off. All of our cars are tin: shoddy, inept. So we have to look at these things. And here's where the real war – the war between the mass of the people and the people who are selling us shoddy goods – that's where the wars are going to be occurring. Then, of course, we'll see the same thing corrupting Russia and Red China. They're going to be destroyed by automobiles, and we're all going to be in the same *meshugana* mess together. Then we'll fall weepingly in each other's arms in ten years and say: "Protect us from the machines!" We'll have to help the Communists against the automobiles.

PIERRE: It's a curious kind of One World vision.

RAY BRADBURY: Oh, it is going to happen, absolutely. The middle classes are taking over everywhere. Finally, we'll wake up in the midst of all our drivel and shoddiness. We'll turn to the philosophers, and then *they* will have to help us redesign the whole thing.

PIERRE: Do you really think, Mr. Bradbury, the day will come when anybody will really turn to the philosophers and request help?

RAY BRADBURY: Yes, I see it everywhere. I see it in the universities. I see it in this wonderful new generation coming up. We talk a lot about the beatniks, but they are a thin shell. We talk a lot about juvenile delinquency, but this is a thin shell. At the core of this fabulous generation there is great creativity, a great excitement, and a great desire to philosophize. They want someone to say: "Excellence is worth while. Quality counts. The job is worth getting done." This is one of the things about the Peace Corps in the last few years. These are the directions for governments to take all over the world. This generation *does* want to work; it *does* want to change the world. It *does* want to boot the old politicians in the behind to get them out of the way. If we can hold up new ideals, find the correct symbols to show ourselves in this rocket age, then they'll get in and they'll do the work. I've seen it happen, in universities where I've visited. The kids come up breathless after I talk about these very things, and they say: "Thank God someone's talking about it."

PIERRE: Interesting to compare this new generation with the one just passed – the safe generation in the late Forties and Fifties.

RAY BRADBURY: Yes, they got kind of lost along the way, and I don't know all the reasons. I blame the middle intellectual age there. Magazines like *The Nation* and *The New Republic, The American Scholar*, and many, many semi-popular intellectual gazettes. They couldn't see the space age coming; and they left the work of dramatizing and being excited about the space age in the hands of a few people. But, suddenly, the space age is here with all of its ramifications, and we have to make do with it. All the religions of our world are changing rapidly; they are going way around back and coming up under the machines so that we are going through a vast age of blasphemy. Now the religions are going to have to come around underneath our blasphemy and reaffirm it. And all of yesterday's blasphemy will be tomorrow's dicta handed down by the Catholic churches and all the other churches of the world. In other words, we are refashioning God into a new image so that he will stay conveniently out of the way. So that we can get the work done of going into space, of landing on God's Moon, of landing on God's Mars, and going places where, a hundred years ago if we had tried to go there, we would have been burned at the stake for doing the job. We're carrying on this kind of ardent mechanical blasphemy on many levels in the world today, and this is what excites the new generation: seeing how each machine, each development is changing our

6

philosophy, changing our religion, changing the family structure, changing our arts.

PIERRE: It *is* an exciting time, isn't it?

RAY BRADBURY: It is. I think it's the greatest age in the history of the world that we're living in. We are privileged to be part of it.

PIERRE: You know, I didn't get around to asking you about your predisposition for Hallowe'en. You've said that you would have loved to have been born on Hallowe'en. Why do you like Hallowe'en so much?

RAY BRADBURY: I suppose when you grow up in a small town – I was raised in Milwaukee, Illinois – rituals like Hallowe'en and the Fourth of July mean a heck of a lot more to you. It is much more basic than in a large city. The whole image of Hallowe'en has changed so fantastically in the last twenty-five years. It's not the same kind of fun. It's become a form of bribery where you go and get candy for not doing anything. Well, that to me is not what it's all about. I like the rawness and the nearness and the excitement of death, which went with the older vision of Hallowe'en. In fact, I've often wanted to do a one-hour special for TV in which I'd make a comparison between Hallowe'en as it exists today and as it used to exist in America. And the way *Dia de los Muertos* is celebrated in Mexico and South America, where they have the sugar skulls with your name on it, or the name of a dead loved one, and they give you a chance to symbolize and live close by death and try to understand this mystery. We've lost sight of it.

PIERRE: The "excitement of death" is an odd phrase to use.

RAY BRADBURY: Yes it is. But children *are* fascinated by it.

PIERRE: By death?

RAY BRADBURY: Absolutely! They hunger for knowledge about it, and that's why horror films have been so successful over the years – not only with children but with older people too. We turn to our religions and our philosophers and our myth-makers to explain the inexplicable to us. *Dracula* is a fabulous example of one way we have of looking at a realistic representation of a thing we can't really see. And a really good horror film helps us make do with this fact for a little while. It is a very important part of existence.

PIERRE: The presence of horror in our lives?

RAY BRADBURY: Absolutely. We have to digest it and get rid of it to go on. We just can't face nothingness. We've got to make something of it. So we can hold death in our hands for a little while, or on our tongues, or in our eyes, and make do with it. This is what we are all up to.

PIERRE: I guess you would disagree with Dr. Fredric Wertham and those parent-teacher groups that are opposed to horror pictures for children.

RAY BRADBURY: Oh, yes, absolutely. I don't like the comic books that are sick; but there are some that deal with death in such a way that they leave the hair-ball in your crop. The dynamic function of any art form is to build attention and then release it to you. The trouble with a lot of things on the American stage, and the international stage – a play like *Who's Afraid of Virginia Woolf*, let's say – is that they take an immense hair-ball and cram it into your mouth, and never give you the right to free yourself from this hair-ball. Well, this to me is automatically uncreative, and some of these comic magazines we're talking about are non-creative and non-tension-relieving because they leave you with the hair-ball. But the average comic magazine or adventure comic knows how to relieve the tension it has built. Then the child can go back to life again with no real illusion.

PIERRE: What do you think is happening to horror? It's becoming a joke. When Abbott and Costello started meeting Dracula and Frankenstein, these horror figures became clowns. Why is this? Is it a good thing?

RAY BRADBURY: No, I don't think it is a good thing. I think it is important to take death seriously and the symbols that we work with very seriously. Now when people get too pompous about it, then you go and prick the balloon with these little silly comics and with satire. I'm all in favour of that. But, if you have a continual bombardment of making fun of a serious attempt to make do with life, then you're in danger of winding up with nothing. And I'm afraid of this. I don't know what the answer is except to go out and make better horror films. I would like to make a really magnificent film that would scare the Jesus out of everybody, with a man like David Lean, who is one of the finest directors in the world.

PIERRE: What produced you? What made you what you are – a writer of horror, fantasy, science-fiction – the best? Who are your heroes?

RAY BRADBURY: My heroes are Buck Rogers, Flash Gordon, Alley Oop, Tarzan, Edgar Rice Burroughes, The War Lord of Mars, Edgar Allen Poe, H. G. Wells, Jules Verne, all the comic strips ever produced, all the films ever made, early radio, Chandu the Magician. I was a member of the Little Orphan Annie Secret Society. I sent away my Ovaltine can tops. I wrote *Chandu the*

Magician. Every night when the program went off the air, I would sit down and write it from memory, so I trained myself as a writer from the age of twelve by writing radio scripts. I got to know *Burns and Allen* when I was fourteen. So I have been deeply involved in all the mass media, which has a wonderful mediocrity; and all the wonderful excellences that are buried in each of these mediocrities. I've taken from each and I've grown with each. And then I've introduced myself to people like Aldous Huxley and Robert Frost and Thomas Wolfe and John Steinbeck. And out of the cross-pollination of all these things, I've made myself into a writer whom I still feel is a great child of our times.

PIERRE: I suppose all of this is what is now called "high camp." The intellectuals have taken over.

RAY BRADBURY: Yeah, and I believe they're the *wrong* intellectuals – the campy intellectuals who couldn't care less about the things that we once loved. They've now picked it up as a dreadful kind of fad, and they're going to go to bed with it for a few months or a year. Then they'll throw it by the wayside. I say to them: "Go away! Go away! You're all frauds. You don't really care about our interests. I find you contemptible. You don't know how to love." I offer an example of the ridiculousness of these so-called wise people: seven or eight years ago I tried to get many producers in Hollywood to make a movie out of an obscure series of books about an obscure hero. The name of the author was Fleming, and the name of his hero was Bond, and they could have got these books – all five of them at the time – for five thousand dollars each. No one would touch them! I thought: "Well, my God, if someone makes a really fine adventure film out of this, it will make nothing but money." But nobody would listen. Of course, now, they're the biggest successes in the history of film-making.

PIERRE: Science-fiction writers are the Cassandras of their time, Mr. Bradbury.

RAY BRADBURY: They are indeed.

CIVIL RIGHTS WORKER

"Most of us look very young,
but we mature fast.
We have, obviously, no choice."

*I met Maureen Murphy in the fall of 1964 in Toronto. I had
agreed to chair a public meeting for James Farmer of the Committee for Racial Equality, and she was one of the last-minute
platform guests. She was twenty-two years old, an attractive,
vivacious, talkative girl who didn't seem to have a care in the
world. Actually, she had many cares: two of her best friends had
been murdered that summer; she herself had been attacked; and
the only real clothes she owned were those she had on her back –
a suit of faded blue denims which she wore unself-consciously.
They were, for her, a kind of badge – the badge of the young civil
rights workers who belonged to the Student Non-Violent Co-
ordinating Committee working on voter registration among
Negroes in the United States South. She had flown into Toronto
that very day, straight from the back country of Mississippi, to
try to raise some money for her cause.*

*I knew nothing of this when, by good fortune, or perhaps by
design, I was placed next to her at a private dinner which pre-*

11

ceded the meeting for Farmer. My first impression was of a chirpy, chattering girl who babbled on with a kind of dogged persistence. It may be that at first this obscured for me the significance of what she was saying. Only after several minutes did it dawn on me that this plump, pink-cheeked girl's tale was pure horror: as terrifying as anything out of Poe or Kafka. She was talking about conditions in Mississippi in the Sixties – about a water-tight society, run by a white power élite, ruthless and unrelenting, where there was no justice for stranger or Negro, where death was ever a possibility and heartbreak almost a certainty.

She readily agreed to appear on television, and I'm happy to say the resultant program brought in several hundred dollars in donations. I began it by asking her to explain to the viewers exactly what was involved in attempting to register Negro voters in a Mississippi small town.

▭

MAUREEN MURPHY: Well, first of all, you go into a community in Mississippi. The community I was working in was Meridian, which is the second-largest town in Mississippi. However, we work out of the town, in rural communities. You go into a community and you try and establish local leadership, and you try and build unity among the Negroes, and you literally go from house to house, from rural shack to rural shack and knock on doors. And we always go in integrated teams.

PIERRE: That is as a Negro and a white?

MAUREEN MURPHY: A Negro and a white student. There are very few whites. Up until this summer, when we had a thousand white volunteers that came into the state, we had very, very few whites in the state because it was much, much too dangerous to send white students in unless it was on a mass basis. I was working in the state last year though, and I was working in the rural communities. You just go into a home, introduce yourself, and try to explain to people the importance of voting – why they must vote and why they must try and break the white power structure in the state of Mississippi.

PIERRE: What kind of an attitude or reaction do you get from these people? How conversant are they with the whole business of voting?

MAUREEN MURPHY: That varies from family to family and from

12

individual to individual. Of course, there's the intense amount of fear that is involved. They've heard of the bombings and the cross burnings and the beatings. It's not so much the workers like myself or the other students that are really the brave people involved, you see; it's the people who have been living in Mississippi and who live there daily who are very aware of the Ku Klux Klan, are very aware, all their lives, of the terror involved and of the consequences of voting.

PIERRE: What happens if they register to vote?

MAUREEN MURPHY: Well, first of all, it's not that they can simply register to vote. When, let's say, a Negro becomes interested in voting, and we finally encourage him to attempt to vote, he must first go to the courthouse, and he must then sign his name to an application sheet, requesting to register to vote. The consequences of this are that his name is published two weeks straight in a local newspaper. Now in a rural community, the people know that they are Negro or they are white. As a consequence, white people see that this Negro is trying to register and attempt to become a citizen with voting rights. Then the Ku Klux Klan usually moves in on this person – threatens his life, tells him not to become involved with us – we are termed the "outside agitators" or the Yankees – and that, if he wants to live and his family wants to live, then he must not have anything to do with us.

PIERRE: Well, have you got *anybody* to register?

MAUREEN MURPHY: Oh, yes, we have. We have gotten people to vote; but many times it's not a great step forward. We get people to vote sometimes out of the pressure from the FBI. They move in and put pressure on the registrar. The registrar doesn't have to give any explanation why people can't register to vote. She doesn't have to explain why she failed somebody. Any time we send somebody to vote, we make sure they are very informed. They know enough to cross every "T," to dot every "I," and to be very well-informed on the Constitution. So we have gotten some people to vote. I registered a man one time and he went down to the court house. He applied and he was accepted. But before he was accepted, he had gone home. That evening several members of the Ku Klux Klan had gone to his house and pistol-whipped him. After he was pistol-whipped, they threatened his family and told him not to have anything to do with us. Well, this man's beautiful really – that's all I can say. He's a marvellous person. Knowing the consequences involved for his life and for his family, he found us and informed us what had happened. We sent workers in to talk to him, and we brought him to the hospital. He then proceeded to go back to the courthouse to vote, and because he was a local citizen, he had so much courage and was very well liked, many people came to vote. They became encouraged.

PIERRE: Did anything happen to him afterwards?

MAUREEN MURPHY: Well, no, you see, because he had said very clearly and openly that if any white man stepped on his property again and threatened his family, he would literally blow his head off. The Negroes took up arms and took up guns. We aren't violent. We cannot carry any sort of weapon to defend ourselves as civil rights workers; but the local people, they say they've lived there all their lives, and most of them have some sort of protection.

PIERRE: Well, now, Maureen, how about the danger to you? Some of your co-workers have been killed. Are you afraid when you're working down there?

MAUREEN MURPHY: I think there would have to be something mentally wrong with me if I was to look at you and say that I wasn't afraid. Of course, everyone's afraid. I'm scared but I can't explain. I don't think I could convey the feeling leaving San Francisco and going to work in Mississippi or the South. Suddenly you're empty. You know that you've got no protection. You know that you've nowhere really to turn to. But you have to learn to function with that fear. Because who are you, as a worker, to approach a Negro who *really* takes the chances, who must go down to the courthouse, who must stand up and vote? You know when you approach him to vote that you fear for yourself. You're scared; but you learn to live with that fear.

PIERRE: What's your situation when you go right into the back areas, which are the real dark areas – not dark in the sense of being Negro, but dark in the sense of civilization – and you're dealing with plantation owners who don't want the Negroes to vote?

MAUREEN MURPHY: Yes, you're dealing with people. You see, it's not only the Negroes who are oppressed in the South. It's the poor white who's also suppressed because of the structure in the South. But you're dealing with the real rural areas of the country where there aren't telephones. There are dirt roads, and there are plantation owners, and the resistance and the harassment that you receive sometimes are extremely intense. For instance, we're walking a dirt road, and when a car is approaching from either direction, we're taught to just automatically step down and walk in the drainage ditches at the side as a precaution. I'm glad that I took that precaution one particular time.

14

PIERRE: Why? Did somebody try to run over you?

MAUREEN MURPHY: Yes. A woman with her children in a car, if you can imagine, tried to run us down. We had just been kicked off a plantation that afternoon. There was another Negro girl and myself, and we were on our way to telephone the office to send out a car. You see, because of lack of transportation, we're just dropped off into the rural area, by ourselves, without any transportation.

PIERRE: And left for the day?

MAUREEN MURPHY: Left to work and walk the fields.

PIERRE: And this woman tried to run over you?

MAUREEN MURPHY: Yes; she approached us from the other side of the road, came over, swerved over, and – we weren't too sure the first time, but then she came back at us. What happened is that there are fences and we jumped the fence, and the woman was – I don't know if you can call it insane – but the woman was really determined to get us. The same woman that afternoon shot at us, and I think that nobody can ever believe that suddenly you're finding yourself in a position that you're getting shot at – and that's what I mean that there's an intense amount of fear, and – and you have that helpless feeling that there's no one you can go to. You can't go to the local sheriff to report the woman because he wouldn't care. He hated us. The local authorities hate us. He would have said it was too bad she missed; so that's what I mean when I say you're helpless. You have only your workers to depend on. You can report yourself to the FBI. But the FBI in Mississippi, they're local agents. Meaning they're residents of Mississippi, and that means they are usually members of the Ku Klux Klan or the White Citizens Council.

PIERRE: You have nowhere to turn?

MAUREEN MURPHY: No; you can phone Washington, D.C., or you can phone the FBI Bureau in New Orleans, but usually they say: "What has occurred? Have you been injured? If you haven't been injured, well. ..."

PIERRE: I want to ask you a bit about James Chaney and Mickey Schwerner, two of the three civil rights workers who were killed this summer. Where were you when it was discovered that they'd been murdered?

MAUREEN MURPHY: Well, at that time I was in New York City. I was sent to New York to talk and try and reach people in New York City to help us with the summer project which was coming.

PIERRE: What did the news do to you inside?

MAUREEN MURPHY: I don't know if it's possible, you know – even now when I'm in a position that I can talk about it. I went through some – well – very impulsive changes, very big changes in New York City when I heard it. I was living in Meridian, Mississippi, and had been working there a long time when Mickey Schwerner and his young wife arrived in Meridian to work with us. All four of us – there was another girl, a Negro girl from New York – the four of us got a home together and lived together and ate together and stayed together for over six months. We literally became – well – like very, very, very close. James Chaney I had known longer. He was a resident of Mississippi. I also became very close with him and his family, so I don't know if it's possible to say what it did to me. I think it's pretty obvious what it would do to everybody. When I heard that they had disappeared – that three civil rights workers were missing in Mississippi – well, at first I wasn't too surprised, because of the fact that many times throughout the year *we* were missing because they changed jails on us. For instance, if you're arrested in Jackson, Mississippi, the local authorities may move you to try and keep us guessing where we've been moved to. They move the students around, but I thought since the summer project was on, the publicity was big and it meant nothing at first. Then I picked up the *New York Post* – just out of curiosity because I was getting my own reports from Jackson, Mississippi. I picked up the paper and I saw that it was James Chaney and Mickey Schwerner and, well, I just was empty. These were trained workers who never get released from jail at night: that's one of the rules. We never would be released from jail at night. There's something wrong if they release you at that time of night. In fact, we would usually protest to stay in jail, and when I knew they were missing and they were *really* missing, then I knew they were dead. There was no doubt in my mind that they were dead. The rest of the country may have felt – well – maybe they're being kept; but it was very obvious to us that they were gone. And that applies to all the workers in Mississippi.

PIERRE: How much do you get paid for this work?

MAUREEN MURPHY: We get paid a subsistence salary of ten dollars a week. For a while we were receiving twenty-five dollars a week; but now we receive a ten-dollar-a-week salary which is sort of impossible. There's not much of a social life in Mississippi, anyway, and you use that ten dollars to buy your food. If you smoke, of course, you smoke. It's generally for everything.

PIERRE: Where do you stay?

16

MAUREEN MURPHY: Many times you stay with families. I stayed with a family up until the time when Mickey and his wife came to Meridian, Mississippi, and when they came, the four of us got a house. Any houses where a lot of civil rights workers live together are called Freedom Houses. Now, many times most of the girls live in a community with families, and the boys live in the Freedom Houses, mainly because the Freedom Houses are very big targets for the Ku Klux Klan to bomb.

PIERRE: What started you doing this? Why do you do it?

MAUREEN MURPHY: Why does anybody do it, you know, why does one become involved?

PIERRE: But you're away out in San Francisco – a long way away. What was it that triggered this decision to go to Mississippi and work for nothing?

MAUREEN MURPHY: It wasn't something that triggered it. It was something – maybe if you say I'm a human being – that had always been against any minority race, in this case the American Negro, being discriminated against. The Negro has not had equal rights, especially in the South. Has always been exploited by the white structure in the South. As far as I'm concerned, he's treated just as bad as he ever was during slavery. He is still treated just like a slave. He still doesn't have any rights in the state. I was active in California in many groups . . . on campuses . . . in college . . . in high school. I had wanted to work in the South a couple of years before, but I wanted to finish my education in college. So when I finished, I applied to work in the South – to simply go down for a few months to try to see if I could be of any help at all. The two months has now led into almost two years. That's another thing, you see. I can't sit here and say to you the changes that I've gone through in the last two years. Maybe I've grown up a lot. Most of us look very young, but we mature very fast. We have, obviously, no choice. You're really working with the real people in the country; you're working with the really beautiful people in the States.

PIERRE: Is it true that some of the Negroes that you talked to didn't know what the word "vote" meant?

MAUREEN MURPHY: Yes. That's what I meant when I said that it's as bad as it ever was in the South. I went up to one man – we introduce ourselves when we first approach people – and I said: "Are you a registered voter?" And he just looked at me as if I was nuts. He must have been about seventy years old. And I said, again: "Excuse me, sir, are you a registered voter?" Still nothing came. So I said: "Do you vote during the election?" I thought maybe he wasn't understanding "registered." He just looked up at me, and he said: "I'm sorry, Miss" – they usually call you Miss still, if you're white – "I'm sorry, Miss, I don't know what you mean. What does 'vote' mean?" Well, this is what I mean about the changes that I went through. I looked at this man standing there in the United States of America, Democracy, land of the free, home of the brave – and the changes that were going through my mind! Here I was, standing in the middle of the country, and the man didn't even know what "vote" meant. I had to sit down. I wasn't sure if I wanted to cry. I wasn't sure if I wanted to scream and run away from Mississippi and go back to San Francisco and forget it, because I was just torn up inside. Well, this is a common occurrence. They only know that the day they get up they work; they get paid two dollars maybe for working from five o'clock in the morning till eight o'clock at night. I mean they know the land they live on and that's it.

PIERRE: Is it true that these Negroes really don't know much about the whites?

MAUREEN MURPHY: They don't know much about whites because, actually, they have no real dealing with white people in the state of Mississippi – other than being run by the whites literally. They only know a white person in Mississippi as someone who rules over them.

THE BLACK VIGILANTE

"The black community has yet
to form a vigilante committee.
This is why we aren't respected
as human beings."

*Malcolm X Shabazz – to give him his full and final name – made
his last television appearance with me in Toronto on January 19,
1965. About a month later, he was assassinated in New York
City. He was thirty-nine.*

*Malcolm X was a black racist, and his background suggests
that he had good reason to be. Born Malcolm Little in Omaha,
Nebraska, he was one of eleven children of an uneducated
Baptist minister. When he was six, his father, whom a group of
whites considered too uppity on racial matters, was found murdered – his head bashed in, his body mangled. The Littles came
close to starvation as a result, and young Malcolm spent his
formative years in a succession of crowded, crime-ridden city
ghettos.*

*He dropped out of school after grade eight and took the only
job available: waiter in a railroad dining room. He hated it and
quit, drifting on to Harlem, where he became a runner for the
numbers racketeers and then a hustler of bootleg whisky and*

*dope. Lanky, energetic, and good-looking, he acquired the nick-
name of Big Red and garnered fat fees from white thrill-seekers
who wanted to be squired around Harlem's vice dens. When
the white police demanded bribes, Big Red peeled them off a
thousand-dollar roll he invariably carried with him. His view of
the white man was thus almost totally satanic: they were murderers, they were sexually promiscuous, they were corrupt.*

*In 1946, his life was suddenly changed. At the age of twenty-
one, he found himself sentenced by a white judge to a ten-year
stretch in prison for grand larceny. And it was in prison that he
first heard the strangely seductive philosophy of a Georgia-born
Negro, then living in Detroit, who called himself Elijah Muhammed, and ran a kind of black Ku Klux Klan based loosely on
the religion of Islam.*

*When he was released from prison in 1952, Little took a Black
Muslim name and dedicated himself to building the movement.
Today it owes its strength and notoriety to his considerable organi-
zational and oratorical abilities. He became the head of the power-
ful New York Mosque and was generally considered to be Elijah
Muhammed's Number Two man and successor.*

*But in 1964, Malcolm X broke with his leader. He organized
a new black activist group, the Muslim Mosque Inc., and its non-
religious wing, the Organization of Afro-American Unity. He also
visited Africa and the Middle East. He was clearly a considerable
force to be reckoned with in the United States' racial struggle. I
remember Dick Gregory telling me that he was the most significant of all Negro leaders and would soon replace Dr. Martin
Luther King as the real symbol of Negro resistance to white
supremacy.*

*This was not to be; but it is interesting to speculate on the
kind of man Malcolm X might have become, had an assassin's
bullet not struck him down, for what he had to say to me clearly
foreshadows the philosophy of "black power" which became the
rallying cry of Negro activists in the summer of 1966. When I
talked to him, Malcolm X seemed to be going through a period of
reassessment. The break with his leader had obviously shaken
him; his journey to Islam had affected him profoundly.*

*He seemed to me to be two men, as so many demagogues are.
On the platform, he was a fiery orator, given to explosive statements under the intoxicating influence of the crowd. In the quiet
of the TV studio, he was a different man – soft-spoken, compara-
tively moderate, almost reasonable – even prepared to hedge. Was*

this just one side of a complex and inscrutable character, or had the break with the Muslims changed him? I began by asking him about his former mentor and the reasons for the rift between them.

⬭

MALCOLM X: Well, he represented himself to us as a prophet who had been visited by God, who had been taught by God, who had been given an analysis of the problems concerning black people in America by God, and also a solution by the same God, and as long as I believed in him as a man, I actually thought that he had been taught and commissioned by God to solve the problems of our people in America. Then I came into the knowledge of something in his own personal life that he admitted to me when I confronted him with it. But when it came to him taking the steps that a man would take to correct this mistake, I found that his own ability to be a man was lacking. When I ceased to respect him as a man, I could see that he also was not divine. There was no God with him at all.

PIERRE: I take it you don't want to discuss this specific thing in his personal life?

MALCOLM X: Well, discussing it might keep your show from going on the air.

PIERRE: All right, we won't discuss it; but there seemed to me at the time that there were other reasons given for your break with Elijah Muhammed. At the time of President Kennedy's assassination, you made a speech that seemed to indicate that you were pleased that he had been assassinated. Certainly at that time, Elijah Muhammed indicated that you had been fired or suspended from the Black Muslim movement. How about that?

MALCOLM X: I had taken a subject as my topic that day – an approach that was designed to show that the seeds that America had sown – in enslavement, in many of the things that followed since then – all of these seeds were coming up today; it was harvest time. At the end of this particular lecture, during the question-and-answer period, somebody asked me what I thought of the assassination of President Kennedy. In line with the topic that I had just been discussing, I pointed out that it was a case of the chickens coming home to roost, by which I meant that this was the result of seeds that had been sown, that this was the harvest. This was taken out

21

of context, and reported in one of the papers, and Elijah Muhammed, who had been waiting for me to make a move that would enable him to suspend me and get the support of the public in doing so, took advantage of that opportunity. He gave the impression that I was saying something against the President himself, because he felt that the public wouldn't go along with that.

PIERRE: How did you feel, personally, about the President's assassination in that connection? Were you bothered about it? Were you angered by it? Or were you jubilant?

MALCOLM X: No. I was realistic, in that being at the forefront of this struggle of the black man in America – in his quest for respect as a human being – I had seen the many-faceted repercussions of this hate taking a grip on the American public. I think that many of the politicians took advantage of it and exploited it for their own personal benefit. So to me the whole thing was a case of politics, hate, and a combination of other things.

PIERRE: There seems to me to have been a fair amount of hate in the Black Muslim movement itself.

MALCOLM X: Well, I won't deny that. But, at the same time, I don't think that the Black Muslim movement and its hate can be classified as the same degree or type of hate you find in the American society itself, because the hate, so-called, that you see among black people is a reaction to the hate of the society which has rejected us. In that sense it is not hate.

PIERRE: I'm not saying that the hate, or whatever it is, isn't understandable. I'm asking if it's effective to fight hate with hate?

MALCOLM X: In my opinion, I think that it is not fair to classify the reaction of people who are oppressed as hate. They are reacting to the hate of the society they have had put upon them or practised against them.

PIERRE: Well, let me ask you about your reaction on another occasion; I'd like to see if you still feel the same way. That's when the plane load of people from Atlanta, Georgia, crashed and 121 were killed. If the papers reported you correctly, you were fairly jubilant about that – because these were white Southerners who had gone to their deaths. Am I right in saying that you had expressed such a sentiment at that time?

MALCOLM X: This was another reaction to the hate that the American society collectively has practised against the black people in that particular country.

PIERRE: Well, how do you feel about it now? Are you sorry you made that kind of statement, cr do you still feel the same way?

MALCOLM X: Well, I would probably not now make the same statement. But I cannot see where I was not justified in making the statement at that time. It was made just after the police in Los Angeles had shot up the Negro community and had killed a Muslim and shot seven others who were unarmed and who had no weapons at all. And the court system, the entire city power structure, seemed to be lined up against the Negro community in general and the Muslim Mosque in particular. I think I was justified. I had mentioned in the courtroom, during the coroner's inquest, that if the court system was not capable of producing justice for black people in this country, then I was thankful, as a religious man, that there is a God in Heaven who could bring out justice in cases like this. A couple of days later, when that airplane dropped out of the sky in France, I didn't think it was a coincidence that it was from Georgia and that practically everybody aboard it was from Georgia. Georgia is a state that has a record for having enslaved and lynched and maimed more black human beings than any other state in America other than Mississippi.

PIERRE: You felt that this was the hand of God?

MALCOLM X: I felt it was the hand of God. I felt that it was a sign. A couple of days later, Billy Graham was holding one of his crusades in Chicago, and he pointed out at the same time that it was an act of God, that it was God's hand doing this. Now, when Graham said this, they didn't call it hate. When *I* say it, then I'm supposed to be a fanatic and an extremist.

PIERRE: Well, of course, he didn't express any jubilation over the death of 121 people. But let me ask you this about your God, Mr. X. Has he got any colour? Is he black?

MALCOLM X: No.

PIERRE: Is he white?

MALCOLM X: As a Black Muslim, who believed what Elijah Muhammed taught, I regarded God just as he taught, as a black man. Having since gone into the Muslim world and got a better understanding of the religion of Islam, I believe that God is the supreme being, and that colour plays no part in his particular being.

PIERRE: In fact, isn't the God of the Muslims and of the Jews and the Christians really the same God?

MALCOLM X: If they believe in the God who created the universe, then we all believe in the same God. I believe in the God who created the universe. Muslims call him Allah. Christians, perhaps, call him Christ, or by some other name. Jews call him Jehovah,

23

and in referring to him they mean "the creative." We are all referring to the same God.

PIERRE: Now, let me switch the subject briefly, and ask you what you mean when you say that the Black Muslims are not militant enough. Your new organization, I take it, will be more militant than the Black Muslims. In what way?

MALCOLM X: Well, the Black Muslim movement, No. 1, professes to be a religious movement. They profess the religion of Islam. But the Muslim world rejected the Black Muslim movement as a bona-fide Islamic group, so it found itself manoeuvered into a religious vacuum – or a sort of religious hybrid. At the same time, the Government of the United States tried to manoeuvre the Black Muslim movement, with the press, into an image that was political instead of religious. So the Black Muslim movement came to be known as a political group. Yet, at the same time, it didn't vote; it didn't take part in any politics; it didn't involve itself actively in the civil rights struggle; so it became a political hybrid as well as a religious hybrid. Now, on the other hand, the Black Muslim movement attracted the most militant black American, the young, dissatisfied, uncompromising element that exists in this country – drawing them in yet, at the same time, giving them no part to play in the struggle other than moral reform. It created a lot of disillusion, dissatisfaction, dissension, and eventually division. Those who divided are the ones that I'm a part of. We set up the Muslim Mosque, which is based upon Orthodox Islam, as a religious group so that we could get a better understanding of our religion; but being black Americans, though we are Muslims, who believe in brotherhood, we also realized that our people have a problem in America that goes beyond religion. We realized that many of our people aren't going to become Muslim; many of them aren't even interested in anything religious; so we set up the Organization of Afro-American Unity as a non-religious organization which all black Americans could become a part of and play an active part in striking out at the political, economic, and social evils that all of us are confronted by.

PIERRE: That "striking out," what form is it going to take? You talk of giving the Ku Klux Klan a taste of its own medicine. This is in direct opposition to the theory of non-violence of Dr. Martin Luther King, who doesn't believe in striking back. What do you mean by "a taste of its own medicine"? Are you going to burn fiery crosses on their lawns? Are you going to blow up churches with the Ku Klux Klan kids in them? What are you going to do?

24

MALCOLM X: Well, I think that the only way that two different races can get along with each other is, first, they have to understand each other. That cannot be brought about other than through communication – dialogue – and you can't communicate with a person unless you speak his language. If the person speaks French, you can't speak English or German.

PIERRE: We have that problem in our country, too.

MALCOLM X: In America, our people have so far not been able to speak the type of language that the racists understand. By not speaking that language, they fail to communicate, so that the racist element doesn't really believe that the black American is a human being – part of the human family. There is no communication. So I believe that the only way to communicate with that element is to be in a position to speak their language.

PIERRE: And this language is violence?

MALCOLM X: I wouldn't call it violence. I think that they should be made to know that, any time they come into a black community and inflict violence upon members of that black community, they should realize in advance that the black community can speak the same language. Then they would be less likely to come in.

PIERRE: Let's be specific here: suppose that a church is bombed. Will you bomb back?

MALCOLM X: I believe that any area of the United States, where the Federal Government has shown either its unwillingness or inability to protect the lives and the property of the black American, then it is time for the black Americans to band together and do whatever is necessary to see that we get the type of protection we need.

PIERRE: "Whatever is necessary?"

MALCOLM X: I mean just that. *Whatever is necessary.* This does not mean that we should go out and initiate acts of aggression indiscriminately in the white community. But it does mean that, if we are going to be respected as human beings, we should reserve the right to defend ourselves by whatever means necessary. This is recognized and accepted in any civilized society.

PIERRE: Let me ask you a specific question again and see if I can get a specific answer from you. There are some people going to go on trial in Mississippi for the murder of three civil rights workers. There are some witnesses who identify them as murderers, but the general feeling is they'll get off. Will you do anything about this if they get off?

MALCOLM X: I wouldn't say.

PIERRE: You don't want to say?

MALCOLM X: Because, then, if something happened to them, they would blame me. But I will say that in a society where the law itself is incapable of bringing known murderers to justice, it's historically demonstrable that the well-meaning people of that society have always banded together in one form or another to see that their society was protected against repetitious acts by these same murderers.

PIERRE: What you're talking about here is a vigilante movement.

MALCOLM X: There have been vigilante movements forming all over America in white communities, but the black community has yet to form a vigilante committee. This is why we aren't respected as human beings.

PIERRE: Are you training men to use aggressive methods? Are you training men as the Black Muslim movement trained the élite core known as the Fruit of Islam? Have you got trainees operating now who know how to fight back?

MALCOLM X: Yes.

PIERRE: Who know how to use knuckle-dusters and guns?

MALCOLM X: Yes, oh yes. The black man in America doesn't need that much training. Most of them have been in the army – have already been trained by the Government itself. They haven't been trained to think for themselves and, therefore, they've never used this training to protect themselves.

PIERRE: Have you got a specific cadre of such young, tough guys working for you or operating under your aegis?

MALCOLM X: We're not a cadre, nor do we want it to be felt that we want to be tough. We're trying to be human beings, and we want to be recognized and accepted as human beings. But we don't think humanity will recognize us or accept us as such until humanity knows that we will do everything to protect our human ranks, as others will do for theirs.

PIERRE: Are you prepared to send flying squads into areas where the Negroes have been oppressed without any legal help?

MALCOLM X: We are prepared to do whatever is necessary to see that our people, wherever they are, get the type of protection that the Federal Government has refused to give them.

PIERRE: Okay. Do you still believe that all whites are devils and all blacks saints, as I'm sure you did under the Black Muslim movement?

MALCOLM X: This is what Elijah Muhammed teaches. No, I don't believe that. I believe as the Koran teaches, that a man should not

26

be judged by the colour of his skin but rather by his conscious behaviour, by his actions, by his attitude towards others and his actions towards others.

PIERRE: Now, before you left Elijah Muhammed and went to Mecca and saw the original World of Islam, you believed in complete segregation of the whites and the Negroes. You were opposed both to integration and to intermarriage. Have you changed your views there?

MALCOLM X: I believe in recognizing every human being as a human being, neither white, black, brown nor red. When you are dealing with humanity as one family, there's no question of integration or intermarriage. It's just one human being marrying another human being, or one human being living around and with another human being. I may say, though, that I don't think the burden to defend any such position should ever be put upon the black man. Because it is the white man collectively who has shown that he is hostile towards integration and towards intermarriage and towards these other strides towards oneness. So, as a black man, and especially as a black American, I don't think that I would have to defend any stand that I formerly took. Because it's still a reaction of the society and it's a reaction that was produced by the white society. And I think that it is the society that produced this that should be attacked, not the reaction that develops among the people who are the victims of that negative society.

PIERRE: But you no longer believe in a Black State?

MALCOLM X: No.

PIERRE: In North America?

MALCOLM X: No. I believe in a society in which people can live like human beings on the basis of equality.

PIERRE: So you have been changed considerably by your visit to the Muslim World and specifically to Mecca. Did this produce violent emotions within yourself? When people lose their faith or change their faith or renew their faith, they usually suffer terrible internal conflicts.

MALCOLM X: Oh, yes. I will confess readily that it's impossible to believe as strongly in a man as I believed in Elijah Muhammed and have him disappoint me – or disappoint anyone else for that matter – and not create a great deal of internal conflict. One of the things that I am thankful for about the religion of Islam is that it is sufficiently strong in itself so that when one broadens one's understanding of it, it gives one the inner strength to face up to some of these crises or tests that one encounters.

PIERRE: There has been talk, I think by you and by Elijah Muhammed, about an Armageddon in the United States by 1984. I'm wondering if you still believe that, and why that particular date?

MALCOLM X: I don't frankly. Much of what Elijah Muhammed has taught I don't think he believes in himself. I say that and can easily defend it sitting opposite him. But, where an ultimate clash between East and West is concerned, well, I think that an objective analysis of events taking place on this earth today point towards some type of ultimate showdown. You can call it a political showdown or even a showdown between the economic systems that exist on this earth, which almost boil down along racial lines. I do believe that there will be a clash between East and West. I believe that there will ultimately be a clash between the oppressed and those that do the oppressing. I believe that there will be a clash between those who want freedom, justice, and equality for everyone, and those who want to continue the systems of exploitation. I believe that there will be that kind of clash, but I don't think that it will be based upon the colour of the skin, as Elijah Muhammed has taught it. However, I do think you'll find that the European powers, which are the former colonial powers, if they're not able to readjust their feeling of superiority towards the darker skinned people, whom they have been made to think are inferior, then the lines can easily be drawn. They can easily be lumped into racial groups, and it will be a racial war.

28

THE ESPRESSO PRIEST

"Everybody's tired of
professional moralizing and
the old type of preaching."

*Malcolm Boyd has all the dark handsomeness of a movie star,
minus the toupée. He reminds one, on first encounter, of Henry
Fonda: the eyes have the same liquid intensity; the voice has the
same flat but honest nasality. I remember that when he came
into the studio in Toronto on November 18, 1964, all the ladies,
from make-up girl to producer, were bowled over. No wonder:
his background is invested with the glamour of the mass-com-
munications media: Hollywood advertising man (Foote, Cone,
and Belding); movie press-agent and executive (Sam Goldwyn,
Mary Pickford); radio and TV producer (Night Beat, Tex and
Jinx).*

*But in 1951, at the age of twenty-eight, Malcolm Boyd, a
former atheist, left all this behind him and entered the Church
Divinity School of the Pacific, which is the seminary of the
Episcopal Church in Berkeley, California. He graduated in 1954
with a Bachelor of Divinity Degree and then attended Oxford
University for a year. He was ordained a priest, earned a Master's*

Degree in Sacred Theology, lived in a French monastic community for a summer, and eventually settled into the post of Episcopal Chaplain to Colorado State University. Here he organized a series of "espresso nights" as an expression of Christian evangelism — and, of course, the newspapers dubbed him "the espresso priest."

Boyd is part of the North American youth movement which is known loosely as the New Left and was born out of the struggle for racial integration. In 1962, Life magazine listed him as one of the hundred most important young men and women in the United States, a member of what it called "The Breakthrough Generation." The same year, Mademoiselle grouped him with Jules Feiffer, Normal Mailer, and others as "A Disturber of the Peace."

Boyd, I think, would accept such sobriquets with equanimity and perhaps with jubilation, for he is a priest who believes the Christian religion is essentially revolutionary. He is deeply involved with the anti-segregation movement. He has participated in freedom rides in the South and racial demonstrations in the North, and he has served his time in jail. He is also a part of the New Left within the Protestant Church. Many of the spokesmen for this revolutionary movement are people like Boyd — former atheists who have left the commercial world and rejoined an ancient institution in the hopes of making it over.

Boyd's controversial views and methods have got him into trouble more than once. He was forced to leave his first campus in April, 1961, after his bishop in a newspaper article clearly criticized him for "some new secular practice being injected into the worship of the church, particularly in the administration of sacraments." The bishop went on to refer, in the same context, to people "who are given over to the non-practice of anything and the wearing of beards and leotards." This was clearly aimed at Boyd and his espresso nights. He resigned his post and became, for the next three years, Chaplain at Wayne University in Detroit. He has since left that campus as well and is now chaplain-at-large to university campuses in the U.S.

Boyd has also written six books and five plays on religious themes. These have caused the same kind of controversy as has his coffee-house evangelism. It was about this evangelism that we began to talk. How about some of the church-operated coffee houses? I asked him. Did they really work?

MALCOLM BOYD: When they're not phoney. I think cl
coffee-houses tend to be extremely phoney because
agenda. They want to convert people on their term
don't want a dialogue – they're afraid of a dialogue. I
the Church can have the guts to get out into a coffee-hou
run by good clean atheists, and get into a dialogue with t
without all the props and all the points, then this is the
this is evangelism to me.

PIERRE: This is the Church getting outside the stained-glass wi
and into the world.

MALCOLM BOYD: Well, it's getting into the world. I think it's
easy to say you're in the world when you're not in the world.

PIERRE: Tell me what's happening in the colleges. Is there a rel
gious revival in the colleges?

MALCOLM BOYD: I'd have to say I think they're quite indifferent
because I think what's very important to students is, of course,
security, the buck, the degree. Then, very important to students –
in a very serious way that a lot of adults don't understand – is sex.
I mean, they're not going to stop to have sex every couple of hours
for relief or something; they're trying to make *sense* out of it, to
relate it to love. A lot of people have great disdain and don't wis
to understand them at all. But they have much more moralit
than their parents do about sexuality. Then they are concerned,
in the United States, about the racial question seriously. Their
parents can't understand the intensity of their interest because
these kids are moral.

PIERRE: What you're saying is that there's still idealism, then?

MALCOLM BOYD: Oh, yes.

PIERRE: But how about the idealism of religion? Do they have
religious bull sessions, as we used to do? "Is there a God? Is there
a Heaven? Should you pray?" Do they argue seriously? Is there
a campus-atheist argument and a campus-religious argument anymore?

MALCOLM BOYD: I don't think this is very important any more. I
think what's much more important is: "Were you in jail in Mississippi? Have you been in a Freedom House? Who from the dorm
was on a freedom ride?" This type of thing.

PIERRE: Well, it may not be important, but I'm sure the church, if it
isn't concerned about indifference, ought to be concerned: Because if the whole of the younger intelligentsia is indifferent to
the Church, then where is the Church in the future?

31

MALCOLM BOYD: I think the Church is completely blind to this situation. I think it's very tragic because I think the Church is prone to keep these little doll's-house, denominational-college centres around. And the in-group – I don't mean to be unkind, but I'm afraid I must be because I think it's important – they come in and have their spaghetti suppers and they talk about the Trinity, which they've had all through Sunday School anyway. What I mean is that there's no sense of mission; there's no concern for the great university out there; there's no concern to touch the nerve of the life of the university.

PIERRE: The intellectuals and most faculty members are estranged at this level. And yet the church leaders, or many of them, keep insisting there has been a post-war religious revival.

MALCOLM BOYD: Actually, a great deal of the religious revival has been fantasy. A great many people have felt that there was a security and a comfort for them in the Church. I've recently written a play critical of the Church. Although I think it's quite positive, some people just throw their hands up and say I'm being negative and angry. I'm angry with love of it, and I think I'm being quite positive. I have a woman say in the play: "I'm so glad the Church is not dead, I don't know what I'd do without it" – meaning the prayer-book, which she may kind of lean on rather than working out the real meaning of prayer (which isn't talking to God in Olde English), or maybe a prayer group, where she and some other ladies are going to avoid the social issues: they may worry about individual sanctity together, yet they will immunize themselves against the real problems of their time and their world. I think there's been some kind of a success-mythology about all this, too. I know that in some areas people are considered rather queer if they don't go to church. I've been told this by a number of suburbanites who attend and don't really know. I happen to believe very strongly and deeply in what to me is the reality of the Church. I consider it to be the Body of Christ. By that I mean that I think it's a living reality that has responsibilities not privileges and a job to do in the world. I think God loves the world. I think the Church has to be in it and love it and work for it.

PIERRE: In your attempt to communicate some of this to the students with whom you've worked, you've got into trouble with your own people, haven't you?

MALCOLM BOYD: Of course.

PIERRE: What happened as a result of the espresso nights that you were holding?

MALCOLM BOYD: They were misunderstood. I think a number of Church people talk about mission and evangelism but don't really want too many people with the wrong deodorant or the wrong ideas or the wrong clothing or the wrong colour of skin or the wrong ethnic background to come in and break up the club.

PIERRE: You were, in effect, a missionary – not to the starving Armenians or the Africans, but to the people in the coffee-houses.

MALCOLM BOYD: Yes. I see the Church as missionary. I think the minute it *isn't* missionary it ought to drop dead. I don't see it as an incestuous in-group interested in its own idolatry. I think at that point people worship religion rather than God, and it does become a club. It *can't* be a club.

PIERRE: What happened to you at Colorado State?

MALCOLM BOYD: I quit. I wasn't fired. But I quit after I was criticized by the bishop, who had not seen my work and had criticized it publicly in the press. It was a little bit impossible to continue there under the circumstances. He had also written that you can't call yourself a beloved child of God if you have matted hair, smell badly, and wear black underwear. I think you can call yourself a beloved child of God under any circumstances at any time, and I'm fed up with the good people – the nice people. The sat back in their churches while several million Jews were de troyed in Nazi Germany, and they always sit back.

PIERRE: But why did you quit? Why didn't you stay and fight?

MALCOLM BOYD: It's a good question. In that case it was all on t line pretty much. I felt I couldn't continue there because of mission. The bishop is the rector of a mission. The vicar isn' rector.

PIERRE: You're really under the thumb of the bishop? Is that what you're saying? You have to take orders – do what you're told? Or is there room for revolt?

MALCOLM BOYD: There's a good deal of room. There's a good deal of room for argument . . . for controversy. In that case, we had a great deal of controversy. We had it, and I felt that in that situation I had to go, and I did. I was just back on that same campus the other day, oddly enough, to visit the students.

PIERRE: Did you get anywhere with the students?

MALCOLM BOYD: Yes.

PIERRE: Did you make any converts, or did that matter to you? It does to Billy Graham.

MALCOLM BOYD: I wonder how we would define converts? I think it's unbelievably vulgar and possibly blasphemous to deal with

33

statistics. I couldn't imagine at some meeting of mine that some-body would say that there were twenty-six converts. I wouldn't know what it meant.

PIERRE: And yet the whole Church deals in statistics. You only have to open a parish newspaper to see them. *We have got so many people at church this year, and that's fifteen more than we had at the same time last year. We have raised fifteen thousand dollars more this year than last year.*

MALCOLM BOYD: The Church feels that it has to have an organi-zation of this kind, at least in many quarters. I believe now that there is a revolution, and that we're going to see a rather complete reformation within the life of the Church over the next few years from several standpoints. You already have experimental minis-tries where you have listening. They're going into certain places, and they're not even talking, until they know what they're talking about. Also, everybody's tired of professional moralizing and the old type of preaching. The world as a whole isn't listening. The Church in some quarters is very, very irresistably and intelligently and creatively coming to grips with this. This is what's new; this is what's exciting! Now, in the United States, some people – and maybe a lot of them – are cancelling their pledges or saying they'll cancel their pledges if the clergyman doesn't say what they want. Okay! He's got to say what they *don't* want. They've got to cancel their pledges, and the structure has to collapse.

PIERRE: In other words, you're saying that the clergyman must stand up to that kind of pressure and say: "Okay! Don't build a new organ. I'm going to say what I feel as a Christian."

MALCOLM BOYD: If the clergyman doesn't, then I think it's a com-plete charade, a complete lie. I see some very exciting things. I was just in McComb, Mississippi, with young student volunteers from most of the different campuses working with Negroes on voter registration. Okay, they're not talking about Jesus; they wouldn't call themselves churchy. But if anybody walks with Christ, they do. If the Church is to have any meaning in the culture ten years from now, they will be among its leaders. But it's going to be a different church. They're not going to come into something that's building-oriented, one-hour-a-week-at-kindergarten moral-ity, a double-standard morality, talking out of both sides of the mouth. They're going to come into something that is existentially real. There's a clear line of morality that makes sense. You *can* admit in public that you don't understand something: we're going to be able to admit that we're all dealing in areas of agnosticism,

34

because, if one is dealing in faith, one is. One isn't dealing with a rigid body of doctrine that cannot be discussed in terms of fluidity.

PIERRE: You are talking about revolution.

MALCOLM BOYD: Yes.

PIERRE: Would you describe yourself as a reverent agnostic?

MALCOLM BOYD: With explanation.

PIERRE: "With explaination?"

MALCOLM BOYD: In other words, I think that there's an element of agnosticism in all of us. I don't think it's a bad word. We've been so prone to say we're atheists or agnostics or we're Christians. What I generally say to students now is that, if they say they're Christian or atheist, I can't accept the term because, if it's Christianity, it's either hand-me-down or emotional conversion – which I don't think they should really talk about yet until they know – and if it's atheist, well, they're much too unsophisticated to know what that means. I think that agnosticism is not a bad word.

PIERRE: It says you don't know everything there is to know.

MALCOLM BOYD: It says you don't know everything. We obviously do not, and I don't think we would want to. I don't know why we want to be so completely lacking in any humility.

PIERRE: I'd like to find out, Chaplain Boyd, what shaped you – how you arrived at what you are today. I know that you used to be an ad-man, that you worked in Hollywood for Mary Pickford, that at one time you were an atheist, and that you, as they say, got religion. Were you always an atheist or, as a boy, did you hold the conventional beliefs of the Christian Church?

MALCOLM BOYD: Well, I wonder what a boy does? I mean, I was an acolyte; I was in the choir until my voice changed; I went to Sunday School. I dispute the Sunday School that doesn't teach you what sin is or who God is – that teaches you stories about Joseph and his brothers, at that level. They do considerably more harm to a person than help. When I got away to college, the meal-ticket phase was over. Obviously I wanted to make my own way and think my life out and work out my philosophy of life. I just became an atheist. I was agnostic – whatever the word might be. Let's just say I dropped the Church completely. I think I felt it was hypocritical; I saw a lot of double-standard morality – a lot of foolishness; I thought I could get along quite well without it. I continued that way after I started to work in Hollywood.

PIERRE: What did the Hollywood experience do to you? Did it have any fundamental effect on you?

MALCOLM BOYD: Funny. A lot of people want me to do a book on the Hollywood experience. I've tried twice, and other books have come out of it. Maybe I never will do this. Maybe it isn't important. Because you're dealing with blacks and whites in a book like that, and I don't really want to; I think life is dealing more with greys. I don't know what happened in Hollywood except that I was a very successful young man and made a lot of money and reputation and suddenly realized that this was rather foolish if I didn't know who I was or what my life was.

PIERRE: Let me ask you about that in this context: you are now, within your Church, a non-conformist. Were you a conformist when you were an advertising man?

MALCOLM BOYD: That's interesting. I guess so. Very much so, I guess, Pierre. I hadn't really thought too much about it in that way, but I guess I was. I think I tried very hard to be a conformist: to order the right lunch, or drink and eat at the right restaurant, and certainly wear the clothes, and be a success, but very much meld into the peer group at the same time.

PIERRE: Well, what happened to you? Did lightning flash from the skies? Did you undergo an ecstatic experience, as so many people who are converted do? Or was it a slower process with you?

MALCOLM BOYD: Much.

PIERRE: What started it? Something must have triggered it off.

MALCOLM BOYD: Whatever triggered it was questioning . . . wondering. Probably a whole lot of things triggered it. As a matter of fact, I'm sure things triggered it that I don't have any idea about. I think these things are deep in us. I do remember we had a penthouse in New York – very high and very elegant. I would look down at people, and they would look like ants, and I kind of wondered where they were going, and who they were, and what they *really* were. I started really thinking a little bit. I didn't have any answers at all, and it didn't seem that the Church could possibly provide them. But then I started going back sometimes, and when I would I tried to slip out during the last hymn. I didn't want anybody to say: "We're having a young adult supper on Wednesday night." Or: "Would you like to sing in the choir?" Or: "Are you saved?" I couldn't really have stood this. I read the Bible, and I read some other things. You know, I think it can be not only very corny but misleading, and perhaps very wrong, to sum this up like woman's magazine fiction, and there's a great temptation to do so. It's just that my life took a rather different direction.

36

PIERRE: Considerably, because you had to quit your job, leave your salary, and go back to university and become a theological student.

MALCOLM BOYD: Right. Yes, I had to learn to study, among other things, and try to learn how to pray. I didn't have a clue, and it was a matter of great concern. Anyway I did.

PIERRE: Well, now, let me find out what you believe. Do you believe the same things that you were taught in Sunday School?

MALCOLM BOYD: The question with me is that I wasn't taught in Sunday School anything that meant anything to me about God. I mean, when I got to college, I had no sense of God as a reality. I had no real sense of sin or Hell or the Church or salvation. I really didn't. I knew a whole lot of stories that were very garbled in my mind, and I knew that they were sort of myths.

PIERRE: Let me get down to the fundamentals of your Christian faith, one of which is the resurrection of Christ. What do you believe about that? Do you believe that Christ literally and physically rose from the tomb, got out from behind the boulder, and was seen on the road – that he was then raised into Heaven and sits on the right hand of God the Father Almighty? Do you believe that?

MALCOLM BOYD: I believe that Christ was always a part of the God-head, that he is now, and that he lived for a certain number of years – I guess we'll call it thirty-three – and that at the end of his earthly life he returned to the Godhead, which is not a physical thing in a certain place, but is obviously (to me anyway) a spiritual entity – a spiritual being in existence. I think that the people he left might very well have been persons like you and me whom he met spiritually as he does ourselves. I certainly don't feel that he physically ascended behind a physical cloud, because there's no place to go. In other words Hell is not so many degrees Fahrenheit, or so many miles below, and Heaven isn't up there. I do believe about Heaven and Hell that we begin living in them a little bit now, probably.

PIERRE: When the Church says Christ lives – how do you mean that? Does he exist as a thinking and functioning entity?

MALCOLM BOYD: I feel that Christ's earthly life was a part of his existence as God. And as Spirit, he possesses feeling and mind and sensitivity, yes. I feel that he is a living being. I feel that we share in his resurrection because it seems to me that what he was proving to us was that he was overcoming the power of sin. And sin, I feel, is separation from God. He was pointing out to us that we need not be separated from God, no matter who we are or what we do. I think that he was able to relate us to God by his

37

life and his death, in a covenant sense, so that we may know who we are and what life is, and we may experience renewal and resurrection in our own lives on a fairly daily or hourly basis. Resurrection, to me – well, I cannot speak of it as an historical entity. To me it is an existential entity. I suppose one could say a mythical entity. Except isn't that word so tragically misunderstood, because people think we mean it's a lie?

PIERRE: Well, people confuse myth and history, I think.

MALCOLM BOYD: Completely. What I am saying here is that sometimes, as in the Creation and the Fall and the Resurrection, we're dealing with a poetical statement of a fundamental truth actually so great and so encompassing that we couldn't possibly deal with it in some historical sense and limit it.

PIERRE: Let me take this a little further. Do you believe that when you die you will continue as a conscious being somewhere? A spirit, a soul? Continue to think and meet friends? That you will remember the past and know what's going on?

MALCOLM BOYD: I don't know about the past. I'm going to will my body to a university so that they can use the organs and the eyes and so forth, and then what's left will be cremated. I certainly don't want the idolatry and the mortally sinful thing of a religious funeral, which I think is as vulgar as you can get. Yes, I think my life has existed prior to this short period here, and will continue to. It's far too complex; *I'm* far too complex. I mean no capricious God dug me up for a few years – up until the plane crashes. I'm here. It's a long deal.

PIERRE: Do you mean that you live through other people in the future?

MALCOLM BOYD: No, I think I live.

PIERRE: You think you *personally* live.

MALCOLM BOYD: Yes. My sensitivity, my creativity, myself, I live, yes. Certainly not in terms of this body. I don't imagine I'll be extremely interested in tomorrow's *New York Times*. I should hope there would be something much more interesting and more significant.

PIERRE: Do you believe that Mary was a virgin – or do you think it matters?

MALCOLM BOYD: To me it isn't central. As a matter of fact, believing that God became man, I think that God could have chosen this particular vehicle had he wished. I don't think it's central, and I think the tragedy of all this is that we stress the historicity, and we get the Christmas crèche and the Jesus in the robes, and some

38

little kid plays in the Sunday School pageant with not a clue as to the meaning of Christ. I do want to say there's one point in the Roman Catholic belief in the Virgin Mary that I have great respect for, and I think we might all learn from. The point is the obedience of Mary to the will of God in becoming the instrument of the incarnation.

PIERRE: If you have doubts here, how is it possible for you to recite the Apostles' Creed, as I'm sure you must?

MALCOLM BOYD: I'm not saying that I don't consider it central. God could have worked in this way. He also had the power not to. I'm not limiting God.

PIERRE: You're saying that you don't know – that in this area you're agnostic. The Apostles' Creed is very positive. It says I *believe*.

MALCOLM BOYD: Yes.

PIERRE: Well, how do you equate that with what you believe?

MALCOLM BOYD: Well, of course, it's quite clear I think, really, that in reciting the Creed we are making a statement of the belief of the Church. What we are doing here – and I'm content to do this – is to join in the historical and existential Church in making the statement of its belief.

PIERRE: Do you think that the average guy in the congregation thinks that? Don't you think he's supposed to think that he believes that?

MALCOLM BOYD: I think he ought to believe it for this reason. When I took my vows to be ordained, nobody made me say: "I will." It was: "I will, God being my helper." I think it would be absurd to ask people to stand up and make a personal statement out of the context of the Church about things which are this complex. As a matter of fact, most people who do so, I'm afraid, don't give it a great deal of thought. In my own case, however, as I say, I do not deny the Virgin Birth. It seems to me that this is quite possible. I don't understand; I must say this – in a world that has killed seven million Jews in Christian Germany and has bombed Hiroshima and Nagasaki, and lives in racial horror in the United States and Africa, and is on the brink in so many ways, and is involved in a sex revolution, there are greater problems.

PIERRE: Than the Virgin Birth?

MALCOLM BOYD: I think so. I feel, maybe, one of the problems of the Church looking inwardly is that it has got to look outwardly. I don't like truisms, but somebody said the Church that's supposed to be *in* the world, but not *of* it, is of it, but not in it. I have a great feeling that it's got to look out from this type of question to man, who is sweating and bleeding and suffering. Actually, there'd be no gospel if it weren't for the world. Then we wouldn't be talking about the Virgin Birth, had God not so loved the world that he decided to take human life upon himself for a few years. I think that the focus upon these questions needs very drastically to be changed.

PIERRE: But you see it's very difficult for someone, who may have a great respect for the Christian ethic but who cannot believe in life after death as you do, or in the Virgin Birth, to recite the Apostles' Creed without feeling hypocritical. This is surely a dilemma of the age.

MALCOLM BOYD: Yes, I find this with students especially, and with people in the Civil Rights Movement, who are acting much more Christian than a number of Christians are acting. More importantly, the Church often doesn't understand what it is saying. I think a great many clergymen and a great many laymen haven't thought it out – at least, this is rather obvious from their style of life. I think that the people who are content to go to a building for an hour a week, and really not make the love ethic a radical commitment in their lives, so that they come out and change the structure of society – I think they're showing that this is something unreal, this is something cut off. Their theology I find quite lacking. Because it's just this: either you can say Christ is the Lord of a narrow spectrum of life called religion, and it's about so wide (I consider this blasphemous), or you can say he is the Lord of life. I feel that *this* is unmistakable – that one comes to this.

PIERRE: And then there's the attitude towards sin. It seems to me that the Church, until recently (and subconsciously still does), equated "sin" with all forms of sex, including marital sex.

MALCOLM BOYD: Most people construe sin, certainly, to be individual, and they certainly construe it to have sexual connotations. We know that. But the horror of it is a lot of people who live so nicely by negatives – they don't do this and they don't do that, nor do they love – have no idea of sins of omission, nor have they any idea of social sins. They don't understand their involvement in the sins of Montreal, Toronto, Ottawa, Vancouver, The Anglican Church, The United Church, The Roman Catholic Church, the school system, the TV industry. Their religion is something terribly personal, and of course I think that *that* religion and Christianity are not synonymous. I think Christianity, seen as an organization, a ritual, a system of ethics of religion, a smorgasbord of religon, is vastly misunderstood. I think Bonhoeffer, the German martyr, before his death, saw something; I think he realized that this is a style of life, that this is a way of life, this involves attitudes, this involves commitments. Here's where I'd have to call myself something of a Christian existentialist, because what is a primary consideration to me is solidarity with other men. You can't say "engagement," you have to say the French *engagement*, I think. I think you have to bring a commitment in here. This is what it's about, I think. It's a dynamic, radical process.

PIERRE: Chaplain, can you be a Christian and not attend church? Is it possible?

MALCOLM BOYD: A Christian technically is baptized. A church is seen as a building. One can certainly be a Christian and not attend the building. Does being a Christian involve some participation in a sacramental life? However I feel that we're going to get away from church building, I think the parish system is probably going to go down like the "Titanic" rather quickly one of these days. I think we're going to have whole new concepts of what it means to go to church and what a Church means. To me, it is the community of the people of God. It isn't a building. It isn't a form of organization *per se*. But no, it's a tough question – one of those real rough ones. But I would have to say you can be a Christian without going to church.

THE SOAPBOX PARSON

"There are too many Bible
study groups and not nearly
enough socialist groups."

*The Reverend Donald Soper, now Baron Soper of Kingsway, but
far better known as plain "Soapbox" Soper, is that typically
British phenomenon, the radical iconoclast who has been render-
ed respectable. The best-known Methodist in the realm, he is
also the first to be made a peer. This has provided him with yet
another platform (the House of Lords) in which to denounce those
institutions that are anathema to him: the Tory establishment,
the bookmaking industry, the tobacco and liquor interests, the
Government of Southern Rhodesia, war, capital punishment, and
trading stamps.*

*But his most effective pulpits are at Tower Hill, where he
appears every Wednesday noon, and at Hyde Park, where he is
to be found every Sunday afternoon, ready, willing, and able to
answer any question put to him. I found it as stimulating to watch
Soper in action at Speaker's Corner as to see Spike Milligan on
stage in the West End. There he was, a black-gowned figure,
wearing a stout leather vest to ward off the February cold,*

43

thoroughly enjoying the give-and-take — a fascinating orator, witty, literate, quick, good-humoured, and eloquent.

It is no accident that he commands the largest crowds. He is as far removed from the mitred archbishops in their ivied chapels as he is from the stereotyped vicars in their snug parishes. Seeing this vastly amusing and thoroughly dedicated churchman, towering above his audience, his cheeks glowing russet in the biting cold, his voice cutting like the wind itself above the babble around him, I could not help but think: "This is a Man!" This is also the Church of the Sixties in its most vital form, pushing out beyond the Gothic buttresses, coming to the people, unafraid of challenge, controversy, or impolitic postures. Soper — the political activist, the ex-alderman, the Christian socialist, the weekly columnist, the broadcaster, TV star, and author — is human proof that the Church, when it wishes, can be a vital, meaningful, and communicative force in a secular world.

The interesting thing is that, until recently, Soper's example has been largely ignored by the bulk of the Church. His peerage, in 1965, came as a tribute to a man who has for almost forty years been pursuing an individual and often lonely course. It all began when a member of his congregation complained that other speakers were making points on Tower Hill but there was nobody to uphold the Methodist faith or answer the charges and arguments made against Christianity. Soper agreed to go himself, even though he felt terribly nervous. When he reached Tower Hill, he saw a man sitting on the wall who looked reasonably friendly. He asked him how to start a meeting. "Get up on the wall," was the reply. Soper clambered up, but no one paid any attention. "What do I do now?" he asked, and his new-found instructor replied: "Clap your hands." Soper began to clap and asked others to clap with him. A crowd gathered; he began to speak. "My memory is a blank after that," he has recalled. "But I know that I began to speak about the faith of Jesus as I had come to accept it and I indicated that there would be neither hymns nor prayers but I was ready to justify that faith reasonably." He's been at it ever since.

A couple of days after watching Soper in Hyde Park, I met him before the cameras in the Westbury Hotel. I began by asking him what questions troubled people most in the decade of the Sixties. What was most of his audience asking him about the Church and about the world?

▢

LORD SOPER: Well, I suppose over forty years – though I by no means know the *answers* to all the questions – I think I probably do know most of the questions that are asked. Broadly speaking, they fall into about three categories: Where do I come from? What am I doing here? Where am I going? But there's a much more local and immediate context to these questions. I should say at the moment the questions that are much more prevalent than any others are: *Is the Church making any contribution to the problems of our age? Atomic energy is here to stay; are we going to live?* You know, that sort of question. And questions, also, about the sort of world which we may or may not be inheriting later on. That's the sort of thing that people ask. They ask you about it in various ways. I mean it's not always "Mr. Speaker"; it's often "Hi, you!" or something like that.

PIERRE: Sometimes I guess they ask you pretty tough questions, which a lot of people consider embarrassing.

LORD SOPER: Yes, they don't feel inhibited, and this is the value, I think, of this kind of speaking: that it is free and uncommitted. You can ask what you like. The trouble about a parson in a pulpit is he's more or less inviolate; you can't get *at* him.

PIERRE: You can't throw eggs.

LORD SOPER: It would probably liven up some sermons if you did; but it's not considered the thing to throw eggs in church. Not that I've had eggs thrown at me at Tower Hill. Though I've been knocked off the perch by an Irishman who had too much lunch. Of course, we had a lot of trouble in the war; but then I was a pacifist and I am still. It wasn't a very agreeable proposition to put and caused a good deal of animosity and I wasn't surprised. But, generally speaking, the problem of open-air speaking is not to answer the questions *you think* people are asking but to answer the questions they *are* asking – and that's a very different proposition.

PIERRE: You've said that you want the Christian Church to take sides. Recently, in the Rhodesian Crisis, the Archbishop of Canterbury did take sides. He was attacked for doing that. Do you think he was right or wrong?

LORD SOPER: I think he was wrong. I think he said the wrong thing to begin with. As a pacifist, I think he said the wrong thing, though I'm not going along with the Conservatives – they're a lot of rascals. They disagreed with him not for religious reasons or for moral reasons at all but for other reasons altogether. Then I think

45

he said it imprecisely. I think it's very important if you're going to talk about questions like war and peace or force that you should say what you mean. And to throw a douche of Holy Water over a word like "force" doesn't really make it any different from shooting people in the head or dropping bombs on them.

PIERRE: The Christian Church really faces a dilemma in the Rhodesian crisis, doesn't it? What are you going to use against the Rhodesians to prevent them putting down the blacks if you *don't* use force?

LORD SOPER: Well, that's really asking the second question. You want to start at the first question. Supposing I was lying very ill, and the only stuff you'd got in a bottle that would help me out of my trouble was strychnine. You wouldn't use it. Now I believe that force is the ultimate evil. I think that violence – that is to say, the force of arms – is ultimately wrong. Therefore, whatever the consequences, I'm agin it. I don't start by saying: "What are you going to do?" I start by saying: "What is poison that I mustn't use?" I know I'm not in a majority. There are quite a lot of Christians, as far as I'm concerned, who haven't seen the light yet; but it *is* a dilemma. But then it's a wicked world, and you can't go on doing evil over a long time, as has been done in Africa – you can't go on exploiting people of a different colour – and then suddenly say: "Now let bygones be bygones; we'll all be good boys now and we'll do the right thing." The trouble about evil is that it paralyzes your ability to do right even when you want to.

PIERRE: In your opinion, then, force is *never* the answer?

LORD SOPER: I would never use the word "force," you see. You're using a certain amount of force to make your voice heard. When you're talking about force, you've got to define it more exactly. I believe that the force that kills, the force that is lethal, the force that is involved in guns, the force that is employed in mass violence, is *always* wrong and therefore – and I derive this from the Sermon on the Mount teachings by Jesus Christ – therefore, whatever is going to happen, I believe this is the *worst* evil. And therefore, before you can start to be constructive, you have to say "no," as I would want to do always, to that kind of armed violence.

PIERRE: You wouldn't believe, then, in unilateral disarmament, nuclear disarmament?

LORD SOPER: Yes, I went to Aldermaston. I stood up. I sat down. All that sort of thing. Although that's only half a loaf, it's better than no bread. I not only want to get rid of nuclear weapons, I want to get rid of the lot. After all I don't think you're any happier if you're blown up by a friendly conventional weapon or a hideous nuclear weapon. If you're blown up, you're blown up. It's the violence itself that I'm agin.

PIERRE: Is absolute pacifism really a viable philosophy?

LORD SOPER: No, it isn't. Not absolute. As soon as you use the word "absolute," of course, you get yourself in an awful mess. Our children during the war were evacuated when we were bombed out. The first week they went to a new school – they were seven and eight respectively, and they were asked to contribute to a Spitfire fund. Well, I'm a pacifist. What could I do? I couldn't expose my kids to my beliefs at their tender age. There's nothing worse for a little child than to isolate that child. So I gave them a bob and got it back from the headmistress the next day.

PIERRE: Well, that's getting around it. You were opposed, then, even to World War II which was allegedly fought against evils of Hitlerism – against the kind of philosophy that would condemn millions of Jews to the gas chamber. What was the alternative to force that Hitler imposed?

LORD SOPER: There was no alternative. If you've fallen over the edge of a cliff, there isn't much point in saying when you're half way down: "What do we do now?" You go to the bottom. And, therefore, when the world got to the stage it did in 1939, it was already over the cliff. I could only make my witness then to something which I couldn't turn into a philosophy or into a program. The program would have had to begin earlier on. But, if you come to think of it, the Archbishop of Canterbury said the other day that we went to the defence of Poland, which we did: which meant that Germany got half of it, the Russians got the other half, and after the war the Russians got the lot. As far as I'm concerned, the tyranny of Stalin, which was provoked and exacerbated by the war, was just as horrible as the Hitler tyranny.

PIERRE: A man in your position is always in a dilemma, isn't he?

LORD SOPER: We are always in a dilemma, and this is part of the struggle. We Christians, unfortunately, have got up in our pulpits and said it's black or white. Quite easy, you just say your prayers and do what you like. As a matter of fact, you can say your prayers till the cows come home, though that's mixing a metaphor; but if you don't realize, wherever you are, you're in some sort of compromise situation, then you never get going at all. Jesus compromised. I know this sounds, horrible, almost blasphemous, but Jesus Christ had meals with rascals like Zacchaeus. He walked on the road with rogues.

PIERRE: And he condoned slavery really – or went along with it.

LORD SOPER: Well, he didn't attack it specifically. He hadn't time among other things. And he also said – and this is very significant – he said that he wasn't going to die outside Jerusalem. If he was going to die, well, he wasn't throwing his life away, he was giving it away. And this calculated sense of making your maximum impact, even though it doesn't always have to mean compromise, is part of the Christian ethic. It's very difficult.

PIERRE: Let me turn now to a slightly different subject, though it's in the same vein. I want to read you two quotes from yourself which interlock. You've said it's quite impossible to have Christianity and Conservatism, and you've said that the capitalist system is the serious and deadly enemy of genuine religion.

LORD SOPER: Yes. That's the style!

PIERRE: I am sure you have shocked a lot of people, some of them Conservatives, by those two statements. Would you like to expand on that?

LORD SOPER: Well, I have never said that a Conservative can't get to heaven. I think he will by a circuitous route in the inscrutable wisdom of God. What I have said is that I believe the Conservative system – the capitalist system – is anti-Christian, inasmuch as the whole basis of capitalism is what is called enlightened self-interest. When you look at that phrase, "enlightend self-interest" is after all only the baptismal name for selfishness. It's no good telling me that you can be selfish and at the same time practise Christianity because the whole essence of Christianity, not that I practise it, is that you *deny* yourself. Now I'm a Socialist. I only wish the Labour Party was – and I believe it will be, one day, perhaps by God's Grace. But what surely stands out a mile is that the whole system is based on fear, greed, and incentive, and these principles are antipathetic to Christianity. We ought to say so.

PIERRE: What about people who say, "But you must have competition to progress?"

LORD SOPER: Oh, I'm all for competition. I'm all for competition within the framework of a co-operative effort. I mean, I'm in competition with other parsons in my own area of London. I think we're in the first league, so to speak – well, perhaps some people would say the second league. But this is competition within a framework. After all, I've watched your ice hockey. Have you a gentleman named Gordie Howe?

PIERRE: Yes, we certainly have.

LORD SOPER: Well, I found that quite often Gordie Howe was in

48

competition with his own side. That competition was in order to produce the best of the side itself – not in order to seek personal glory.

PIERRE: Let me ask you, in this context, if there is now operating any economic system which you consider compatible with the Christian view?

LORD SOPER: There is a good deal in the socialist system that operates in the Scandinavian countries and, though it sounds pretty ghastly to say so to some people, there's a great deal in Communism. I'm not a Communist and I've got an American visa to prove it. But, then, I'm certainly of the conviction that many things the Communists do are nearer to Christianity than many of the things the so-called Christians do. For example, it does seem to me that a system which endeavours to establish a common responsibility and endeavours to stimulate a common end is a preferable system to that which is atomistic and individualistic. Though I deplore the violence of Communism, though I deplore its lack of liberty (not that they are the only people who lack liberty), yet at the same time, in the overall patterns of life, in many places, such as China, I would think a good deal of what is happening today is nearer to the Christian gospel than anything that happened in the old days.

PIERRE: Dr. Soper, are there some occupations that are considered respectable by society which you would consider unfit for Christians?

LORD SOPER: I think there are. The manipulator of money, the entrepreneur, the middleman, the uncreative exploiter of the affluent society – I think he is intrinsically a scoundrel. That is to say, I believe he is acting in a way that is deleterious. I have no one in particular in mind, I'm happy to say, yet I think this is an anti-Christian occupation. I don't believe, therefore, that the entrepreneur, the middleman, is a Christian, and I don't think he ever can be. There are other sorts of occupations which I think are menial and therefore are un-Christian in the sense that they are undignified – you can't invest them with any sense of vocation. That is why the scientific revolution is the greatest potential boon to humanity, because you can take those jobs away from individuals and do them so that individuals are not involved.

PIERRE: I take it you're not one who believes that work is necessarily ennobling?

LORD SOPER: Oh no, it's the sort of thing that I can watch for a long time and feel quite happy if I don't have to do it myself. I think "work" is far too vague a word. When I first started my ministry in the Old Kent Road in London, where you know they "knocked 'em in the Old Kent Road," I found fellows who used to lean on a shovel for the local borough council for three or four hours a day and you might call them lazy. But the moment they came home, they were absolute beavers for work at their own rabbit hutches and that sort of thing. Now, work is occupational, and it depends on the kind of occupation as to whether it's pleasurable or not.

PIERRE: Surely work is what you don't want to do but have to do to make a living. Isn't that a pretty good definition?

LORD SOPER: Well that wouldn't do for me because I wouldn't really feel that I *had* to work.

PIERRE: Perhaps what you do isn't in that definition "work" at all. It's what you *like* to do. I'm talking about drudgery.

LORD SOPER: Drudgery, of course, is the thing for which the scientific revolution can be the answer. But drudgery is also the unremunerative work – the work that has no end product that is worth having.

PIERRE: But hasn't the Church paid a good deal of vocal service to this myth that work is a wonderful thing? "Work for the night is coming – when Man shall work no more."

LORD SOPER: Yes. That's very interesting.

PIERRE: Hasn't it supported the capitalistic system in this?

LORD SOPER: Of course: the idea that work is a very good thing for the underdog, a very good thing for the labouring classes because it keeps them in their places – but work for the other fellows is rather undignified.

PIERRE: I suspect that your Church has helped to get across the idea that leisure is naughty.

LORD SOPER: Yes, Satan finding work for idle hands to do.

PIERRE: Exactly.

LORD SOPER: Oh, you're a good socialist! I approve of this sort of activity. You see, when I think of work, I think of a contribution you make to the community in which you live, which not only enriches that community but enriches *you* as well. And, of course, this is the Christian ethic. The Christian ethic is you don't work for its own sake. You know the pre-Raphaelites said "art for art's sake." What sort of nonsense that was! There's no such thing as "art for art's sake." There's no such thing as "work for work's sake."

PIERRE: Let me change the subject and talk about Britain as a republic. I think you've expressed some fairly trenchant opinions on this.

LORD SOPER: Ah, yes. Well, a Christian, of course, must intrinsically be a republican.

PIERRE: The Anglican Church and the Archbishop of Canterbury wouldn't agree with that.

LORD SOPER: No. Well, we'll deal with them a bit later on. Surely what one has to start by asking is whether primogeniture is a virtue. I can't think that it is and I'm a life peer. I wouldn't be a hereditary peer. I'd never have been asked to be. I don't believe that you can build up a society in which, for instance, because you happen to be the son or daughter of your father and mother, therefore you enjoy the privileges and responsibilities other people don't have. This is idiotic. It isn't so much immoral as stupid.

PIERRE: Well, do you think it would be possible to elect a Queen or a King and still retain the Royal idea?

LORD SOPER: I would like us to have all the panoply. I'm all for soldiers, if they haven't got anything in their guns. I think there's something to be said for all the panoply and pomp. I like it. And I think this would be an excellent sort of system. I don't care very much what you call the person or the representative, provided that that representative epitomizes the community in which he or she lives, but does not by any virtue or primogeniture or birth have powers or authorities. That's the point.

PIERRE: Well, now, what would you do about the Royal Family if you had dictatorial powers in this country? Would you abolish them?

LORD SOPER: I wouldn't abolish them in the sense of sending them to St. Helena. I think they would probably be very glad to be rid of the job. And, therefore, if I could facilitate a decent holiday for them, or if you like, a more remunerative sort of occupation, I would. This is rather frivolous; what I mean is this: we've got a very good Queen at the moment. She does do too much racing, but apart from that I have no objection, provided that the Royal Family does not persist in being the focal point of the class system. That's what's really wrong with it.

PIERRE: She represents the class system?

LORD SOPER: She represents the class system; she can't help it.

PIERRE: Let's go back to the Archbishop of Canterbury. In your definition of the word "Christian," is the Archbishop of Canterbury a Christian?

LORD SOPER: Well, I have never defined the word Christian.

PIERRE: You must know what you mean when you use it.

LORD SOPER: I do. I was going on to say that I believe he's a saint in the New Testament sense of the word, which is a man who's been saved.

PIERRE: Let's leave it at that. I asked you a moment ago what you would do with the Royal Family if you had dictatorial powers. If you had dictatorial powers within the Christian Church, how would you change the Christian Church?

LORD SOPER: I would try to transfer the emphasis from metaphysical doctrine to moral behaviour. The early Christian Church was distinguished not so much by what it said about the next world, about God and about metaphysical matters, as by what it said about the business of living. And the early Christian Church was of course a Communist society. I think those theologians who've said that this was a mistake are in real trouble; because if the first thing that the Christian Church did on the reception of the Pentecostal Grace was to make a mistake, then I think there's something wrong with Pentecostal Grace.

PIERRE: I think you once said you wouldn't mind declaring a moratorium on all Bible reading. Why did you say that?

LORD SOPER: Oh, I think the Bible for many people is more trouble at the moment than it's worth; and for many people who *don't* read it, it's more trouble because of people who do. You see, you can quote from the Bible anything you want. If you want to make up your mind to have some slaves, or you want to run a war, then you find the Bible and look up the appropriate text. We've had enough of these evangelical jamborees with people telling us what the Bible says. The Bible says any darn thing you want it to say, and therefore it's an impossible guide. It's a magnificent servant of the Christian faith, but it's an intolerable master. And therefore, I said, not too seriously, that it would be a very good idea if we scrapped the Bible for a year. You see, there are too many Bible study groups and not nearly enough socialist groups.

PIERRE: You also said that if you had these powers you would compel every minister to preach every other sermon on a political text rather than on a religious one.

LORD SOPER: Yes, I think that would do them good. And it would do the congregations good. They'd have to vary their reading in order to get their sermon.

PIERRE: What does your ideal world consist of?

LORD SOPER: I don't know my ideal world. . . .

PIERRE: It wouldn't include the Beatles, from what I hear.

LORD SOPER: I'm not particularly impressed by the Beatles, no. I was brought up on Fats Waller and Jelly Roll Morton. I used to play jazz, and I thought that when my children grew to the age when they would appreciate their father's performance they'd think that I was fine – but not a bit of it. They think that I'm a square. Two of them are Beatle fans, but the other two have seen the light. They are very interested in music, and I wish I knew them better. I find it very difficult, this gulf. I think there is a very real gulf now.

PIERRE: This is one of the problems we all face.

LORD SOPER: I think it's a very serious problem. Somehow we've got to try and get inside this somewhat curious attitude. They're tremendously honest and frank, and they're not nearly as covert and hypocritical as my kind of world was. But they are the first secular generation, and this is what's really wrong. Their morals seem to me to be a superstructure without a foundation, and their children, I think, are not even going to get the superstructure.

PIERRE: One final question, Lord Soper. You rub shoulders with everybody. What's worrying people about the Church today in this country?

LORD SOPER: I wish more people *were* worrying. Those who do worry about the Church worry because they see the Church on the edge of life instead of at the centre. They feel that the Church is irrelevant. They don't necessarily disbelieve or believe. They're very dubious about many of its doctrines, but principally they don't really think that it makes much difference. And deep down in their hearts they wish it did.

PIERRE: What you're saying is that people don't care, and this must worry you.

LORD SOPER: It worries me a lot.

THE CHURCH
AND THE PILL

"I thought: 'Is this God
being very tactful?' "

*In the summer of 1965, my producer, Elsa Franklin, filed away
for future reference a newspaper feature about a Roman Catholic woman psychiatrist who had defied her Church and been
publicly refused Communion because she had opened a birth-
control clinic at Wallasey, near Liverpool. Later that year, when
the TV program crossed the Atlantic, we persuaded this woman
to come to London for a television appearance.*

*Dr. Anne Biezanek's background is a singular one. She was
raised a Quaker but became a convert to Roman Catholicism at
the age of nineteen. Her new faith seems to have been inexorably
intertwined with an adolescent interest in Poland, which occupied
her during the war and immediate post-war years. She felt a
great guilt over Poland and the Polish settlement – a guilt fed by
the poems of Chesterton and Belloc. Shortly after her conversion,
she married a Polish ex-officer, Jan Biezanek. He had been a
Judge Advocate in his native country but, unable to practise in
Britain, had become a steward in the merchant navy. To Dr.*

*Biezanek, Poland was identified with "the perfect religious con-
dition." Even for a convert, her faith seems to have been extreme.
She told me when we met that until very recent years she had
felt the United Nations to be the work of the devil.*

*Obviously she has been through a trying emotional experience
of lengthy duration, and one which, no doubt, will be duplicated
to a greater or lesser extent in many a Catholic domicile as the
Sixties roll on. When I met her, however, she was the picture of
glowing health – a strapping and comely country girl of thirty-
seven, with ruddy cheeks, an enviable complexion, and seven
children back in Wallasey.*

*I suspect that in the transcript that follows a fellow psychia-
trist might find some fascinating clues to a complex and, perhaps,
still-troubled personality; but I must say that she answered my
own questions in a robust and forthright fashion, without any
false emotion or hesitation. Here was a woman, one felt, who had
thought things through over a long period of time. Indeed she has
recently described her experience in a book of her own:* All
Things New.

*We began by talking about her career in psychiatry, and the
difficulty of pursuing that career as the babies began to arrive,
one upon the other.*

☐

DR. BIEZANEK: I was quite ready to abandon that actually. I was
prepared to abandon it as the family increased. The difficulty was
that my husband, as an exile, had increasing difficulty in making
his way. You know, we hadn't a home.

PIERRE: Now the first thing you did when you were faced with this
kind of a problem was to go to your priest.

DR. BIEZANEK: Yes, I did. I asked the advice of the chaplain at the
hospital where I was working.

PIERRE: What advice did he give you?

DR. BIEZANEK: He advised me to see a good priest.

PIERRE: Wasn't *he* a good priest?

DR. BIEZANEK: Well, he said I should see someone really good, a
holy man and an intelligent man.

PIERRE: A spiritual adviser?

56

DR. BIEZANEK: Yes.

PIERRE: Now I understand that he told you that you must obey this man implicitly.

DR. BIEZANEK: Well, he said, if you want this direction to work. . . .

PIERRE: . . . You must obey him?

DR. BIEZANEK: Yes. He said it's no good going to find a good and spiritual priest and then pleasing yourself. I mean, you couldn't have it both ways.

PIERRE: Yours was the problem of having an unknown number of children and still trying to work.

DR. BIEZANEK: Yes. It was the problem of trying to hold down a responsible job upon which our home depended because, you see, our house went with my job.

PIERRE: So what did the spiritual adviser say: "Quit, don't take a job, stay home."

DR. BIEZANEK: No, he didn't because he knew we absolutely depended upon the job and my income.

PIERRE: He couldn't say: "Stop having children," could he?

DR. BIEZANEK: No, he couldn't, really, and he didn't even suggest it, because he knew the circumstances of my marriage. He knew that my husband and I were a couple that really needed one another, and he wasn't so irresponsible as to say that that wasn't necessary. His line was that God would send children when he thought best, and I should continue with my job, and God would provide everything that was necessary.

PIERRE: But God did *not* provide in your case, did he?

DR BIEZANEK: No, no, he didn't. He provided children, yes.

PIERRE: But he gave you a great deal of mental unease.

DR. BIEZANEK: Well, more than that. I mean he provided me with a complete physical and mental breakdown.

PIERRE: What do you mean by "mental breakdown"? Were you confined in an institution, or were you just sick?

DR. BIEZANEK: Oh, I was sick, and it was suggested to me that I should go to an institution, and I went for the sake of my parents and family.

PIERRE: As a psychiatrist, can you diagnose your own condition at this time? Was it worry, guilt, what?

DR. BIEZANEK: No, I was beginning to be able to diagnose. This was nine years ago, and I'm only just beginning to get it into perspective. It was physical exhaustion because I was anaemic; I was losing a lot of weight.

PIERRE: A lot of children running around underfoot?

DR. BIEZANEK: Yes, I had three children under four. I was feeding the baby, and I was miscarrying. I was in a full-time job. I was up two or three times a night with my children. I was up two or three times a night perhaps with my patients. And combined with that, I was resisting the idea that I was breaking down because my spiritual director had said this would work. God had to see me through; therefore, I mustn't fail God.

PIERRE: Did he talk about martyrdom?

DR. BIEZANEK: Oh yes, he did indeed. He said that he knew wonderful Catholic mothers who had been told by doctors that if they had another child after they had ten or eleven they would die; and he said that they had accepted that as martyrdom. That, he said, was fine Catholic spirituality. When he said this, I was beginning to have my first serious doubts, because I didn't hear of any of these martyrs being sung. In fact, I was seeing a lot of them not quite dead in the mental hospital I was working in.

PIERRE: Did this cause you to turn away from your husband sexually?

DR. BIEZANEK: Well, that happened later. You know, quite a lot of good Catholic wives say to me, with some irritation: "Well, couldn't you have learnt some self-control?" Well, what I'd like to point out is that, by the time you've had a lot of children quickly, and you're run off your feet all day, to give up sex would be a positive blessing for a woman. It's not the first thing she wants. What she wants is a night's sleep and time to eat and all that. I mean she's not looking for sex, but it's a question of fulfilling her obligations as a wife. You see, a woman can say to her husband: "Let's give up sex," and he'll say: "Yes, let's." But sex is what, in fact, happens.

PIERRE: It's really like saying: "Let's give up marriage," to a certain extent, isn't it?

DR. BIEZANEK: Well, it could be. But I think if the couple has been married for a number of years and has shared a bed and has developed a habit, I think it's quite impossible to say, "Give up sex."

PIERRE: Now, you finally decided to quit your job, and then you came to the much more difficult decision, as a Roman Catholic; you decided to take the birth-control pill.

DR. BIEZANEK: Well, this happened quite a lot later. It happened two babies and a nervous breakdown later. I had two nervous breakdowns.

PIERRE: So it was quite a while before you came round to that point?

DR. BIEZANEK: Oh, yes. I had begun to get sort of a bit sticky in my thinking. I'd made my private observation about these unsung martyrs; but I still couldn't see a way out, so I gave up my job. I thought: "Well, the first thing I must do is to concentrate on looking after the children I've got and being a full-time wife and mother. Let's see if we can play it this way, if it will work." We lost our home, of course, when I lost my job. My parents gave us a home in their house. For the next two or three years, I suppose, most of that time I was really recovering mentally and physically from the last breakdown. But then, of course, I did have more children and more miscarriages.

PIERRE: You have a total of seven children?

DR. BIEZANEK: Yes. It was when the seventh was conceived that my parents said that they had had enough. Their house wasn't very large, and they were really frightened for me because they could not see what the future was going to be. It seemed to them that I ran a very good chance of dying.

PIERRE: But the Church is quite prepared for you to have twenty children?

DR. BIEZANEK: Well it's not quite fair to say the Church, because some members of the Church would say: "You should separate from your husband because, obviously, as long as you two are living together, you're going to breed." Others would say: "The thing that you must do is to learn self-control or practise a rhythm." Then I'd point out that my husband was away at sea a lot of the time, and he used to come home at odd moments, and one can't practise rhythm under those circumstances, even if it was reliable; and then those people would say: "Well, perhaps you should separate from your husband." Then other people used to say: "Well, what you're needing is more faith in God." So I would think: "Well, I really haven't got a problem; I *must* have more faith in God."

PIERRE: So you were going through a mental argument with yourself. At what point did you make the decision that you would take the pill?

DR. BIEZANEK: I didn't just suddenly do this. This all took place over a period of two or three years. The seventh baby was born, and following that I began to realize that I was heading for my third nervous breakdown. I knew that this would be for keeps, because I didn't have any further resources to draw on. I mean I knew now that any arguments such as more faith, more effort, or working hard, or concentrating more on the duties of the household, all that sort of thing were useless. I knew that I was doing that to my fullest capacity. I thought to myself: "I'm strong and I'm competent." I didn't have an awful lot of money, but I was told by many people that I ran a home very well, and my children were very fine children. And I felt that I was making a reasonable success of my job. But I knew it was getting too big for me even *without* more children. You see, I wasn't sleeping sufficiently because the younger ones cried at night. My husband was away most of the time, so I didn't have any help from him. I had very little money. I began to notice that I was losing weight again, that I was shrieking at the children, that I didn't want to have anything to do with my husband when he came home. I began to sort of dread the prospect of him walking through the door. It was a sort of situation that I would have to respond to, and I didn't want to. I began to remember that, in fact, was what the psychiatrists had said to me five years previously and three – I began to think about that for the first time. At first, you see, I had regarded this as an insidious Protestant brainwash, to try and get me to do something that was immoral and offensive to God. But I began to think: "Well, perhaps I should just look back over what they said and think about it." And I began to see that they hadn't actually wanted my harm at all. They'd put a certain pressure on me to use the pill, but only in so far as they had stated an opinion. I thought: "They haven't, in fact, fed me the pill by stomach pump or anything like that. I am free, and they wish me well." They wanted my health, those men, and it took me two or three years to realize that they weren't trying to get to me. I began to think: "They're right. I *am* going to break down. I recognize the signs." If I went into mental hospital again on the same wicket – that the Catholic Church teaches truth, and that it's contrary to God's law to use birth control, and that by resisting it I was being a martyr to the faith – then I'd go into that mental hospital, and I'd stand in a corner and I'd stare and see visions of Christ appearing, and I knew I'd be doing that for the rest of my life. Because it's what suited me. You see, I would be turning my back on the world and on my responsibilities, which were seven children. I thought: "Now, this is the most dangerous moment of my life. I must do something about this." I saw my doctor, who said that he thought the pill would be a good thing. And I thought: "Oh, yes, the pill!" Of course, whenever I'd thought of birth control, I'd thought of things like sheaths. I thought they were very rotten sorts of things.

60

But the pill! I thought: "Is this God being very tactful? You know, sort of *offering* me a pill? I could swallow a pill, couldn't I?" I thought to myself.

PIERRE: You were able to come to terms with your religion?

DR. BIEZANEK: Oh no, not quite that. I was a long way from doing that. But I thought: "I can physically swallow a pill." But I couldn't physically do anything else at all, you see. I'm incapable of it, and so I got this prescription from the chemist. That was a nasty moment, too, going into the chemist to get a prescription made up for birth-control pills because I was very conscious of being a model Catholic – going to church every Sunday with my large sort of model family. I felt I had been fighting this great battle against sexual corruption, you see. And here was I going into a chemist to get birth-control pills. I felt probably the chemist was talking about it and telling his assistant. It would get all round the grapevine and everyone would know. And I thought: "Even if they do, it can't be helped; it's what I've *got* to do." I brought the pills home and put them on the mantelpiece, and I looked at them for the next fortnight because I didn't have to start taking them for a fortnight. Then I frantically wrote to *all* the Catholics I knew – a number of priests and educated Catholics – explaining what had come upon me, and could they think of any alternative to my situation, because if they could before May 25, when I had to start and take them, I would be very pleased. Most of them didn't answer, but some wrote back and simply said they were sorry to hear I was turning my back on my faith which, of course, wasn't an answer to my question. But I felt pretty narked about that – that this was their attitude . . . friends . . . Catholic relations . . . who had never come up with any concrete proposal of any kind.

PIERRE: It was no solution for you.

DR. BIEZANEK: No solution. I said: "I'm being destroyed, you see, by this." This taking the pill I regarded as what was going to destroy my soul. I felt: "Oh, well, all right; my soul has got to be destroyed. But I've got to look after these children. I've got to do this." *But can you people suggest a way to save my soul for the faith?* Not one of them could suggest any way at all.

PIERRE: Now, the Church, in effect, has really publicly called you a sinner, which is a pretty rough thing for a devout Catholic to be called in public?

DR. BIEZANEK: Well, I don't think really it's true to say that the Church has called me a sinner. My bishop has implied it, but I do think one has to distinguish between the hierarchy and the Church.

PIERRE: All right. Now I'll let you finish your story about starting the birth-control clinic.

DR. BIEZANEK: Well, when I started taking these pills, the parish priest said he couldn't give me Communion. For several months I was terribly upset about this. I was furious and bewildered. I couldn't work anything out, but as a result of taking the pills my health began to improve. I began to put on weight. I stopped shrieking at the children. I began to realize that, in fact, my life was saved, and the home was saved, and the marriage was saved. Then I thought that the parish priest was wrong in saying that I couldn't receive Holy Communion. What I'd done I'd done for the best of motives, and I felt: "God is with me, manifestly with me." And I went and told him this and said I was coming back to Communion, and it was up to him to refuse it to me if he chose. But he didn't refuse it me, and for the next year I went to Communion with my family, though I was on the pill.

PIERRE: The interesting thing is that the Church did not refuse you Communion as long as this did not become a *cause célèbre*.

DR. BIEZANEK: Well, I went to see the bishop, you see, and I said: "Well, I'm a doctor, and I know from my own experience that this is a very important health matter with women. It nearly destroyed me mentally and physically, and when I begin to practise again, as I will be able to now – now that I've stopped having babies – I will have to take this matter up as a doctor with my patients. I'll have to tell them, if they want to know, why I don't have any more children. I won't and I can't pretend to them that my husband and I are abstaining when we're not. I'm going to tell them the truth: that I think that perhaps for them the pill might be the same answer as it's been for me." I said to the bishop: "I think you should know this – that I think this, and that I am receiving Communion." He just gazed at me and said that he couldn't approve of what I was doing; it was against the law of God. I said: "Well, that's your opinion; what I want you to know is that I have a different opinion." And the more I thought about it, the more important I thought the issue was. It had saved my life, and I'd nearly been destroyed. I thought: "There will be other women who don't have my education, who don't have my resources, who perhaps would benefit by having someone like me to advise them; because I'd had no one who understood what it was like to be a Catholic in this position, to advise and help me." And that's why I decided to open a birth-control clinic. There wasn't any publicity attached to that to start with. I simply let it be known amongst a few people I knew in the town that I was prepared to give this advice, and I gave it. The newspapers came to hear of this and interviewed me. They asked me if I would speak to them, and I said yes, because I had nothing to hide.

PIERRE: I think the point we should make, Doctor, is that you never sought publicity.

DR. BIEZANEK: No, I didn't. It's just that I've nothing to hide. But that's how it's come about, and it just so happens that what I say people seem to find interesting.

PIERRE: Of course, it's interesting. Surely every Catholic, sooner or later, is going to face up to the kind of dilemma that you faced up to.

DR. BIEZANEK: Well, anyway, it got into the papers, and then I had a short interview on television, and following upon that I was refused Communion in the Church. And then the papers asked me if there had been any reaction, and I said: "Well, yes, unfortunately I have been refused Communion, and the parish priest has told me I must write and apologize to the bishop." I wrote to the bishop and asked him what sort of apology would be deemed adequate. I wasn't quite sure what I had to apologize for – perhaps he would tell me. He said what I was doing was contrary to the teaching of the Church and would have to stop if I was to receive the Sacrament. "Well," I thought, "that's *his* opinion." The fact is the position hasn't changed in the last year I've been running this clinic and going to Communion. I don't think he's answered my question. What is my crime, for which I must now be deprived of the source of all life?

PIERRE: But why wouldn't you be happier in the bosom of the Protestant Church? Why the Catholic Church?

DR. BIEZANEK: Because I *am* a Catholic, you see. I am what I am because I became a Catholic . . . because I kept the Catholic faith . . . because I believe what the Catholic Church teaches about the Christian religion.

PIERRE: But you don't believe everything the Catholic Church teaches. In certain areas you are going against their teaching.

DR. BIEZANEK: Yes, because I don't really think this is part of the teaching of the Catholic Church. It's become so.

PIERRE: The Pope himself at the United Nations has made it pretty clear where he stands.

DR. BIEZANEK: Well, in this matter he is but one individual – one Roman Catholic. He's saying what *he* thinks.

PIERRE: He's not infallible?

DR. BIEZANEK: No. It's never been taught that the Pope's infallible in every matter. It's only if he's speaking infallibly, but no Pope has yet spoken infallibly on this issue.

PIERRE: I know one of the reasons you feel able to carry on in the face of so much clerical opposition is that you have received so much support, in this country and elsewhere, from other people, especially Catholics; I want to ask you now whether you don't feel perhaps you're a better Christian?

DR. BIEZANEK: Yes, I think by being refused Communion so often (because I've often gone for it and not been given it), I've been obliged to look for God elsewhere than in the Blessed Sacrament. It's not that I don't believe he's there; it's just that it's a waste of time me looking there. I've been obliged to look for him in the souls of my fellow men. And, you know, I often feel I find him there.

THE UNINHIBITED
ATHEIST

"I am prepared to accept
the existence of ANY God."

*One of the five million interesting things about Gordon Sinclair
is that he found himself well launched into a brand new career as
the Sixties opened. He has had several careers, including two distinct periods of national prominence. He was a major figure in
the Thirties when, as a globe-trotting reporter for the* Toronto
Daily Star *and* Star Weekly, *he caught the public imagination with
his uninhibited and highly personal journalism. When he turned
to radio, his audience became, largely, a local one. It was* Front
Page Challenge, *the* CBC's *long-running, high-rated weekly panel
show that gave him a national platform once again. By the Sixties,
Gordon Sinclair – opinionated, blunt, abrasive, and unpredictable
– had become an imperishable Canadian institution.* Why? *What
was there about this free-wheeling, loud-spoken, and ungram-
matical ex-newspaperman that caught the public's fancy and made
him a better-known figure than the Prime Minister?*

*There are several answers. One is that Sinclair plays no role:
he is himself and there is no one else like him; and the nation*

65

understands this. Someone once confronted Sinclair with a list of factual errors he'd committed in his reporting. He merely shrugged: "Well," he said, "that's me." For he is a man without pretense, projecting no false image: his gaudy costumes, his wild irrelevancies, his utter lack of pomposity, his fondness for Old Stepfather, his hatred of fluoridated water – all this is the real Sinclair, on and off camera.

He is exactly as old as the century itself – and he refers to himself constantly now as "the old man" – but he is, in actuality, a small boy. His confidence, sparkle, and zest are those of a teenager. In the seventh decade of his life, he manages to fit the mood of his times far better than some who are half his age. In recent years, especially since he has become a national figure, he has publicly cultivated two aspects of his personality: his abiding delight in all matters monetary, and his abiding contempt for so-called Biblical truth. One might suspect that his periodical recital of his personal worth, his endless fears about the stock market and the state of taxation, and his continuing curiosity regarding the affluence of panel guests would make him a Silas Marner in the public's eye. Far from it – his audience delights in this intoxication with money. One might also suspect that his regular attacks on the concepts of God, Heaven and Hell, his bullying of priests, missionaries, and bishops who appear as panel-show guests, and his constant reiteration of his own free-thinking beliefs would cause him to be pilloried in a God-fearing nation. If this was ever true, it is not true in the Sixties. The new mood of the "listening church" is such that even the prelates love him – or pretend to. When the Suffragen Bishop of Toronto appeared on Front Page Challenge, Sinclair was the only panelist able to call him by his first name. "Hi, Harry!" said Gordon. "Hi, Gordon!" said Harry. They had lunched together the previous week.

By being himself Gordon Sinclair has made iconoclasm pay off. He has become a legend in his own time and – dare one say it? – a "grand old man." When he appeared on my program in September, 1965, I chided him with this. The label, I suggested, could easily destroy him. The public adulation could render him so lovable that he would become ineffective.

▢

GORDON SINCLAIR: Oh, I don't think you need to worry too much. I still get a lot of hate mail and books and pamphlets on religion, you know. "Have you read this?" and all that.

PIERRE: You told me when you came to the studio today that the switchboard at CFRB, where you do your daily newscast, was already lit up because you had reviewed a book by Billy Graham. You didn't like the book?

GORDON SINCLAIR: No. It's called *World Aflame*, and it's an absolute cliché from beginning to end, Pierre. It says the same things that Aimee Semple McPherson said, that Pastor Moody said, that Billy Sunday said. You know: "Take heed, man! Because the world is at the end of its rope . . . the world is coming to an end; and your only hope and salvation is at the throne of Jesus." He never comes to grips with anything practical at all. It's supposed to be about the world and the people of the world, but does he look at racial segregation? Or over-population? Or hunger and war? Not at all! Not at all! It's just emotion. It's a dreadful book. If he made a mistake in sending me a copy for review, and I reviewed it in the way I did, then I think they should take the consequences. That's all there is to it. You don't ask favours when they review *your* books.

PIERRE: No, I don't. How long have you held your present religious beliefs? You must have gone through a change at some time.

GORDON SINCLAIR: I was brought up in a most devoted home. I taught Sunday School, I taught the Bible. My being at odds with religion really started in 1931, when I first went to India and saw this enormous suffering. A lot of people said it was from the death of my daughter. This is not true at all. I went to India in 1931; my daughter died in 1942 – eleven years later. So it had no connection whatsoever.

PIERRE: When you finally die, I'm told there's not going to be a gravestone on your grave.

GORDON SINCLAIR: No, I'm opposed to gravestones as being a sort of a supreme ego. It's stupid. I oppose gravestones for anybody. I took care of the funeral of my parents and of my daughter, and I certainly wouldn't put a stone over them.

PIERRE: Will you have a religious service of any kind? What will happen when Gordon Sinclair finally leaves this earth? What instructions have you left behind?

GORDON SINCLAIR: Well, I've asked that there be no religious service. In fact, I've asked that, in the death notice in terms of myself, they simply put the name "Alan Gordon Sinclair, June 3, 1900," and then dash, the date that I died. This is what I've asked. I wouldn't be surprised if these desires are sort of overcome, I don't know. I have many friends, you know, in the ministry.

PIERRE: I suspect half the preachers in town will be fighting to bury you.

GORDON SINCLAIR: Well, a lot of them have said they'd certainly be glad to do that. I know a lot of clergymen in a personal way. I go to their homes and they come to mine and we visit and we argue.

PIERRE: When you buried your daughter, did you have a religious service at that time?

GORDON SINCLAIR: Yes, we did. My wife at this time did not share my agnostic viewpoints and wanted a religious ceremony, and we did have one.

PIERRE: Will she have one for you if she outlives you?

GORDON SINCLAIR: My wife now, to a large extent, shares my views but doesn't like to talk about them. She gets a few crank calls on the telephone which bother her. We've got a phone that's right in the book. Anybody can look us up. There used to be, you know, five Gordon Sinclairs in the Toronto phonebook.

PIERRE: I'll bet the other four were mad at you.

GORDON SINCLAIR: Yeah. Well, they're all out, and I'm still there.

PIERRE: Do you fear death, Gordon?

GORDON SINCLAIR: Oh, not at all.

PIERRE: Are you in any sense a hypochondriac about your health? It's been said that you are.

GORDON SINCLAIR: Oh, this is not true at all. I'm relieved of all the worry of whether I'm going to go to Heaven or whether I'm going to go to Hell. I'm convinced that there is no Heaven and never was and never will be, and I'm equally satisfied there's no Hell and never was and never will be a Hell, and that death is the end and there is nothing else. I will live on in my sons and my grandsons, and this is a good way to have it.

PIERRE: You know, it's interesting that in this country you're able not only to voice the opinions of an atheist but also, really, to prosper by them. I wonder if this would be true if you were operating in the United States as a radio commentator, television personality, and journalist?

GORDON SINCLAIR: I would say emphatically not. I'm just niggling here, but I rather reject the word "atheist" on this ground, Pierre. An atheist, as I understand it, is a person who does not believe in the existence of any god. Well, I am prepared to accept that there are all the gods that the different outfits say there are. In other words, they go from A for Allah, B for Buddha, C for Christ, right on down to Z for Zeus. The Christians have three. The Hindus have 220. I'm prepared to believe that these people are honest when they worship their god. Therefore, what I am is perhaps a Deist.

PIERRE: It's not that you don't believe in *any* gods; you believe in *all* gods?

GORDON SINCLAIR: That's right. I accept them all. And, therefore, it's stupid to say, *as* a Christian, that we have three gods – one of them is a ghost – and that the people that believe in Allah are stupid fools. And that Allah does not exist. Because, I say, they're all around. Accept whatever one you want.

PIERRE: Well, in that sense, you're the most religious man around.

GORDON SINCLAIR: I guess so.

PIERRE: You believe in more gods than anybody else!

GORDON SINCLAIR: Well, then, don't let them call me an atheist.

PIERRE: You've got your tongue in your cheek, Gordon, and you know it. Come on.

GORDON SINCLAIR: Okay.

PIERRE: Tell me more about the kind of angry phone calls and crank letters you get. I know you're much more sensitive than you like to let on. I suspect you're always personally upset when you get a really rough letter.

GORDON SINCLAIR: I don't know about "always"; but certainly I *have* been hurt and I *have* been angered and I *have* gone to the management of CFRB and I've said: "I don't want any more of this. I don't have to submit to this." This would be on days when you get it right, left, and centre. You get stopped on the street. You get nasty letters. You get dirty phone calls. And your family gets other dirty phone calls at home. You might be tired or kind of beat. You get all of that in one day. You say: "To hell with this; this is not my job; I don't have to put up with this." But then you'll go dozens of days in which the mail and the phone calls and even the stopping on the street are all friendly. And I get much more that's friendly than is unfriendly.

PIERRE: Has the friendly mail and the friendly reaction been increasing lately? I suspect it has been. You've become a sort of institution.

GORDON SINCLAIR: To me, it's a regional thing, Pierre.

PIERRE: How do you mean?

GORDON SINCLAIR: I am a national figure now through *Front Page*

Challenge and magazines and so on. They know me all across the country, and currently – as a matter of fact, for almost two years – I've been getting a steady stream of abusive mail from Saskatchewan and quite a bit also from Alberta. Now this could be that Manning, the Premier of Alberta, is a very religious man who conducts a Bible society; perhaps he's got his people there conditioned, and they aren't conditioned to accept my type of guy. But I get a lot of abusive mail from those two provinces. I get some from rural Ontario, and that practically ends it.

PIERRE: Is most of the abusive mail based on your religious beliefs or lack of them?

GORDON SINCLAIR: Nearly all now. It used to be on other different things – that I was cocky, that I was arrogant and over-confident and egotistical. Well, the big point is, as you know, of course, I *do* believe in myself. My own personal slogan is: "To thine own self be true," with emphasis on the "self"; and I believe that. I believe "he can who thinks he can." I can beat anybody some days in my mind. I can lick 'em. Well, all right, this is an attitude that angers some people. But that kind of an anger seems to be dying out.

PIERRE: I sometimes feel that you're very proud of the fact that you've gone as far as you have with so little formal schooling.

GORDON SINCLAIR: Well, I don't know if "proud" is the word, Pierre. But it's the truth that I went to a high school for nine months. I thought I was doing all right, but a recruiter was allowed to come along to the high school where I attended – Riverdale in Toronto – and seek employees for the banks. This was in World War I. They wanted young men to go into the banks as clerks to relieve the older men who were going to war because they wouldn't, at that time, take any girls. One of them made me an offer: come into the Bank of Nova Scotia. My mother thought it would be a pretty fair idea, so I went at the salary of $25 a month and I stayed with the bank about a year, and I never went back to school. Now I have done quite well, but it couldn't be done today – you know that. The academic level must be there.

PIERRE: Have you ever regretted that you didn't finish high school and go on to, say, university?

GORDON SINCLAIR: Yes, I have. I've regretted it several times but, of course, I don't know how I would have turned out.

PIERRE: Maybe you wouldn't have been as successful in your terms.

GORDON SINCLAIR: It's quite possible. I was a very aggressive young guy. I was going to make my mark, and I don't know that I would have been the other way. Now I used to sneak into the University

70

of Toronto. I was transferred to the bank at Queen and McCaul and frequently had to deliver drafts up around the area of the University of Toronto, and there was one professor there who absolutely fascinated me. That was James Mavor – a huge man with a great beard, a most fascinating man. He could tell an anecdote better than anybody I know in Canada except Greg Clark. Jimmy Mavor was terrific, and I used to sneak in and listen to him.

PIERRE: Gordon, you were once described in print as "a man without sympathy, feeling, or religious beliefs." Do you agree with that quotation?

GORDON SINCLAIR: Oh, no. I have such sympathy that I sometimes cry. And feeling! I have all kinds of feeling, of course. That was a stupid remark. The fellow, whoever wrote it – I don't remember who it was –

PIERRE: You don't know who wrote it?

GORDON SINCLAIR: No.

PIERRE: Gordon Sinclair wrote it in an article in *Maclean's* in 1948. A piece about Gordon Sinclair by Gordon Sinclair described Gordon Sinclair as "a man without sympathy, feeling, or religious beliefs." Now, why did you say that then . . . ?

GORDON SINCLAIR: I have no idea.

PIERRE: . . . If you didn't believe it?

GORDON SINCLAIR: I have no idea, but I might possibly have believed it in 1948: I might have felt like saying: "Well, I don't have feelings; I'm superior to feelings," or something, but I have no idea, no. I have no idea at all. I can break into tears if I hear "O Canada."

PIERRE: But not "God Save the Queen?"

GORDON SINCLAIR: Oh, no. That's quite different.

PIERRE: You once told June Callwood that, "I am not close to any-one."

GORDON SINCLAIR: I think that's true.

PIERRE: Not even to your wife and children?

GORDON SINCLAIR: Well, I don't think so. I don't say this as bragging. I don't say this as being a loner for the purpose of being a loner. But I think, at heart, I'm a loner, yeah.

PIERRE: Does this mean that you can't unburden yourself of your true feelings to your closest, most intimate friends, and relations?

GORDON SINCLAIR: Yes, "can't" would seem to be the best word, yes, although I've not seriously tried. But I don't, no. I don't un-burden myself to people.

PIERRE: Not even to your family? Do you find a barrier between yourself and your children, then?

GORDON SINCLAIR: I think we have an excellent relationship. And yet there might be a barrier there, yeah.

PIERRE: Of course, you're not unique in this. I think many parents these days find they have a barrier. But how about yourself and your wife?

GORDON SINCLAIR: I think there's lots of things we hold from each other. I have a good relationship with Gladys, too. We quarrel and disagree, and we have all sorts of things we do together. We're quite companionable, but I don't think that we reveal everything to each other.

PIERRE: Probably very few married couples can say that they do. Maybe it's a good thing they don't.

GORDON SINCLAIR: I think so. We live almost separately in the same building, but we each have our own apartments. We have a big house, and the children have been gone for quite awhile, and when the children went, we each had our own apartment made over, and we live separately with our own quarters.

PIERRE: Why did you do that?

GORDON SINCLAIR: I guess it was my idea. I think it's a good idea. We're together in the living room and dining room. We have our meals together, and so on. We play cards together, cribbage, and so on; but actual living quarters, they're quite separate.

PIERRE: Gordon, I'm not going to ask you how much money you make, partly because everybody seems to know these days.

GORDON SINCLAIR: It's a corny question.

PIERRE: I think I was the first to ask it, six years ago, on *Closeup*. That started the whole money bit.

GORDON SINCLAIR: You started me on a whole lot of trouble. We agreed at that time that I wouldn't duck any questions, and I didn't. You asked me about religion and money, and it got me into a lot of a bind. I'm still in it, I guess.

PIERRE: Sure you are, and you're prospering. But I'd like to ask you something about your *attitude* to money. It seems to me that in you there's a basic insecurity – even though you have so many hundreds of thousands in the bank – that you still don't feel that you have quite enough for your own security. Or have you reached that point now where you feel you've got enough?

GORDON SINCLAIR: I may be insecure. I don't really know. But I feel that the yardstick for success in Canada, 1965, is money. This is the thing by which you're judged. I have suffered in the past for

72

want of money. I was turned away from the Hospital for Sick Children twice – the only twice I went – I was personally turned away, and I was personally present with my dying daughter when she was turned away because we didn't have instant cash. My daughter was dying on a Sunday morning at about twenty minutes to twelve midday, and the temperature was twenty below zero. She was left on a stretcher in the foyer of the Hospital for Sick Children because I didn't have cash. Now this is Toronto. And so I have a high regard for money. And I am determined that I'll have money. I've had it a long time, this determination. And I've got the money, and I make no apology for it. I think the most dreadful thing is the mealy-mouthed rich man – he's a poor little Uriah Heep going around pretending he's nothing. A poor, little, shrinking violet. Well, I am not.

PIERRE: You drive a Rolls-Royce.

GORDON SINCLAIR: Yes, I do.

PIERRE: Do you think that the fact that you drive this Rolls-Royce and the fact that you are now known to be reasonably wealthy has changed your image in the eyes of, say, the business community or the people to whom money means a great deal?

GORDON SINCLAIR: No, it's changed my image in the eyes of *my* kind of people: the newsboys, the barbers, the truck drivers, the cab drivers – these are my kind of people, and they respect me. And this is the thing that I didn't really expect. I thought when I got a Rolls-Royce that they would look on me as a kind of a snob that stepped out of my class. Instead of that, they take the attitude: "By God, one of our guys made it." Yeah, and they're very friendly. I have never had an undesirable crack made in my whole life by anybody of that type about the Rolls-Royce, or the fact that I've got a half a million dollars, or something like that. I have had from people of a somewhat more elevated social stature than myself, the odd crack – sort of: "Who do you think you are?" Or, "A Rolls-Royce doesn't give you privileges," or something. Well, I know it doesn't give me privileges, and I'm certainly not socially graceful, and I'm not likely to be – but my kind of fella, he likes me for it.

PIERRE: Does the Rolls-Royce help you or hurt you with traffic cops and parking people?

GORDON SINCLAIR: When I first got it. I got it on the nineteenth of August, 1961, trying to beat the Ontario Sales Tax which came in eleven days later. A three-percent sales tax on a Rolls-Royce would be pretty high, so I thought: "If I'm ever going to get one, now is the time to get one." And I did. Now, in the first ninety days after that, I had four summonses, and I was convicted four times. The maximum number of points you could lose in Ontario at that time was twelve and I lost nine just bang, bang, bang. I thought this was stupid. I'd been driving an automobile since 1916. Now that's quite a record. In 1916, I was sixteen years old, and I drove a Rio and I drove a Gray Dort – cars that have vanished. Well, I had never from that minute to now had an accident. I'd driven cars in Europe, I'd driven cars in Asia, I'd driven cars in South America, and in this country, and yet I was about to be deprived of my right to drive. I think it was the Rolls, there. My member of the Ontario Legislature was the then-Minister of Transport, Leslie Rountree. I said to him: "Les, look what you're doing. You're going to ground me on this thing, and I've never had an accident from 1916 to this second; so this is a stupid law." He raised the points to fifteen.

PIERRE: I wonder if he raised them for Gordon Sinclair?

GORDON SINCLAIR: I don't know. It would maybe get him in a bind if that's what happened.

PIERRE: Still talking about money, Gordon: You were very poor as a kid, weren't you?

GORDON SINCLAIR: Oh yes, we were very poor people. My Dad never earned over forty dollars in his life and seldom got up to forty dollars. There were three years when he was on the black list. The most punishing thing, the most evil, wicked, monstrous thing in this province was the black list, whereby industrialists could say: "This man is an agitator." My Dad was listed as an agitator, and he could get no job at all. Blacklisted: that meant starvation for his children, and I was the oldest of his children. He had to leave the country.

PIERRE: Agitators, as we have seen from the record of Gordon Sinclair, are treated a little better in the society of the Sixties.

A WITCH
IN SUBURBIA

"I can assure you
it's nothing like
the Women's Institute."

Something very strange has been happening recently in Great Britain. A pantheistic mystical religion, which pre-dates Christianity and is called "witchcraft," seems to be on the rise. It may be significant that as Christianity – at least in its newer manifestations – becomes more and more a religion of intellectual belief, witchcraft, a religion of direct personal emotional experience, becomes more and more intriguing, even to non-witches.

During a trip to England in November, 1965, my producer asked one of our London researchers to find a witch who would be willing to appear on the program. Thus was I introduced to Mrs. Lois Pearson, a comely, dark-haired English housewife who lives in the suburb of St. Alban's with her husband and two children.

On meeting Mrs. Pearson, a stranger would never know that she was a witch. She is a soft-spoken, highly intelligent woman, who expresses herself extremely well. Though middle-aged and inclined to plumpness, she has retained her good looks and could be described, I think, as sexy. More, she has the quality of making you believe the most outlandish stories. Of all the far-out people I have talked to on television — mind-readers, astrologers, mediums, flat-earth believers, and Christian fundamentalists — she, and she alone, is the only one I've come anywhere near believing. She didn't quite convince me that there is such a thing as witch-craft, save in the minds of the would-be witches, but she did convince me that she is herself *convinced. Whatever Mrs. Pearson may be, she is, in no sense, a phoney.*

PIERRE: I'm interested to know how you *know* you're a witch. Did somebody tell you? Did you just decide to become one? Or did you just find out? Are witches born or made or what?

MRS. PEARSON: Witches are born. You can't be made into one. It's something which you're born with, and it's something you have to make the best of just like a birthmark.

PIERRE: How did you know you were a witch?

MRS. PEARSON: Because I've been recognized by other witches. This is one of the proofs.

PIERRE: What do you mean "recognized"? On the street?

MRS. PEARSON: No, not necessarily on the street. What it really means is that I was born with certain hereditary powers – the power to foretell the future, and to look at a person and in a very few moments be able to assess practically everything about him: what sort of a life he's led, what sort of a person he is, and what sort of things are going to happen to him in the future. Also I have the power to hold an object for a few minutes – this is called psychometry – and deduce from this object the sort of people who have owned it, the sort of people they were, and the sort of things that happened to them during their lives. Also to be able to enter into at will a transcendental experience. Now these are things which happened to me as a very small child. I was aware of small children who were not obvious to my parents or to other people, and I used to talk to them and play with them and gradually, as I grew older, I was able to do other things. I was able to sort of foretell what was going to happen in my family. If someone was going to die, I knew about it, and during the course of time I

76

became acquainted with other people who had these gifts, and I was recognized by them as being one of them.

PIERRE: If you met a stranger who's a witch would you know?

MRS. PEARSON: Yes.

PIERRE: Instinctively?

MRS. PEARSON: Instinctively I would know.

PIERRE: Would the stranger know about you?

MRS. PEARSON: Yes, probably.

PIERRE: Tell me about your family, Mrs. Pearson. You said this is hereditary. Does this mean there are witches in your past?

MRS. PEARSON: Usually it runs in families. My grandmother was Spanish and she had the reputation of being a witch. Unfortunately, I never knew her because she died when my mother was eleven. But I often heard of her from the family, and when I was very small, I was told that if I didn't behave myself I would grow up to be a witch like my grandmother, and I did.

PIERRE: What's the male equivalent of witch . . . wizard, is it?

MRS. PEARSON: No, we just call them witches.

PIERRE: I've heard the word "warlock."

MRS. PEARSON: Yes, but we don't really use this term.

PIERRE: Has either of your two sons inherited this tendency?

MRS. PEARSON: I think my eldest son is inheriting it. The signs are there. But I don't talk to him about it.

PIERRE: Does he know you're a witch?

MRS. PEARSON: Oh, yes, they both know. They just accept it.

PIERRE: Is witchcraft tied up with black magic?

MRS. PEARSON: No, it isn't. This is a popular misconception. Witchcraft really is a pantheistic mystical religion which embodies the worship of life, and life is personified by the Mother Goddess. She is the female principle of life, and the male God – the Horned God – is the male principle. And these two together represent life which witches worship. We know that we are alive. We don't know really what happens to us when we die. But we know that at this present moment we are alive. Consequently, we worship life – the life around us, the beauty of the countryside, the sun, the birds, the trees. We talk about the Goddess, but the Goddess is a symbol, and we can as easily worship the Deity in a beautiful flower or a blade of grass. Just as Roman Catholics in the Church have figures of the Virgin Mary or Christ on a crucifix, they don't worship the plaster images, they worship the idea behind them, and in witchcraft we worship the life force, the idea behind the Goddess.

PIERRE: Are you also a Christian?

MRS. PEARSON: I'm not a Christian. I'm pagan. I can't be a Christian and a witch.

PIERRE: How about your two sons? Do they go to church?

MRS. PEARSON: They go to church occasionally, but they're being brought up virtually as Christians because, I think, there's a great deal of good in the Christian religion. I'm not anti-Christian, not by any means. I think that Christianity provides a yardstick for living, and this is essential to children. My youngest son is not going to be a witch, I can see that. But my eldest son, I think, will be. He has a tremendous power over animals, and sometimes he tells me that he's able to influence the masters at school, if there's a question been asked and he knows the answer. He concentrates on the master and persuades the master through the power of his own will to ask him for the answer. I said to him: "I wish you'd influence the master to give you better marks in maths, then."

PIERRE: Can you read his mind? Is this possible for witches?

MRS. PEARSON: Yes, we do read people's minds, but we don't make a habit of doing this because this is prying.

PIERRE: Is it hard to do? I mean, is it tiring?

MRS. PEARSON: It is very tiring. It's something you have to settle down to and you have to have terrific concentration. The majority of people can't concentrate on one simple subject for more than a minute. But when witches are trying to do something, they have to concentrate on a thing for up to two or three hours and force their will into it.

PIERRE: In witchcraft, the females seem to be more important than the males.

MRS. PEARSON: Well, it's a matriarchal religion, you see, and the women always take the chief part. I have a coven of witches – a coven of thirteen – and I'm known as the high priestess, but I usually don't use this term. I'm usually regarded just as the leader of the coven. And the women take the chief part. The women raise the power, and the men act as an earth for it. There are many ways of working magic. If you belong to a coven, it doesn't give you any particular privileges except that you are able to work with other witches. But many witches don't bother to join covens or to mix with their own kind. They're quite content to work on their own.

PIERRE: This is a priesthood without a congregation, isn't it?

MRS. PEARSON: It is a priesthood without a congregation.

PIERRE: Every witch is a priest?

MRS. PEARSON: It used not to be like that. I believe that in the Stone Age – it goes back to the Stone Age – and in this country before the advent of Christianity, witchcraft was *the* religion.

PIERRE: Was this tied up with the Druids?

MRS. PEARSON: No, the Druids are different. But we believe witchcraft was the religion of the country and that the witches were the priests and the priestesses. Now we're a priesthood without a congregation. We're content to be so.

PIERRE: Is there any common denominator for witches? Are they the same kind of person?

MRS. PEARSON: Well, no, you could sit next to a person on a bus and not know that he or she was a witch. In an average coven, you would find quite a mixed selection of people. In my own particular coven, for instance, I have a doctor and a nurse and a university professor and two housewives and someone who is in television. They're quite a mixed bag.

PIERRE: You know, you make this coven sound like the Women's Institute.

MRS. PEARSON: Oh, I can assure you it's nothing like the Women's Institute.

PIERRE: But you sit there and talk about it, looking like a normal, ordinary, everyday woman. . . .

MRS. PEARSON: I am.

PIERRE: But you don't look like the conception of a witch that my three-year-old daughter has: somebody in a pointed hat with long hair, a beaked nose, a broomstick, and full moon behind.

MRS. PEARSON: This is another popular misconception. Witches are quite normal people. They're very well-balanced, and they're not mental in any way. They have to be well-balanced to do what they have to do.

PIERRE: How many witches are there in the world, do you know? How many in Britain? Do you have any idea?

MRS. PEARSON: I have no idea. I couldn't even guess at it. You see, witches are very insular. They don't normally associate with other people, and they don't go around saying that they are witches. Probably just their relations and very close friends know. Very few people know that I'm a witch. I have friends that haven't the slightest notion that I'm a witch.

PIERRE: They'd probably be pretty upset if they knew that you were.

MRS. PEARSON: I don't know that they'd be upset, because the sort of people that I take for friends are usually the sort who would accept the fact that I was a witch. They would probably be rather surprised, let's say that.

PIERRE: To put it mildly. I'd be surprised if any of the young ladies or middle-aged ladies that I know turned out to be witches, but maybe they are. But this seems to be very peculiar to Britain. I don't think we have many witches in Canada.

MRS. PEARSON: Oh yes, you have. Oh yes, there are witches in Canada. I've been in communication with some of them.

PIERRE: How do they find you, and how do you find them?

MRS. PEARSON: Well, this is very strange, you see. There isn't really any explanation for this. You just do meet each other. As if it's preordained, you meet each other under the strangest circumstances. I came across a group of witches when I was on holiday in Cornwall. I hadn't the slightest idea that they were there.

PIERRE: How did you find them?

MRS. PEARSON: Well, I used to frequent a little beach which was very private, and on my way down there, there was an old mill, and one day I saw a notice outside inviting visitors to the mill, so I thought I'd like to go this particular day. I went in there, and I was met by a very charming lady. She took me around, and I noticed to my great surprise there were many relics there, and swords and witchcraft tools which I recognized. And I didn't admit to her that I was a witch, and she didn't admit to me that she was, and we fenced with each other for quite a long time. We talked generally about it, and she said that I obviously knew quite a lot about it, and she thought that her husband would like to meet me, so she left a notice on the car one day: would we go up for dinner one evening? When I went up to the house, I was very, very surprised to see a gentleman whom I had passed quite frequently on the path down to the beach. When I'd passed him I'd taken particular note of him, but he was always alone, and I was usually alone, and I didn't like to sort of speak to him. But I had a very strange sensation each time I had passed him, and when I met him, of course, I realized why. He was a witch.

PIERRE: Suppose I find out that I'm a witch and I want to find a coven. How do I do that? Or does the coven find me?

MRS. PEARSON: I don't know, quite frankly.

PIERRE: How did your members find you?

MRS. PEARSON: Well, some of them were introduced to me by other people, and some of them just wrote to me out of the blue. It's very strange, you see, I can't explain this. It just happens as if it's meant to be. People just contact each other over a period of time, and then they become roped into coven activities.

PIERRE: Now, what does a coven do? Is it true that it meets at the time of the full moon?

MRS. PEARSON: Yes, witches always meet at the time of the full moon.

PIERRE: Outside?

MRS. PEARSON: In the summer we meet outside, but in the winter of course, when it's rather inclement, we meet indoors.

PIERRE: Whereabouts outside? In a forest?

MRS. PEARSON: In a forest, or in some sort of special glade. We have lots of open spaces in this country.

PIERRE: In a circle?

MRS. PEARSON: Well, we work within a nine-foot circle, and witches work within a circle to conserve the power, unlike cabalistic magicians who work inside a circle to protect themselves from the things which materialize outside. As high priestess, I start in the East and with a sword I draw a circle. In the centre of the circle, there's an altar, and on the altar there's usually water and salt and several tools, and at each quarter of the circle there will be a candle. When we work indoors, the candles at the quarters of the circle are to represent the fires which we would normally have if we were working outside. After I've drawn the circle, I consecrate and bless the salt and water, and I go round the circle sprinkling water. This is to purify it, and then I purify myself. At this stage, I take a sword or a witch's knife – a black-handled knife – and I draw down the power, after having drawn a pentacle at each corner – I call them corners, but they're points of the circle. And then I bring the other witches into the circle, and the business of the evening begins. Each one of them is purified in turn, and then we start whatever we have to do.

PIERRE: What do you have to do?

MRS. PEARSON: Well, the main preoccupation of witches is and always has been the pursuit of mysticism. There are certain breathing rituals which we have which induce a trance state. Now this sounds probably absolutely fantastic to you, and if anyone was sitting here talking to me about this, I just wouldn't believe them, but by a certain method of under-oxygenation or over-breathing, and knowing what to do at a certain stage, we can go into a trance.

PIERRE: I've gotten dizzy from breathing too hard.

MRS. PEARSON: That's right, yes. It's the same sort of thing, but it goes on in excess of what you have experienced. We enter into a trance-like state, and we have the power to leave our bodies and to overlook people. Now if you read books about the old witch trials, you hear about cat familiars – animal familiars. In the old days of witches, this is where the significance of the animal familiars comes in. The animals were trained; they weren't just household pets, they were specially trained to watch over the witch's body while she was out of it.

PIERRE: That's why a witch is always shown with a cat in Hallowe'en pictures?

MRS. PEARSON: That's right, yes. But in this day and age, you see, we have our friends around us. If we work in a circle, we have friends, and they watch over us so we don't need the animals to see that we're all right.

PIERRE: Where are you when your body's lying in a trance state in the circle?

MRS. PEARSON: Not necessarily lying.

PIERRE: Standing, you mean?

MRS. PEARSON: No, we work under comfortable conditions. To get into this trance-like state, and to get out of your body, you have to be in a comfortable position so that you can dissociate yourself from your body and forget about it. If you're uncomfortable or cold, you couldn't do this. You asked me where I am. Well, it depends on what I want to do. If I want to see what is going on in a different town or what is happening to a certain person, then I will myself to be in the presence of this person, and I can watch them and see what they're doing.

PIERRE: Do they know you're there?

MRS. PEARSON: It's interesting you should say that. It depends on how receptive people are. I have been present in a room with somebody, and I've seen them look round, you know, as if they're conscious of something. And when I've said to them on a later occasion, "I saw you at such and such a time on such and such an evening and you were doing so and so," they're absolutely amazed.

PIERRE: You realize that everything you're telling me is very hard to swallow.

MRS. PEARSON: Well, I don't mind. You can believe it or not.

PIERRE: Well, the interesting thing is that you have no axe to grind as some of our guests have. You just came to the program because we asked you. Witches normally don't even seek publicity. I think you only came on this program because it's not being shown in England, only in Canada, isn't it?

MRS. PEARSON: That's right.

PIERRE: What do you think of Sybil Leek, for instance? She's on television a lot.

MRS. PEARSON: Well, I don't know Mrs. Leek, quite frankly. I don't know whether she's a genuine witch or not.

PIERRE: Ah. Some scepticism there. Here's a question I must ask you: How do you know what to do as high priestess? Who teaches you? Where do you get these rituals?

MRS. PEARSON: Ah, this is interesting. Now, we have a book. I have this book, which was handed down to me from my grandmother. It was kept in the family amongst various odd papers, and it contains several rituals.

PIERRE: What's it called?

MRS. PEARSON: It's called *The Book of Shadows*. And it's a beautiful book. It's got poetry and lore and the history of witchcraft and how to make various tools and the use of various herbs and things. Our rituals are taken from these books. But the thing is this that, when you reach a certain stage in witchcraft – when you're sufficiently developed – you don't need all the impedimenta of witchcraft; you can work. I'm quite capable of just sitting down in a quiet room and inflicting or projecting my will onto somebody without the use of tools or drawing a circle. I can work alone, because I'm pretty well advanced, but I'm not so advanced as some people. I work under a guru or a teacher. She is a woman who lives in East Anglia, and she's a much more developed witch than I am. She doesn't teach me anything; she helps me to remember. You see, witchcraft isn't a question of learning anything; it's a question of learning how to remember. This may seem very strange to you, but witches believe in reincarnation, and we believe that if we were witches in a past life we'll be witches in this life. To learn how to work witchcraft again and to work our spells, we have to remember. And no one can teach us; we must learn for ourselves.

PIERRE: Tell me more about this book. Who publishes it? Is it available?

MRS. PEARSON: Oh no, it isn't published. It's written. My book is written in the handwriting of my grandmother.

PIERRE: Are there many copies of this book around? Do all the witches have one?

MRS. PEARSON: Every witch . . . every witch is entitled to have a copy.

PIERRE: How does she get it?

MRS. PEARSON: She copies it from the ones belonging to other people. You see, when someone discovers that they think they are a witch, strange things happen to them, and they're not quite sure what they are. Then, eventually, they contact people who can explain to them that they're probably hereditary witches, and they're asked if they'd like to join in a coven and we have an initiation ceremony. Now the initiation ceremony is very strange in that it really doesn't consist of anything very much. What happens is that they're taken to some sacred place, with which this country abounds, at a certain time of night, and they're left there completely alone, and after about two hours they're collected. Now if they're genuine witches, they're full of happiness, and they know that they want to joint the coven. If they're not genuine, they'll usually say, well, thank you very much, it's been nice knowing you, I'll see you again.

PIERRE: Did this happen to you? Were you taken to a sacred place?

MRS. PEARSON: Yes, I was.

PIERRE: Was it spooky?

MRS. PEARSON: Well, I'm afraid I can't go into exactly what happens. I know what happens, and I know that people have identical experiences, but I can't go into what happens.

PIERRE: It's a secret?

MRS. PEARSON: It's a secret, yes.

PIERRE: Do you believe in the spirit world?

MRS. PEARSON: Yes, I do. If you mean by the spirit world, do I believe in the life hereafter, yes, I do.

PIERRE: Do you believe in ghosts?

MRS. PEARSON: Yes, I do believe in ghosts.

PIERRE: Have you ever seen one?

MRS. PEARSON: Yes, I have.

PIERRE: Who?

MRS. PEARSON: I've seen my mother. I've seen lots of the members of my family who have died.

PIERRE: Have you seen your grandmother who was a witch?

MRS. PEARSON: Yes, I have.

PIERRE: Have you talked to her?

MRS. PEARSON: No.

PIERRE: Have you ever talked to a ghost?

MRS. PEARSON: You don't talk to ghosts by word of mouth – you communicate mentally. Telepathically.

PIERRE: Do you communicate with other witches telepathically?

MRS. PEARSON: Yes.

PIERRE: Over great distances?

MRS. PEARSON: Over great distances, yes.

PIERRE: How often?

MRS. PEARSON: Whenever I have the need to.

PIERRE: What are the big festivals? Witches in my scheme of things are tied up with Hallowe'en.

MRS. PEARSON: Hallowe'en is one of the great festivals. There are actually four. Candlemas, May Eve, Lammas, and Hallowe'en.

PIERRE: What's Lammas? I never heard of that.

MRS. PEARSON: Lammas is August Eve. It's really a harvest festival. The Christians have taken it over as a harvest festival.

PIERRE: What do you do on these big festival occasions?

MRS. PEARSON: Well, we have a ritual for this particular occasion, and then we usually have a party. A general get-together, and we have drinks, and we just enjoy ourselves. Sit around and talk, play records, dance.

PIERRE: Sounds awfully suburban for witches to be bobbing for apples and that sort of thing.

MRS. PEARSON: Well, what do you expect us to do?

PIERRE: Well, I expect you to do what witches have traditionally done, I suppose, all through history. What you're really telling me is that witch trials of the past were genuine. That there *were* witches. We've always thought that the evidence was faked evidence, and that they were just strange, unfortunate women.

MRS. PEARSON: Quite frankly, I don't know whether they were genuine or not. It's impossible to tell from all the literature that's been written. Much of it is contradictory. I think some of them were obviously genuine; others were not. There was a lot of hysteria at that time. And for reasons of its own, the Church wanted to get rid of the witches because witchcraft was a rival religion.

PIERRE: From what you say, it was. Is it true that witches sometimes work naked? Without clothes?

MRS. PEARSON: Well, some covens do work naked. I don't. My coven doesn't work naked because we don't find it necessary to do it. We work more on a mental level; but you see different covens are at different stages of development, and if they work on a physical level, they raise power. The witches who do work naked say that they raise power from their own bodies, and that the wearing of clothes would impede the production of this power.

PIERRE: How do you feel after you come out of a trance? Are you tired? Elated? How?

MRS. PEARSON: I feel very tired, as a rule. Before a general meeting, or before some sort of work that I'm very anxious to do on behalf of other people, I fast for three days. I'm allowed to drink, but I have to be well past the first stages of hunger, and usually I'm very, very tired. I'm all right after a night's sleep, you know, but I'm normally very, very tired after a session.

PIERRE: You say you're here to help people, but I understand that they have to ask before you can help them.

MRS. PEARSON: That's so, yes. I'm not allowed to offer my services. I have to be asked to help.

PIERRE: Have you helped many people?

MRS. PEARSON: Yes, many, many, people.

PIERRE: In what way?

MRS. PEARSON: Oh, there are so many cases. The one which comes to mind is a particular friend of mine who had an unfortunate love affair with a man. He went to America. But before he went – well, he was quite a stinker – he relieved her of several hundred pounds. When he got to America, she wrote polite letters to him asking him if he would mind returning this money. It didn't have any effect. She asked me if I would help her, so she gave me a sample of his handwriting and I concentrated on this for a matter of hours. I got through to him very quickly, and within about a week, I'm happy to say, a cheque arrived for her of several hundred pounds.

A CHILD
BEFORE HIS TIME

"In freedom of speech,
the accent is on freedom,
not on speech."

*It was said of Lenny Bruce that he execrated all that is unctuous
and sanctimonious in our society from Santa Claus to small "l"
liberals. He was a man who attacked the real sacred cows to his
personal cost, while others attacked the pretend ones to their personal benefit. He preached that sex is not dirty, that drug addicts
are not criminals, and that homosexuals should not be persecuted.
He said that "every man who professes to be a man of God and
owns more than one suit is a hustler – so long as there are people
in the world who don't have any." Kenneth Tynan, the British
critic, praised him as an impromptu prose poet "who uses words
the way a jazz musician uses notes," but few critics were as
ecstatic. Others called him an egotist, a vulgar, tasteless boor, a
hard-core pornographer, and a sick comedian for sick comedians.*
 *Bruce attacked the most sacred taboos of the Judaeo-Christian
society: those short, explosive words that are the commonly
accepted shorthand for longer, more euphemistic phrases dealing
with matters sexual. Because he believed these words derive their
strength from being taboo, he tried to devaluate them by constant*

87

public use. It was this that got him into a peck of trouble and made it virtually impossible for him to perform anywhere in the United States, Canada, or Great Britain (from which he was barred in 1963).

Bruce's career reached its peak around 1961. Then it went steadily downhill to the point where he was destitute. Over and over again he was hauled into court. Over and over again he fought back, his head bloody but unbowed. He became a man obsessed with the law. It consumed his waking hours and haunted his sleep. Toward the end of his life, he talked of little else; his friends, bored and exhausted, had deserted him; his social life, he told me, had been destroyed.

In the mid-Sixties, he seemed less a child of his time than a child before his time. Just as Lady Chatterley's Lover, *the cause célèbre of an earlier decade, seems mild fare today, so I suspect will Bruce's taboo-breaking monologues seem relatively innocuous to a coming generation. Though he was virtually out of business when I interviewed him, his personal following remained impressive. It is no accident that, without the advantage of any TV appearances, the recorded monologues of this essentially moral and unvengeful man have — when available — consistently outsold those darlings of the Critical Establishment, Mort Sahl and Jonathan Winters. The Critical Establishment wanted no truck nor trade with Bruce, the idol-smasher. But there was an enormous if largely incoherent underground movement that considered him one of its high priests. Bruce, who saw so much so clearly, understood all about this and the reasons for it, which is why he didn't blame the critics for disliking him. "It's not their fault they don't understand," he said. "Each generation is incoherent to the next. They can't help it. They're old."*

Bruce rarely appeared on television. Most of the time he wasn't wanted, and when he was he often declined. He had turned down a much fatter fee from another Canadian program just the week before he agreed to appear with me. It was, I believe, his last appearance before his death in August, 1966. The comments I heard about him in Hollywood, where we taped the program in February were discouraging: "You'll be sorry . . . he won't show . . . wait till he starts talking dirty . . . you'll never get it on the air . . . who can understand him? . . . he'll put you down. . . ."

But Bruce, arriving on the dot of time, turned out to be a mild-mannered man who, without histrionics, obscenities, or self-pity, calmly set out to discuss with me his trouble with the law.

Since he had once been described as a man with a message for humanity who was willing to risk jail for it, I began by asking for his comment.

◯

LENNY BRUCE: I don't know if it is a message for humanity, but my point of view is that under our constitution no American citizen is born with an original sin. Therefore, the burden is *not* upon any of the citizens in our country to prove that our speech is beyond reproach, but respected and protected by the constitution. The difficulty I've had is with the people who confuse themselves with the authorities. Which I believe is a quasi-religious point of view.

PIERRE: Well now, let's go back a moment and get some statistics here. I think I'm right in saying that back from 1956 to 1960, you made well over one hundred thousand dollars a year, whereas last year you only made about two thousand dollars, which is obviously quite a change in your life. You're almost broke. You've spent about one hundred and fifty thousand dollars in lawyer's fees. Is this correct?

LENNY BRUCE: Yes. Most of the money I've earned, in the courts – fighting with these people who act under the collar of the law, without the authority of it.

PIERRE: There have been nine charges against you over the past three or four years. Seven have been for obscenity and two for narcotics. Now you still have not gone to jail on any of them. I think you have been acquitted on all but one.

LENNY BRUCE: Well, there is a difference between going to jail: I have gone to jail on *all* of them, but there has been no judgment. I've appealed and I've won my appeals. But it has been a trial by ordeal. It's cut a lot of my income out, changed my social life, and changed my point of view on stage.

PIERRE: Now the two charges against you for narcotics were for using drugs, and yet you claim you're not a drug addict – that you don't use drugs except for medical reasons. Is this not correct?

LENNY BRUCE: The problem I had there was that the peace officers who had arrested me had arrested me previously on charges of obscenity. They then decided that the medication that I had, although it was prescribed by a doctor, was fooling the law.

PIERRE: What do you mean by that?

LENNY BRUCE: It's the only conclusion I can make. Again, that they have not a truly religious view but a quasi-religious view that the law is something that is out to trap you. They don't realize that it is created by We The People. They think there is a good and evil in the law instead of a right and wrong in the law – that the people who enforce the law are the goodness and anybody who has a prescription for any medication is obviously fooling the law because they are not supposed to have that unless they are in the hospital.

PIERRE: You suffer from a nervous disorder that requires certain drugs?

LENNY BRUCE: I never use any narcotics; I use a stimulant called methedrine which is listed as a dangerous drug. It is the same drug that the astronauts take.

PIERRE: And you carry around with you a doctor's letter saying that you require the drug?

LENNY BRUCE: Yes, and their opinion was that I was just doing that to trick the law.

PIERRE: And it's your belief that, if you hadn't been up on the obscenity charges, there would have been no narcotics charges against you?

LENNY BRUCE: That's really where it's at.

PIERRE: Then let's talk about really what we are here to talk about: the seven charges against you for obscenity which really get down to your use of four-letter words in night clubs, don't they? Or do they?

LENNY BRUCE: Well, they really don't. The law is very precise on what is obscene. I think that anyone will take judicial notice of the fact that what art is is a *portrayal*. For instance, if I was now to take a motion picture of *you* as an artist, all that anyone could judge would be my art as a motion-picture producer depicting another artist at work. And, since all art is just another portrayal of another art, what happened in my case is that a peace officer would view my art and then go before a grand jury or magistrate and would say: "Here's my resumé of Lenny Bruce." And the magistrate would watch the peace officer be a comedian and he would say: "That stinks!"

PIERRE: The peace officer would be doing your act in court?

LENNY BRUCE: Yes.

PIERRE: But you weren't allowed to do your act in court?

LENNY BRUCE: Well this was *before* the court case. This was on the complaints made against me. The peace officer says: "I saw a man who did an obscene show." The magistrate says: "Well, if you have the evidence. . . ." The peace officer says: "I can do it

90

for you." And he does the show. The magistrate, in effect, says: "That's a *terrible* show" and has me arrested for the peace officer's act. The irony of it is that I have to go to court and defend the peace officer's act. That's why, in the last case, I refused to appeal: I don't want to win the right to do another comedian's act.

PIERRE: Let's get this clear: if something is considered art, it can't be considered obscene. You say that what you are doing is art. Even if it requires the use of certain taboo words, those words may be part of that art as, indeed, they are in books like *Ulysses* and *Lady Chatterley's Lover*. But you can't let somebody else do your act and still call it art. And that's what the police officer does when he gets the summons to haul you into court?

LENNY BRUCE: Which is against the law.

PIERRE: And that's really the irony of the whole thing?

LENNY BRUCE: The reason it's against our law came from the British law. It was a case called "Regina versus Hicklin," and at that time there was a book called *The Confessional Unmasked*, and the judge was the Lord High Cockburn. It was in 1869. He ruled that the test of obscenity was its effect on *the most corruptible mind in the community*. And that was the test the American courts adopted until about 1931. In 1931, when *Ulysses* came up, Judge Wolsey, and Judge Learned Hand in another case following, said: "I don't think that will be a good American system – to judge the work by the most corruptible mind in the community. Because if we use that for a standard, all the literature in our country will be directed at the most corruptible mind in the community." And, he said, instead of that we had better have it directed at the *normal, average man* with the normal, average sex instincts – and not use the isolated excerpts. Rather, *judge the work as a whole*. In this way, no artist will ever be judged on somebody *else's* work. That is the clear rule, and the Supreme Court has held to that rule. And people who don't agree with the Constitution – people who again have a quasi-religious view – continually interfere with that.

PIERRE: You know a lot about the law.

LENNY BRUCE: I've spent the last two or three years now reading about ten hours a day. First, the United States Constitution very thoroughly; then all the laws that were passed to enforce the provisions of the United States Constitution; then all the people who violated the Constitution – their arrests, their cases, and their appeals, their exceptions, and every footnote.

PIERRE: This has changed your life, hasn't it?

LENNY BRUCE: Oh yes, I have a much different view of the law.

PIERRE: When you were first arrested in 1962, allegedly for an obscene act, did you think you were guilty?

LENNY BRUCE: Well, the first time I was arrested for obscenity, I was ashamed. Because I never dreamed that the man who was arresting me didn't know the law! Because when a man says to you: "You're under arrest for violation of 326!" and he is a law enforcement officer, you assume that you *must* have violated the law. But after I was arrested for the second and the third time, I started *reading* the law, and I realized that I was not violating the law. I realized that the California legislature passed the law. I realized that We The People are the law! Any law that's on our books today, we agree to it either by not voting against it or by voting for it, and that the only people who enforce the law correctly are the people who do enforce it correctly.

PIERRE: You've had a rough road, and yet you don't feel very bitter about this. Instead, you seem more intrigued and interested.

LENNY BRUCE: I think you get sort of depersonalized when you start to read. From reading, especially now, I believe we are the most successful country in the world because we worship a charter, a blueprint – the United States Constitution. In some countries that are ruled by a religious faction, they can hand out franchises, like Howard Johnson, and each person can use the franchise in his own way. In our country, you can't. You go right to the charter. The charter is correct; it is precise. If it's not there, it's just not right.

PIERRE: Now tell me what happened. Is it hard for you to get work? Because of the charges against you?

LENNY BRUCE: Like what happened to me in England: I liked England, and I was very well received by the press; but then, when I came back to this country, I was arrested. I was arrested in town A, and if towns B, C, and D don't arrest you, they are not doing their jobs. That's the big problem we have in our country: unfortunately we elect people on their record. I think that law-enforcement officers should be treated like the postman. They shouldn't *have* to be keeping busy all the time. We demand that the man do his job and keep busy; and when the crime rate drops – which it has in this country because the welfare is up and the economy is up – it results in a lot of false arrests. The poor police officer is put in the position of doing his job when he's not *required* to do his job. Because he's of short tenure, and that's what he's elected on. You find it with a [civil rights] demonstration.

How do we have law in our country? Well, let's reduce it to the very first law. Let's say we all made an agreement; we said: "We'll sleep in area A; we'll eat in area B; we'll throw our garbage in area C. Because that's the rules." Everybody agreed on it. Everybody went to sleep. Then, say, some guy woke up and he got a face full of garbage. So he says: "What's the deal here? I thought we had a rule: A, B, and C." So they discovered that although they had the rule, there was no way to *enforce* it. So then they had to get somebody to enforce the law. So they said: "All right; this is what we'll do: if anybody throws any garbage on us while we're sleeping, he gets thrown where the garbage is. But the problem is that we have to do business with these people so *we* can't throw them where the garbage is. So we'd better get somebody else to do it. We'll get some 'law-enforcement officers.' " And they said: "Look, we're trying to get some sleep, but people are throwing garbage on us. So if anybody throws any garbage on us while we're sleeping, *they* get thrown in the garbage. *But don't do it in front of me — because I want somebody to be the bad guy, and I've got to do business with these people, and you've heard me say a lot of times that it takes a certain mentality to do this work.*" So when the demonstrations come, that's the way the law is. You can't change the law without repealing it. So you've got a poor peace officer with a stick in his hand, and fifty thousand people throwing rocks, sticks and stones — and the thing stopping them is *him*. In fact, he is really doing the job of a public servant, but people always sort of want to beat the devil. The newspapers — they can only sell papers, you know, by showing what they *assume* is the bad guy. This creates, you know, a bit of a problem.

PIERRE: Now, Mr. Bruce, let's talk about the business of taboo words — the so-called four-letter words that you do use. What is their purpose? Is it necessary to use these words?

LENNY BRUCE: Well, first of all, I never talked about sex on the stage. I discuss religion . . . I criticize the authorities . . . but sex, that's not my point of view, that's not my interest. The way I do my act is that I portray many different characters throughout many different regions. I do the dialect of the regions; therefore, I do the portrayal of the character. To have each character speaking like a Cockney, but talking as an Italian, the people would think I was absurd. So the character has to be real. And that cliché about freedom of speech doesn't mean you can go far in a crowded theatre. Because the stage is make-believe: you can kill Christ on stage, and no one takes you away at the end and puts you in jail. It's make-believe! The mistake is to believe that the American theatre is an instruction for morality, which it is not. The reason the Supreme Court is very concerned with the First Amendment is that it is the only strength our country has. In freedom of speech, the accent is on freedom, not on speech. It's the right to get it across, to communicate – the right of the reader to read it and the person to say it. In other words, a discussion on syphilis is not an instruction to get it. A country can only be strong when it knows all about the bad – the worst, worst things. When it knows about the bad, then it can protect itself. The country that only knows all about the nice things about itself ends in failure, as Hitler did.

PIERRE: What you're saying is what is being argued on behalf of novels – that in dialogue, to be realistic, you must let the character speak the way he would in real life – in the army, say.

LENNY BRUCE: Well, anywhere they speak Jewish, they speak *Jewish*. And if they speak a *verbotten* language, then they speak a *verbotten* language.

PIERRE: This right has now been won by the authors who write the printed word.

LENNY BRUCE: It's never been *lost*. That's the thing: the protection has always been there. There's been a misreading. Actually, it's a handful of insurance attorneys who don't practise law. They feed upon all of these cases. There's a lot of money to be made in pornography. Let me tell you where the money is made: there is a whole department devoted to pornography. And none of these pornography cases is ever brought by the people. They are always brought by the police officer. So what we have is an army of peace officers searching about in cellars for pornographic books. They find the books – they're *supporting* all of the books – and then it goes to court. It's a bunch of nonsense! It's an obscenity circus! The people are not concerned with it; and it costs a fortune. And, of course, there's the fact that each book costs five dollars and it comes from some kind of a fund. We end up with a dirty-book tax fund to support these cases, which is nonsense. People who are so on the band wagon for cleanliness really don't realize what's happening.

PIERRE: Let me ask you this, in this connection: Is there such a thing as obscenity, and if so what does it mean to you?

LENNY BRUCE: All right, "obscenity," in the dictionary sense, is entirely different than "obscenity" in the legal sense. The reason those things have to be different is that none of us voted on the dictionary. When we agree on the *legal* sense of the word, that's where it's firmed up and nobody can change it. Now, the legal meaning of "obscene" is that, first, you have to take the thing, judge the matter, whatever the work is – whatever the medium of expression is. And the law writes with sort of parenthetical statements: such as "obscene" means "to the average person" – which refers to the earlier case we talked about, "Regina versus Hicklin" – and in the second parenthetical statement – "applying contemporary community standards." Of course, realizing that a judge that doesn't get out much, doesn't see too much – might perhaps be a little Victorian in his standards – they keep warning the laws to provide for exceptions. Obscene means again "to the average person applying contemporary community standards"– that must be the predominant appeal. That's what we are really talking about: to be "obscene," it must appeal to the "prurient interest." That means that if the work is dedicated to do nothing else but to upset the happily married couple, then the people decide they don't want it. And that's what "obscene" is. You see the difference between the artist who depicts life and the artist that takes out a piece of life and predominantly pushes that point across for just one reason: to exploit that part of life that is considered forbidden. There is no artist's work that ever gets into court because, if it *is* art, the court doesn't look at it. You see, that's the mistake of all these cases: that the right of property has to be forfeited before the trial starts. The bad thing has to *happen*. In other words, somebody had to bring the work before the judge and say: "Here it is; here is the bad thing."

PIERRE: Somebody had to decide that without recourse to anybody but himself.

LENNY BRUCE: Yes; "Here is the contraband." When it is decided that it *is* contraband, then the trial starts.

PIERRE: Do you think it is necessary for us to have an obscenity law at all?

LENNY BRUCE: Any law that we have on our books is necessary.

PIERRE: You accept that?

LENNY BRUCE: Oh, yes. In other words, *we* make the law – the people. And the way to solve any judicial abuse, any legislative abuse, is right at the polls. The only way you can argue it is to vote against it, and that's where it's at. All of our laws. So there's nobody can say: "Well, what do you think about our law?" They have to *obey* the law.

PIERRE: So you don't object to the law. You object to the way it has been used.

LENNY BRUCE: Yes, but unconstitutionally applied. The law is crystal clear, and these people who abuse it are very dissatisfied with the law.

PIERRE: How do you earn your money now? How do you support your child and your mother?

LENNY BRUCE: Well, I haven't in the last six months.

PIERRE: Is this mainly because you have occupied yourself with the law, or mainly because you just can't get work? Your albums aren't selling; you can't get people to buy them? They won't stock them and put them in their windows?

LENNY BRUCE: Well, no; I'm a fugitive from justice from New York, which I intend to solve by going to Federal Court and bringing these people to justice.

PIERRE: You can't work in the New York night clubs?

LENNY BRUCE: Yes, and that's what has happened all over – just through hearsay. The people whose duty it is to preserve the moral fibre of the community are naturally not put upon to search around and see if I got a fair trial. If they just *hear* about it that there may be a danger to the community, it may be their duty to keep me out – which is understandable. The fact is that they would have no idea that I've been arrested nine times maliciously without provocation. It wouldn't seem reasonable until that point is brought out. The way to bring it out is in the proper place, and that is in court. I intend to go into the Federal Courts and sue these people under the civil rights act.

THE GATE-CRASHER

"If you want anything bad
enough, you'll get it."

*When the Beatles first hit Toronto in September, 1964, utter
chaos reigned. I know, because our production offices happen to
be across the street from the Maple Leaf Gardens, where the
Beatles appeared, and on that memorable and slightly terrifying
afternoon, you couldn't get near the front door. If you were inside,
you couldn't get out. If you were outside, you couldn't get in.
As for the Beatles – they were virtually incommunicado. The
backstage area was policed by private guards and about one
hundred City of Toronto policemen. Even the president of the
Toronto Musicians' Union wasn't allowed in. The Mayor himself
tried to meet or maybe just touch a Beatle. He didn't have a
chance.*

*World news vanished from the papers for a day or two, and it
was only a matter of blind luck that my eye was attracted to a
small item, in the midst of all the major Beatle copy, about a
young man from San Francisco who had successfully wangled
himself into a series of Beatle concerts and press conferences*

without paying or showing a pass. *I wanted to meet that young man.*

By this time, the Beatles and their retinue had swept on to Montreal, and Fred Paul, the young man in question, had apparently been swept along with them. I asked my staff to try and track him down and see if they could persuade him to return to Toronto to appear on my television show. The tracking down took two days. The persuading took two seconds. The phone was scarcely back in its cradle, it seemed to me, before Fred Paul was with us – an incredibly smooth-spoken teenager in a sharp, three-button suit carrying a smart, black attaché case. The case turned out to be full of photographs of himself with people like George Harrison and Richard Nixon.

I learned later that his television appearance with me was only his second on TV; but his performance – and I think I can call it that – was far superior to that of many seasoned politicians and entertainers. My first question, which dealt with the number of Beatle concerts he'd crashed, revealed that he was an old hand at the game.

○

FRED PAUL: Well, I would say now we're into about twenty-five performances, and some places they do two performances.

PIERRE: You go to both performances, do you?

FRED PAUL: Oh always, both.

PIERRE: You must know those lyrics by heart.

FRED PAUL: Oh, I know every song they do. The timing and everything.

PIERRE: You have succeeded in getting into twenty-five Beatle concerts without paying a nickel?

FRED PAUL: Only once, in San Francisco, I had to pay; I paid twenty dollars to get down to the front.

PIERRE: This was the first time?

FRED PAUL: The very first time.

PIERRE: And from then on you've never had to pay?

FRED PAUL: Never.

PIERRE: How do you do this?

FRED PAUL: Well, you know, there's really not just one mode of operation.

PIERRE: Well, tell us some of the techniques.

98

FRED PAUL: Well, you know, I'll rent a limousine service — a Cadillac, you know — from one of the big passenger limousines, as I did in Milwaukee. I got about seven people to come with me. They paid a dollar each to defray the cost of the limousine, and we pulled up to the stage-door entrance. I don't know what happened, but they just opened the gates for us, and I told everybody to get out of the car quick, you know, and go right straight through, and we all paraded to the back stage area where the Beatles' limousines were, and there we waited throughout the entire show.

PIERRE: Now let's get this straight. You mean that just the act of getting out of a Cadillac establishes an aura over you which cows officials, is that right?

FRED PAUL: Right.

PIERRE: Do you dress in a certain way?

FRED PAUL: Well, I always have a suit and tie on, you know, or a sport coat and tie, with my attaché case and everything.

PIERRE: I suspect that attaché case is pretty important.

FRED PAUL: Yes.

PIERRE: It's very official-looking. I suppose you grip it in a brisk and business-like way?

FRED PAUL: Oh yes, and I use a quick and fast pace, you know. Sometimes I just go through so fast before they realize who just went by. They don't even bother because they've got to deal with someone else who might crash in.

PIERRE: What do you say if you're accosted?

FRED PAUL: Well, I usually say, "I'm with the tour." Then they'll say: "Where's your identification?" and I'll say: "Do you *really* want me to go through this whole case and find it?" And they say: "No! No! Go ahead." Then, maybe if I rip out one of the pictures with the Beatles, they say: "Oh, that's fine. That's good enough."

PIERRE: How are you at getting in on atomic-bomb sites?

FRED PAUL: Well I have never tried that yet, but I probably will, you know, some day.

PIERRE: Yes, I'm sure you will. What are some of the other techniques that you use?

FRED PAUL: Well, there was a cab driver who came into the hotel where the Beatles were staying in Seattle and said: "I'm here to pick up someone from the Beatles' party." And I said: "That's me." So he drove me out the gates and I said: "Stage-door entrance!" He was a real professional guy. He says: "Now, I've been a professional driver for eight years, and we'll get you through there — no problems, no mobs." He says: "We're going to roll up the windows here and protect ourselves." Oh, he played the whole role, and we got there, and he said: "I have a member of the Beatles' party here." And you know all those teenagers are standing out there and banging on the windows of the cab and everything so this guard, to protect me, he and the cab driver opened the gates and we drove right to the stage door. Then this Burns man grabbed me and brought me right back-stage before I knew what was happening.

PIERRE: The guy who is supposed to keep people *out* was helping you in?

FRED PAUL: Oh, they've done that several times. Escorted me back when I didn't know where the press conference or the stage dressing rooms were.

PIERRE: Now you haven't got a reserved seat or anything. So where do you sit?

FRED PAUL: Well, this is another unexplainable thing. At three or four of the performances, I've just taken a seat in the front row, and for some reason that party never shows up. I don't know why. I can't understand it.

PIERRE: It's always people who have front-row seats who don't show up.

FRED PAUL: Isn't that funny? Here's a whole crowd of thousands and thousands, and this one front-row centre seat never shows up.

PIERRE: After you, Maple Leaf Gardens will never be the same again.

FRED PAUL: Only one man in Cincinnati — who heard me on the radio in the afternoon, he happened to be the promoter or something like that — heard that I was going to crash the gates. He was ready for me, you know, but one of the press officers was there and said: "He's to go in, he's to go in," as though he had seen me before. Evidently this man thought, well, there must be a mistake then; I must be someone else. So he let me go right through.

PIERRE: I get the sneaking suspicion that you're quite a lot of use to the Beatles. There are a lot of extra news stories about you.

FRED PAUL: Well, you know, they always introduce me at every press conference, as of late. You know, Derek Taylor, who is their press agent, has been marvellously kind to me. He'll introduce me, and before you know it I've got five or six interviews going at one time, even in the midst of the Beatles' press con-

100

ference. I don't think they liked that too much, so I don't do that any more.

PIERRE: The very fact that you became a famous gate-crasher made gate-crashing easier, is that right? A celebrity within the celebrity?

FRED PAUL: This is true. People recognize me in hotels, and they're constantly badgering me to get autographs, and can you get me in, and can you do that, and can you do this? I took one girl with me one time, but she was so much of a problem I just don't bother with it any more.

PIERRE: How old are you?

FRED PAUL: Eighteen.

PIERRE: You're going to find, as you go through life, that girls continue to be a great deal of –

FRED PAUL: A bother, yeah. Financially and otherwise.

PIERRE: This brings up a pertinent question. Why in the name of all that's holy would anybody want to see twenty-five Beatle concerts? I can imagine seeing one, two, or even three or four, but twenty-five of them at eighteen!

FRED PAUL: Well, you see, I plan to write a book about all this, so it all makes the book more interesting each time I crash a gate, so to speak. I still don't like that term; I'd rather be called "uninvited guest" or something like that, you know. Gate-crasher, that doesn't sound very, you know, professional.

PIERRE: But how did you get it? Was this just started as a lark when you first saw the Beatles in 'Frisco?

FRED PAUL: I wanted to meet them after seeing their movie; I was thrilled with their movie. People who have never acted in their lives – no theatrical background, they did a marvellous job, really. I saw it five times, as a matter of fact.

PIERRE: Now tell me, you've observed Beatlemania first hand?

FRED PAUL: Oh boy, it's unbelievable.

PIERRE: What is it?

FRED PAUL: It's . . . I don't know if you can put it into words. In a way, I can see where these girls might go out of their minds or completely potty, as the English people put it. Here are their heroes, whom they've listened to on records, observed on television, read about in newspapers, seen in the movies, here they are right in front of them, and they just seem to lose all control. One girl, I don't know how she did it, but she threw herself right over the orchestra, right bang into the stage, and even this didn't stop her. She was going through all these gyrations when they were taking her away.

PIERRE: How do you feel personally as a teenager about your fellow teenagers when they go on like this? Are you disgusted, saddened, amused, or elated?

FRED PAUL: Oh, I think it's hilarious.

PIERRE: You enjoy it?

FRED PAUL: I just like to watch them, you know, because how anybody could go so completely balmy. . . .

PIERRE: Is it always girls who do this, or do boys do it too?

FRED PAUL: I've never seen a boy actually try to get on the stage. I've seen them rush the stage. One time another gate-crasher, he got backstage somehow, and he used the backstage entrance to get on the stage.

PIERRE: Upstart, eh?

FRED PAUL: Yeah, they got him off quickly then.

PIERRE: Amateur.

FRED PAUL: Amateur, oh yes, he was very unprofessional. I would never do that. I would never do that because it would ruin everything. That's common sense. They, you know, get them out as soon as they do this.

PIERRE: Well, now, you've sort of got an official aura around you: briefcase, neat suit, and Cadillac. Don't they try to attack you and try to tear pieces off you?

FRED PAUL: This only happened one time when I got out into the crowd in Seattle, and I had a key from the Edgewater Inn where everybody knew the Beatles were staying. They said: "Grab him! Grab him!" and I had, you know, some pictures and all that. I had shown them to one of the girls who said: "He's got their autograph! He's got their autograph!" So the only refuge I could take was to get into the Beatle limousine itself, and for some reason the Beatles weren't in the car, just me – and the chauffeur let me in the car. We had a motorcycle escort and everything. You know, I felt like the President or somebody. And they were all banging on the windows and they tore off the aerial and ripped off the back lights and stomped on the roof, and it was really quite frightening, you know. Here I'm just sitting there observing all this, you know. And even though they realized that I wasn't a Beatle, they thought that I must have something to do with them – maybe Brian Epstein. I've been asked: "Are you Mr. Epstein?"

PIERRE: The Beatles' manager.

FRED PAUL: Yes. I've met him also, and he's also been very nice to me. And you know, he's a very sophisticated man, but he's taken time to listen to my unusual story also.

PIERRE: How can you afford the time and money to cross the country in the wake of the Beatles?

FRED PAUL: Well, this is a great question also.

PIERRE: What's the answer?

FRED PAUL: The estimated cost of this tour is now at twelve hundred. And I have no car. I was going to buy a new car this year but I have this instead of my car.

PIERRE: Sort of a hobby?

FRED PAUL: Well, yes. I have no other extracurricular activities: nothing which involves that much of an expense – no car, no insurance. I don't go out much when I'm home and, so far, girls have had no real interest for me, because they're never exciting enough, you know, they're always too –

PIERRE: Say, what kind of a kid are you?

FRED PAUL: Well, they're *not* exciting enough, you know. Lately I've found some that would say: "Can I go with you, can I do this with you, you know, go on a trip with you." But they always . . . they jumble everything up. All fingers.

PIERRE: Well, that's not necessarily bad. Look, I understand that this is not new to you, this business of gate-crashing. You've got a whole history of it. This is only your second television appearance. And you're cool as a cucumber. Is this part of your stock-in-trade?

FRED PAUL: You have to be.

PIERRE: What are you going to be, a public-relations man?

FRED PAUL: Either that or I'd like to get into managing a group, or in radio and television.

PIERRE: Tell me about how you began all this business of meeting celebrities and having your picture taken with them all.

FRED PAUL: Well, four years ago, during the 1960 Presidential Election, Ambassador Lodge came to our hometown of Sarasota, Florida, where I was living at the time. It was my feeling, then, that here's a man who's our ambassador at the U.N.: he's come to our little bitty town; yet all the schools are open, all the businesses are open: there's really no honour for this man. He might be our next Vice-President. So I said, well, I'll at least go out to meet this man. So I left school that day and went out, and the Governor was there, LeRoy Collins, whom I've also met. I attended a luncheon with him earlier this year, and the mayor was there and the senatorial candidates and all that sort of thing. And it just worked. Actually, the first one to shake his hand when he came off the plane was me. And I didn't know what to say, and that's the truth. I didn't know what to say, so I said: "On behalf of Sarasota Junior High School, welcome to Florida!" And he smiled and his wife came down, and I didn't have any flowers or anything and then, finally, the other people took over, and I walked with them right back to the podium.

PIERRE: You mean when this plane landed you just ran forward?

FRED PAUL: Everybody else ran, so I did too.

PIERRE: You got to the outstretched hand before anybody else?

FRED PAUL: First one, right on the bottom of the stairs. There were even girls there with great big signs, "We Love You" and all this, and they stayed behind, and I got up and, you know, shook his hand.

PIERRE: This tells us something not only about the age we live in but also how to get ahead in this curious world.

FRED PAUL: You know, we're living in a time now – and this is my confirmed opinion–where if you want anything bad enough, you'll get it. Now people think success for the Beatles was overnight. It wasn't. They pounded . . . for at least five years, every day, sometimes six hours a day, three concerts or four a day, for five dollars, ten dollars, fifteen dollars, till success finally came to them.

PIERRE: What does your family think of all this running around?

FRED PAUL: Oh, they think I'm a first-class nut!

PIERRE: I guess they do.

FRED PAUL: These people here probably think I'm a nut, too.

PIERRE: Your family haven't been able to stop you. Have they tried?

FRED PAUL: Oh, no.

PIERRE: What was this? Was it hero worship in the beginning, a desire to be seen with celebrities, to meet famous people?

FRED PAUL: No, not really. Because I've even spent time reading books about great men, great men such as Billy Graham and people who have left an impact on this world. And I don't idolize these people. Well, I do in a way, but yet I don't. I find ninety-nine percent of your successful people came from very small backgrounds, and it was only through determination that they got to this height in our world today.

PIERRE: How did you get into the last GOP Convention?

FRED PAUL: Oh, brother, that was really a lollapaloosa!

PIERRE: How did you do this?

FRED PAUL: Vice-President Nixon's car came up, and there was such a surge forward of people that if you were going in one direction you just couldn't do it. So I just joined in with this constant flow, and Representative Bill Miller was there, and they all just kept

slowly filing past. Then they started weeding them out, you know
– I mean ones with special passes. And this one man came and
was very, you know, insistent that we have the proper credential,
and these Burns and Pinkerton men were arguing with him, so I
just went right in behind *them*. I couldn't be bothered with all
that waste of time. I got right inside. Senator Goldwater was
there, and the Vice-President was there, and General Eisenhower
was there, and everybody.

PIERRE: How did you get your *picture* taken with Nixon though?

FRED PAUL: Well, you know, he was walking towards the area where
the luncheon was to be, and so was I. I'm always ready for a free
meal. And I just said to him: "Can I have your autograph?" and
bang before I knew it everybody was shooting this picture. I guess
they thought, you know, human interest or something like that.

PIERRE: You get your picture taken with as many famous people as
possible?

FRED PAUL: Well, I try to. It's good for my memoirs.

PIERRE: You're only eighteen, and already you're writing your
memoirs? How did you meet Eisenhower?

FRED PAUL: Well, he walked in. He had quite a bit of guard around
him. All I did was walk up, and I think I said, "Mr. President"
or something; I said: "I'm a great admirer of yours, it's quite an
honour to meet you, sir." And he signed the thing for me and
that was all.

PIERRE: You should be in the newspaper business.

FRED PAUL: Well, I could get the story. I'll tell you I can get the
picture. Some of these photographers, you know, it kills them
because even the ones in the official entourage have been refused,
and there they can see me in the press box or see me in the front
row. I can just see them boiling right there, you know.

PIERRE: I can see them boiling, too.

FRED PAUL: They almost boiled on me one time.

PIERRE: How do you mean?

FRED PAUL: Well, in Atlantic City I had my own photographer there.

PIERRE: Your *own* photographer?

FRED PAUL: And he was in the front row, but he was all cleared.
He was cleared by Derek Taylor, and I had him in the front row.
And these other British people who were travelling – *The London
Daily Express* and all this – wanted to get pictures. And I said:
"I'm sorry, that seat's taken. My photographer's here tonight to
get pictures." Oh boy, I heard about that for days. They were
going to get off the plane if they continued to allow me to do this,

but now we've all become very good friends. They admire that. In fact, some of them have said: "I think we'll be on tour with you next year."

PIERRE: I wouldn't be at all surprised. Nothing surprises me after hearing —

FRED PAUL: There's only one gentleman there who's really given me trouble. That's the representative of the *Liverpool Echo*. He's been simply ugly. And this man has no reason to be. I had to vouch for him one time, so he could get into the Beatles' suite, and they said I hurt his pride or something like that.

PIERRE: You vouched for him!

FRED PAUL: Yeah, for him. I was on the eighth-floor steps, and he was just coming up, and the guards tried to stop him.

PIERRE: He's probably worked for twenty-five years for that newspaper.

FRED PAUL: Well, he's worked the Beatles on all their tours. I said: "That man's with the official party," and they said okay fine. After that he never spoke to me.

PIERRE: No, I bet he didn't. What's the toughest piece of gate-crashing you've ever done?

FRED PAUL: Oh, let's see. There was one where I had a bit of a problem. Well, they told me Montreal would be a problem, but that was no problem.

PIERRE: Could you speak French?

FRED PAUL: Yeah, the stewardess gave me the words. "*Je suis avec le tour*," or something like that. "I'm with the tour." And I just said, "*Comment ça va, comment ça va?*" to everybody, which means "hello" or something, and you know they went along with me, and that was all — no problems. That was the easiest one. About the hardest one was the Saddle and Sirloin Club here in Toronto. I got through everyone but this one Burns or something, one private guard. He said "You're not cleared with me." And I said: "I have a letter and everything." He said: "You're not getting by here!" I said: "How do you think I got cleared with all those other twenty-five guards?" And he almost had me, you know, ejected. But, finally, Derek Taylor came along and got me through. That was about the hardest press conference to crash.

PIERRE: There'll be heads rolling in the Burns Detective Agency after this revelation.

FRED PAUL: I'm a great Goldwater man, and the only thing that bothered me was: here was all this protection for the Senator and for a man like General Eisenhower; yet one person such as I could get in. I know there were those who got in who didn't belong there. You know, this might happen some day with the President of the United States.

PIERRE: Well it did in a way, didn't it?

FRED PAUL: It did, yeah, that's one thing that I have great feelings on.

PIERRE: You're a Goldwater man. I thought kids were radicals. But I suppose *he's* a radical to you.

FRED PAUL: At the convention, every young person I talked to is a Goldwater fan.

PIERRE: What's happening? When I was a kid all the kids were Socialists.

FRED PAUL: I don't know. We're all radicals today. The way we're living, how can we help but be radicals?

PIERRE: No, I think we older people are the radicals, and I think you kids are the conformists. You know, really, you all dress alike and you all think alike and you all scream alike at the Beatles.

FRED PAUL: Oh, I never scream at them.

PIERRE: No, you don't. And I wouldn't say that you were a typical teenager, or, really, that you were a conformist. What you've said suggests you're not.

FRED PAUL: No, I consider myself very separate from the average teenager. I've never met another one like myself. Maybe at Bellevue or some of our better places I might meet a few, but up to this point I haven't.

PIERRE: Are teenagers really in revolt against the adult world, as we are told?

FRED PAUL: No, I think it's completely opposite. I think that adults have forgotten what their younger heroes were really like. My mother has told me about Rudolph Valentino, and the way she describes him you'd think he was the greatest man that ever walked on this earth.

PIERRE: No, he wasn't. Harpo Marx was.

FRED PAUL: All right, all right. And who was the other fellow, huh? Frank Sinatra?

PIERRE: Oh, that old broken-down man that we occasionally see in the movies. Yes, I remember him.

FRED PAUL: And then Elvis; 1950 was his day. But this is the day of the Beatles. Maybe in 1970 it'll be someone else. You don't know who it will be. So this is their hero, this is their representative, and that's why when they see him it's like seeing the President really. The President is our representative as a nation, but for the teenagers this is their present leader, and they're going to go all out to give them the royal welcome.

PIERRE: I hear your next plan is to go to the Inauguration of the President of the United States. What will you wear for that?

FRED PAUL: Well, I thought I'd get a tux and top hat, Cadillac, no briefcase but, you know, the whole thing.

PIERRE: How close are you going to stand to the President?

FRED PAUL: Well, you know, I want to say hello and all this and, you know, mingle around.

PIERRE: That's all.

FRED PAUL: I just want to have a brief chat, that's all. Give him my love, even if it's the wrong man.

PIERRE: How do you come by this self-assurance?

FRED PAUL: It's something that you have to develop, and this world is a highly competitive world. Certainly in your business you know that if you're going to make it in radio or TV you're going to have to let everyone know that you believe you have the talent and the ability. They'll eventually see it.

PIERRE: At your age I was a nervous kid.

FRED PAUL: Oh, I am usually.

PIERRE: You are?

FRED PAUL: But I can't ever sit still.

PIERRE: But when I was your age, I couldn't open my mouth.

FRED PAUL: Well, I was very active in church, and I've given a lot of — I don't want to call them sermons — but, you know, I've spoken to church congregations on juvenile delinquency and things like this, so it's something that's developed, I think. You know, I talk all the time, like a broken record my mother tells me, and so after a while I guess it becomes natural. You know, doing what comes naturally like the song.

PIERRE: Well, I have the distinct feeling we are going to hear from you again. Remember the name: Fred Paul.

FRED PAUL: Buy the book! Tell them to buy the book!

I WAS A

TEENAGE ADULT

"I would think the kids today
wouldn't get
broken-hearted very readily."

Murray Kaufman is a dapper man with a ravaged face who happens to be the world's most famous disc jockey. Tom Wolfe dubbed him The Fifth Beatle, and Malcolm X and his followers did him the signal honour of appropriating one of the several phrases he's invented: "It's what's happening, baby!" When he stages one of his rare personal appearances, he consistently breaks all records and outgrosses all competition.

Murray the K, to give him his professional name, is a man in tune with his times – or at least a sizeable segment of his times. He has an uncanny ability to know in advance who or what is going to go over big with the kids. Bobby Darin, Johnny Mathis, and Paul Anka all owe much of their early recognition to this prescience.

I first read about him when he did a national television show for Sargent Shriver's Office of Economic Opportunity, to which he is the official radio-TV consultant. The show, which outdrew network competition, got groans from congressmen but applause from the people to whom it was directed – the nation's youth.

So I read up on Murray the K and discovered that he likes Vivaldi, once managed Mickey Mantle and Willie Mays, played in Our Gang and Eddie Cantor comedies as a kid, and was a high-school drop-out who went back. I also began to suspect that he might, like Malcolm X, be two people: quiet in private, raucous in public.

And so, it turned out, he was. Very quiet in the studio: soft-spoken, intelligent, unflamboyant. Until I asked him to don the beat-up straw hat that has become his public talisman and talk into the microphone, just as he does at his home station WINS.

"You'd better look out!" said Murray the K, giving the sound engineer a moment's warning. Then, twisting in his seat and hunching forward, he became a different kind of man with a brand-new voice.

"Hi, everybody!" cried Murray the K, as the windows rattled, "this is Murray the K coming to you like it is, baby. Tonight we're gonna play some what's happened sounds for you out there! Sounds that are definitely what's happened and including some blasts from the past – some golden gassers. Some newies, too! So get ready, 'cause we got a mess of stuff for you! Papa's got a brand-new bag!"

The interesting thing was that even Murray the K's accent changed. He sounded like Elvis Presley. I asked him why he'd adopted it.

▭

MURRAY KAUFMAN: Really, I don't adopt it – it's being from the South. Whenever I talk loud or express myself in any kind of excitable manner, the Southern flavour sort of comes back.

PIERRE: You also talk a different language. You're using words there that I don't understand. "Golden gassers" – what was all that?

MURRAY KAUFMAN: Well, actually, these are some phrases that I coined. "Blasts from the past." When something is a blast, it means it's great. And from the past is, of course, self-explanatory. So that's what we call the "Goldie" – the record that we used to refer to as a million-seller record. Hits from years gone by that still have the appeal today.

PIERRE: They tell me you've made up a whole new language.

MURRAY KAUFMAN: Like, *Measurray.*

PIERRE: What's that?

110

MURRAY KAUFMAN: "Measurray." Actually, if you'd say "Murray" and then use the Measurray language, Murray is Measurray. And if it's "Pierre," it's Pieassierre.

PIERRE: Oh, I used to do that when I was a kid.

MURRAY KAUFMAN: That's the old carny language, which we adapted. We gave out something like seven hundred and fifty thousand explanations in a little dictionary form. We understand that some teachers here, in a lot of the high-schools, to get their students to study Spanish, would teach them their Spanish lessons in Measurray.

PIERRE: Well, now, I think we'd better have you explain why you are called the Fifth Beatle.

MURRAY KAUFMAN: Well, I think if I had planned it, Pierre, it never would have come about. But I had played the Beatles' record in New York before it was ever played in the United States. I think the winter of '63, and nothing happened. I mean just no reaction. I had my Christmas show, which is the "In Person" show I do four times a year, and then I took off down South for a vacation. While I was there, in a matter of ten or twelve days, the Beatles exploded – just exploded on the scene. Like, most of the people said: "Where did it happen from?" Actually, I was hip to them about a year before. My wife knew about them because the fashion magazines – *Vogue* and *Harper's Bazaar* and magazines like that – were writing about them. They were causing a stir in Europe and creating a lot of clothes styles. So the station called me in Florida and said: "We want you to come back because the Beatles are coming in," and I said: "But I don't know them. I mean I've had some contact with them, but I don't know them." They said: "We just want you to cover it. Would you go to the airport?" So I went down to the airport and I had my tape machine, and the newsreel men were in the back and a couple of interviewers – you know, ready to put them down – were there and a couple of other disc jockeys. When they came into the press conference, the people really tried to put them down. Of course, the Beatles in their own inimitable style turned it around the other way and put the newsmen on. I started talking to them about a friend of mine who had come over on the plane with them . . . and then I think we talked the same language . . . and they had heard about Murray K.

PIERRE: You were very close to them at this point?

MURRAY KAUFMAN: I was the first one in line up in front, and I was crouching down under the platform, and then I stood up. Now all of a sudden the boys became interested in what I was saying. They forgot about the rest of the entire press conference. Fellows from the networks were hollering out: "Tell Murray the K to cut it out," and this and that and the other thing; so Ringo was saying: "This bloke said to cut it out!" So they started putting the press on, and we just had conversation. They said: "What are you doing later?" And they invited me up to the room and the rest is history. We just became sort of very good friends. I travelled with them to Washington and then to Miami. I roomed with George. Paul and Ringo were next door, and George and I were in this other room next door, and then Cyn Lennon was with John. Cyn made that trip to the United States. And I sort of acted as their host while they were in this country, and then they invited me to England when *A Hard Day's Night* was on, and I was their guest there for about two or three weeks. Every time there was a rumour about the Beatles – and it was spread all over the air waves and all – the kids got to know to listen in, because I would not make a comment until I found out what the truth was.

PIERRE: I'm trying to think what kind of an experience it would be to travel with this madhouse.

MURRAY KAUFMAN: Unbelievable. You get numb after awhile. You don't believe it. Everything gets out of proportion. Now, in my own little world here, we have this at our shows when I make personal appearances. Since the Beatles, it's become even more so, because the gals, particularly, know of the close association.

PIERRE: You must have peculiar eardrums.

MURRAY KAUFMAN: Yeah, you do, but it gets to a point where it reaches such a tumultuous amount of decibels, I guess, that your ears completely leave you. I mean, it just becomes like a wave. The sound is something else to describe, because it reaches such proportions that the Beatles themselves find it hard to believe that it's happening to them. They're in the midst of it and you're in the midst of it and you don't believe it's happening. It's happening out there . . . it's like some dream – but you're not really in it.

PIERRE: Are you frightened by this kind of enormous mob psychology?

MURRAY KAUFMAN: I'm only trying to give you my own experience to explain how the boys must feel. I think they have a much better sense of humour about it. They come out and they say: "Hey! It's great! Isn't it wonderful?" They really enjoy it. Like at Shea's Stadium, John said: "I wish they had been a little closer so a couple of them could have broken through." He likes to see that happen. That turns them on. I remember going out there and hearing this, and then I remember standing on the stage and becoming . . . well, after awhile, you become sort of at ease at it, you know; there's a rapport between you and your audience. And I said to myself: "Now what is this? This is happening to *me*. Why am I getting this?" You can look at it that way because it becomes very unreal to you after awhile.

PIERRE: Well, it can do one of two things to you, Murray. It can either give you a sense of humility, or it may give you a sense of ego and a feeling of power that is larger than life, and which might in the end destroy you. Do you think about this?

MURRAY KAUFMAN: Listen, the Beatles have a power that's all over the world.

PIERRE: Absolutely.

MURRAY KAUFMAN: Whatever power – if you call it that – whatever influence I have here, I have been trying to direct in a different manner – against adults who have closed minds, who don't realize that there is a social revolution, a music revolution, without any representation of the young point of view (and I'm talking about up to the twenty-five-year-old) in the press. None whatsoever. One day things will explode, as they have many times already here in the United States.

PIERRE: You're talking about the Negro riots in Harlem and Los Angeles.

MURRAY KAUFMAN: Riots for one, right. And other situations too. They're gonna turn around, the adults, and they're gonna say: "Why, where did *this* come from? How did it *happen*?"

PIERRE: Which is what they said in Los Angeles when the Negroes revolted. But what you're saying, though, is there is going to be a youth explosion. A violent one?

MURRAY KAUFMAN: Well, I don't know whether it becomes one on the intellectual level or it becomes one where there's actually a physical revolution. But there is definitely, you know, something on the horizon. People better listen now. The only thing that's getting the adults to listen – all those people at agencies and newspapers – to even take any mind is (again a horrible thing) the Almighty Dollar. All of a sudden they found out kids have money and can be exploited. I mean, half of the population is under a certain age in the twenties – I think it's twenty-two or twenty-three. Now, they don't realize that rock-and-rollers no longer exist. People who use that term "rock-and-roll," it's sort of aged. It started in '51, '52 with Bill Haley! This is thirteen years later – it's over. I think the English sound is over and by that I mean the dominance of the English scene. Of course, the Beatles will be on the scene and, of course, there'll be a lot of others, like Herman's Hermits, who will make good records and all, but the overall dominance is over.

PIERRE: How do you know what's happening in the world that we've been discussing – the new world of youth?

MURRAY KAUFMAN: Well, I guess, how does an editor who's in charge of foreign affairs know what's going on around the world? You make it your business. You have an antenna that's attuned to youth. You're out in the field, whether it be the Bedford-Stuyvesant section of Brooklyn, which is the Harlem of Brooklyn, or whether it be Shaker Heights in Ohio. I've been to these places, and I get to talk to the young people first hand, and I get to meet those people who now are shaping the expressions. There is a new musical expression on the horizon. The older people – who call it rock-and-roll, who can't understand it and can't get with it and naturally have to put it down (because if you can't understand it you must put it down), I have news for them; *these are the good old days*, and they'd better realize it soon. Because there has never been a wider gap between the young people of the country and the older generation than there is now; and that gap is widening every day. They say: "Well, we don't understand them. What is it that they want?" And yet they don't *want* to listen. I don't say that the younger generation should run the country. But in order to realize all the energies and imaginations and force and drive of youth, you have to understand them by setting out communication lines. You have to be able to receive and understand what they are saying. Because the youth *have* something to say. And if you're going to suppress what they have to say, it's like putting it in a pressure cooker. One day it's going to explode.

PIERRE: Why is there such a difference today? When I grew up in the Thirties, I don't recall that I felt there was a gap between myself and the adult world. Nor was youth that cohesive in the Thirties. There were no "teenagers." We were just called kids. There was no teenage market. Is it the money?

MURRAY KAUFMAN: No, I don't think so. I think, let's face it, we're in a television age, a jet age, an atomic age. You learn things faster . . . quicker. The kids are getting around. They travel more, they understand more.

PIERRE: The audiences are getting younger, aren't they?

MURRAY KAUFMAN: That's right.

PIERRE: What's your audience? When you get on that radio, what age are you covering?

MURRAY KAUFMAN: Well, actually, when I talk, I talk to one person. I never look at it as an audience.

PIERRE: How old?

MURRAY KAUFMAN: I have in mind someone in the twenties.

PIERRE: That old?

MURRAY KAUFMAN: Yes.

PIERRE: I would have thought that the Beatles, for instance, would appeal to kids of between twelve and fifteen.

MURRAY KAUFMAN: Do you know who the Beatles really turn on? They really turn on the older people. They get the biggest kick out of them.

PIERRE: That's why they're out with the kids, I'm told.

MURRAY KAUFMAN: Well, in certain parts in England, I think. Because parental approval meant that it was no longer a kick for them, and they went to the Rolling Stones.

PIERRE: Now when you talk of a *social* revolution among youth, exactly what do you mean?

MURRAY KAUFMAN: Well, in utilizing the songs, for example, there's a song that's very big here in the States called "Eve of Destruction." They say these are protest songs. They are, in a way; but they are also saying more. There is a song called "All I Want to Do" by Sonny and Cher; if you listen to the lyrics of that song, it's saying something that it didn't say in the Thirties or the Forties or the Fifties. The "Oooh, Oooh, Baby, Baby" sound is out. They're really saying something.

PIERRE: What are they saying?

MURRAY KAUFMAN: "All I want to do: I don't want to hypnotize you, I don't want to sympathize with you, I don't want to meet your kin or anything, all I want to do is be friends." It isn't like: "Stand Beside Me" and this and that. What it's saying is "All I want to do is be friends with you." The songs have returned to the lyrical, and they really are saying something. And from the various tones of the lyrics, you can get a *feeling* . . . because of its immense immediate popularity . . . because of its complete involvment with the audience that it's reaching. Look at the tremendous success of Sonny and Cher who, back in June, were really nothing. Just in two months they've been sensational. I met them in June, and I fell in love with what they had to say. Now, if you and everybody else around the country, in our country or Canada or wherever it may be, would just *listen* to these lyrics: listen to "I

115

Get No Satisfaction." It's saying something, you know. *I get no satisfaction because you don't smoke the same kind of cigarettes as me.* Each and every lyric has something to say. It's not a parody, but really an explanation of their outlook of various phases of our life . . . love. And you find that the teenagers towards sex are much more sophisticated, much cooler. Of course, in England, they're *very* cool, more so than in the United States.

PIERRE: What do you mean by "cool" in that context? Unenthusiastic? Not so fervent?

MURRAY KAUFMAN: Yes.

PIERRE: Less emotional?

MURRAY KAUFMAN: Well, maybe in any outward showing of emotion.

PIERRE: They're not wearing their hearts on their sleeves anymore?

MURRAY KAUFMAN: Yeah, and I would think the kids today wouldn't get heart-broken very readily, you know, with a boyfriend, etc.

PIERRE: They *wouldn't*?

MURRAY KAUFMAN: Not as much.

PIERRE: Is this a good thing?

MURRAY KAUFMAN: I don't know. I don't think I would like to offer a comment. I think it's a very personal thing.

PIERRE: What's the attitude of kids towards religion? Do they believe in a personal God as kids have in the past?

MURRAY KAUFMAN: Some do.

PIERRE: But is there a change?

MURRAY KAUFMAN: I think so, yes.

PIERRE: What is the change?

MURRAY KAUFMAN: I think that they're a little confused. I think that there is a controversy between what the Church is saying and what they're reading. I think they're very confused about it.

PIERRE: Are they equally confused about the leadership of their country? Is there a disillusionment or a cynicism going on?

MURRAY KAUFMAN: I think in England a disillusionment is a more readily built-in liberalism, as far as being able to live with all kinds of parties and pressure groups. Here, in the United States, they go on emotion, you know. If they're taught "Hate this!" or "Don't like that!" well, they'll go along with it.

THE TEENAGERS' TYCOON

"You just can't relate
or communicate with somebody
who doesn't understand."

*Even though he lives in a twenty-one-room mansion and wears
expensive clothes, Phil Spector doesn't really look or act like a
typical American tycoon. It's true he has a chauffeured limousine,
but the licence plate bears the inscription: "Mary Poppins Is a
Fink." It's true he has beautifully engraved calling cards; but there
is only one gold-embossed word on each: JESUS. Tycoons are
usually graying at the temples, and they have a well-fed, well-
barbered look about them. Spector is positively cadaverous, and
as for his hair – it falls down around his velvet coat lapels in ring-
lets. On the day I met him, beside the swimming pool of Hollywood's Ambassador Hotel, he was sporting, among other articles
of clothing, a velvet-brocade waistcoat and a ruffled shirt with lace
cuffs. Nor was his mien in the best traditions of the U.S. Executive Suite. Where was the hearty grin, the steely eyed glance, the
firm handshake, the aura of confidence and corporate strength?
Spector made a couple of flip comments,* sotto voce, *looked at
the ground, and turned away.*

117

Yet this is a powerful man and a significant one – perhaps more significant today than Floyd Odlum of Atlas Corporation. Spector represents a new kind of businessman, tapping a new and burgeoning market. He knows exactly what he is doing; he understands his market thoroughly; he spares no pains, effort, or sweat to produce a product that is, in his terms at least, as near to perfection as he can make it.

At twenty-six, with five production companies under his wing, he is a millionaire several times over. He has been in that class since 1961, when at the age of twenty-one, he had made his first million clear.

He did it in less than two years. When he was sixteen, he was just another high-school kid playing the jazz guitar in clubs at night. A year later, inspired by an inscription on his father's tombstone, he had a solid hit on his hands: "To Know Him Is to Love Him." It sold a million copies and became an all-time teen classic. It netted Spector twenty thousand dollars, but after the sharks were through with him, he saw only three thousand of it.

For two years he marked time, working in Los Angeles as a court stenotypist. Then, at nineteen, he moved to Manhattan. His objective: a job as a U.N. interpreter. The night before the interview, however, he fell in with a group of musicians. He has been in the music business ever since.

His first attempts to crash Tin Pan Alley were abortive. Then he wrote another hit, "Spanish Harlem," which gave him enough leverage to land him a job as an A & R (artists and repertoire) man with Atlantic Records. By 1961, he was a free lance record producer, song writer, director, and entrepreneur. Without looking back, Spector marched resolutely into the jungle of the recording business and emerged with a den full of trophies.

How did he do it, this pale-faced boy with the limpid eyes and the hollow cheeks who seems so insecure? Partly by reversing the big companies' shotgun style of producing a dozen teenage records a month and hoping one would catch on. Spector's method was to produce one record at a time, then push it as hard as he could. In four years, he turned out two dozen records which he wrote, arranged, and produced himself. He sold twenty million of them. The skinny kid with the guitar had somehow captured the heartbeat of his own generation and bested the adult world at its own game.

I had heard that Spector was a kook, and he certainly looked like one. I had heard that he often refused to give straight answers

*to questions and, certainly at the outset, his replies were flip
enough. But as my talk with him progressed, it grew more serious.
Though his idiom is new, Spector, like the songs he writes, does
have something to say. Somebody once wrote that "nobody gets
a bigger kick out of himself than Spector." It sounded to me like
a good place to begin, so I asked him if he enjoyed being himself.*

◯

PHIL SPECTOR: It's nice. My psychiatrist gets a lot of fun.

PIERRE: Your psychiatrist?

PHIL SPECTOR: Oh sure. I pay him all that money. The police get a
lot of fun – everybody gets a lot of fun. It's okay. I don't know;
there's great displeasure in being *anyone*. I haven't decided who
I am yet – as I don't think anyone has.

PIERRE: At the age of twenty-six you don't know who you are?

PHIL SPECTOR: No, no. Who is anyone? You know? I'm always trying to be something. Everybody is. You go on forever trying to be
someone that we can look back on and say, you know, good or
bad, or wasted or well-spent.

PIERRE: Who are you trying to be?

PHIL SPECTOR: Someone offering something, someone doing something constructive, creative.

PIERRE: In your field in the music business?

PHIL SPECTOR: In life.

PIERRE: Let's talk about the music business. You've said: "I function well in a world of hostility." Were you referring to the music
business?

PHIL SPECTOR: Just as a basis for being successful, on an emotional
level, in the music industry – which is a very competitive and
extremely angry industry because there's so much competition.
You have people going at each other all the time. And society
has been extremely hostile to people like myself. I'm not talking
about financially, I'm talking about emotionally. I can thrive very
well in a hostile world and function much better in an antagonistic
interview than in a friendly one.

PIERRE: You've said also that ninety-five per cent of the music
business is heavily infiltrated by morons.

PHIL SPECTOR: It's gone up since I said that. It's on the rise every
day.

119

PIERRE: Tell me about this. You call these people greedy and vicious. You've indicated you've had trouble yourself – that a lot of young kids have trouble in what appears to be a cut-throat business.

PHIL SPECTOR: Well, of course, it's a business that was created by an era which is slowly dying off. That fat cigar-smoking individual, who's being run by people like myself and others, he's holding on tight to his old ways. Many people said: "You can't do this, you can't do that," but you can do anything. There was a time when the industry was controlled by major labels. No longer. There was a time when one record producer, Mitch Miller, controlled everything. No longer. Now the industry has opened up, and there's room for everyone. A lot of people are extremely angry about this.

PIERRE: Are you saying that in the old days there was a master-slave relationship between a large record company and a recording star?

PHIL SPECTOR: There was a master-slave relationship on the part of the major labels and anyone who tried to make a hit. You couldn't get in the industry unless you were with one of these. It's like England today; you can't really start your own record company in England. You have to be distributed by one of the three majors, and that's the way it was in America. It has changed considerably.

PIERRE: Then there must be an awful lot of resentment in the music industry over people like yourself – indeed, of youth in general – who have, in a sense, taken over and gone their own way?

PHIL SPECTOR: Yes. It's because of that that you have such a high amount of, let's say, freaks. Because the normal is to just stay and compete and see . . . and then, if you can break through, you break through so big that you get called a freak. It's always the absurd that comes through. Who is it that said, "The freaks shall inherit the earth?"

PIERRE: A lot of people, I would guess, would consider you a freak.

PHIL SPECTOR: Oh, boy! Side-show edition! I don't know about those people.

PIERRE: Do you get called this by the adult world?

PHIL SPECTOR: Every now and then there is a brave individual who will come along with a mighty pen and write something.

PIERRE: You have succeeded on the level that really counts in our society, haven't you, which is the financial level? You've made it.

PHIL SPECTOR: Our society is such, unfortunately. I don't respond to the name callings. It doesn't mean anything. I don't have the time.

PIERRE: Now let's talk a bit about why you've been successful. People talk about "the Spector sound" in music. What is the

120

Spector sound? You handle all this music yourself, don't you – you produce it yourself?

PHIL SPECTOR: Yes, yes: I put marshmallows on the microphone. No; what *do* I do? It's not a sound; it's a style. It's comparable to Bergman's style in the movies or Stanley Kubrick or Polanski or anybody. It's a style; and because it's musical, they call it a *sound*. Basically it's a Wagnerian approach to popular music. That's what the basis is.

PIERRE: What do you do – add more of certain kinds of instruments?

PHIL SPECTOR: If you're familiar with Wagnerian operas, it's a steady, large, overpowering flow of sound: you're not really quite sure what's doing it, but you can always hear a big chord behind whatever: behind the singer, behind the soloist. This is built from Wagner – the idea, the concept.

PIERRE: You enjoy classical music?

PHIL SPECTOR: Very much.

PIERRE: A lot of people would think that strange because you're in the popular field.

PHIL SPECTOR: Who is it said a knowledge of syphilis doesn't mean that you have to get it?

PIERRE: Do you personally also enjoy the music that you produce?

PHIL SPECTOR: Oh, very much so.

PIERRE: How long does it take you to make a three-minute recording?

PHIL SPECTOR: From about four to six weeks. Sometimes longer.

PIERRE: How much time would be involved with the actual artist playing the music and singing?

PHIL SPECTOR: Most of the time is spent *after* the artist leaves – in putting it together, editing it, creating the right sound.

PIERRE: A song that takes two or three minutes on a popular label – how many times does the artist play that for you so that you have that on tape?

PHIL SPECTOR: Oh, that could be any amount of times; there is no number.

PIERRE: Twenty times?

PHIL SPECTOR: Sure.

PIERRE: One hundred times?

PHIL SPECTOR: It could be. It depends. Until you get the right performance that feels as though it responds emotionally correct.

PIERRE: Then you take that performance – the one you like – and you fiddle with that for, as you say, four to six weeks?

PHIL SPECTOR: Yes; not necessarily. People believe that you use mechanical gimmicks, but it has nothing to do with that. It's just

121

working with it, playing it back, playing it through many, many times, until you're sure, and then making a change and then listening to it many, many times, and then making another change. It's like editing a film. To actually shoot a scene takes ten minutes, you know; but to edit it – maybe overdub a voice because the actor turned away. There's many, many things you have to do.

PIERRE: Then what the kids hear on the record isn't necessarily what they would have heard if they'd heard those recording stars in the studio?

PHIL SPECTOR: That's correct. Quite different. What they're hearing is what we try to call popular art-form music rather. . . .

PIERRE: Then you really are the most important man in this?

PHIL SPECTOR: Well, I think the producer of any piece of art is – whether he is a painter or a director of movies.

PIERRE: What you're saying is that you are really the artist working with the raw materials which are the people who play guitars and sing?

PHIL SPECTOR: Well, I put it all together. They're not necessarily that raw. I work with very talented people, and what I try to do is get all the talent out of them and get all the emotion out of them – tell them when they've gone too far and tell them when to stop and tell them when they haven't gone far enough.

PIERRE: Now, you write the songs and you produce them and you arrange them. Do you also distribute them?

PHIL SPECTOR: Yes, I do.

PIERRE: You've had a lot of trouble with distributors, as everybody has.

PHIL SPECTOR: Oh, yeah; but we carry a big axe usually. It's a very rough business. It's the only business in the world where the distributor calls you collect for your product. You try to call Thom McAn for his shoes and you call him collect and you know what you'll get.

PIERRE: I am told a lot of young kids who should make a lot of money don't get it.

PHIL SPECTOR: Well, it's very difficult. In order to make a hit record today on an independent label, you have to build up a reserve, and you have to keep making hits. With the competition of eight hundred records a week coming out, that's difficult. You only have a top forty. Forty records that are hits; so it's very, very hard. And that's why many companies go out of business, and the kids who may be hits go out of business with them, and everybody goes to court.

122

PIERRE: Let's talk about the content of these hits. You say that your lyrics appeal to modern youth because modern youth is dissociated . . . because they have a feeling of not belonging . . . because they have a yearning to be free, to be needed, to be loved.

PHIL SPECTOR: Certainly. I think we all do.

PIERRE: How about you? Do you have this feeling?

PHIL SPECTOR: Sure. I think every normal person (which is a very ambiguous term) has that need.

PIERRE: Yes, but if that was true of all people in the same degree, then your lyrics would also appeal to elderly people; but they really appeal more to young people than to any other group in society.

PHIL SPECTOR: Well, I don't know any more. I used to think that, too, until I went into a discotheque and I saw all adults; till I went into a taxicab and heard them listening to a pop music station; and then I went all over the world, and I saw everywhere in the world the same people listening to the same kind of music. Everybody has their right to like country and western, classical, and different varieties. But if you have one music that's so outstandingly popular throughout the world – is it *just* children? Is it *just* teenagers?

PIERRE: Is the music popular because of the sound or the beat, or because of what the words say?

PHIL SPECTOR: I think because it causes the same emotional response in all the people – and a certain freedom. It's taken away a lot of the anxieties of life, a lot of the barriers that used to exist. Society is changing; and with it a certain relaxed kind of music has taken over, just like a relaxed kind of dancing. You no longer have to go to Arthur Murray to learn to dance – to be successful at a party. You get out on the floor and do whatever you want to do. It's the same kind of thing with music. All kinds of music are accepted. We have the extremes from the Beatles to Frank Sinatra to Dean Martin. They can all make hit records today.

PIERRE: From nuns to nineteen-year-olds.

PHIL SPECTOR: Right.

PIERRE: What are you saying in your lyrics?

PHIL SPECTOR: Well, all the people who have listened to the music I hope have listened to the words. I'm just saying what I feel, what I believe. I think the Beatles say it, I think Bob Dylan says it, I think everyone who is writing today is saying what they *feel*, as well as saying what they think.

123

PIERRE: What do you feel and what do you think? Are you essentially a happy guy or a sad guy? Could you describe yourself?

PHIL SPECTOR: Emotional. I don't know if I'm sad or happy. I have a lot of conflict.

PIERRE: You mentioned your psychiatrist a moment ago. I know one of the reasons you hated to leave New York was because you didn't want to leave him.

PHIL SPECTOR: It takes a long time to create a rapport with someone, especially on such a personal level – someone you haven't grown up with, someone you don't know.

PIERRE: Why do it at all? Why do you need a psychiatrist?

PHIL SPECTOR: Oh, I think the whole society needs one.

PIERRE: You think everyone of us should have one? Is this because you need somebody to talk to about yourself?

PHIL SPECTOR: No; it's because there is such frightening conflict in today's society – such fear and trepidation around – that it's just very difficult to live a normal life. Professional guidance can't hurt. I'm not saying every psychiatrist is a god, but professional guidance can't really hurt, and someone to talk to can't really hurt. I don't think you can cure cancer by yourself. I don't think you can cure mental illness by yourself. Mental illness is really the extreme, but most of us suffer from mental illness to some degree. It's very difficult to exist in society today. Money is the criterion and respect and long hair is out and this is in. You see, children grow up and parents look at them and say: "Well, *you're* nothing, so it's a reflection on me. Shall I slap your face down?" The whole theory is that when a child of eleven years old – a little boy – sees his sister and he wants to make love to his sister and he feels very upset. He says: "Oh, my God, I'm very disturbed; what'll I do?" and he even becomes a homosexual because he gets no help and he can't tell anyone. And if he went to a psychiatrist, the psychiatrist tells him: "Look, *every* little eleven-year-old boy wants to do that; it's normal." You don't have anybody telling you. Parents can't do it because their generation didn't communicate.

PIERRE: We're really on the subject of the barrier between the generations, aren't we?

PHIL SPECTOR: That's what it is; that's what it is. This generation will raise a healthier generation because the introduction of psychiatry has become a very common thing. There are so many things coming along for the mind . . . drugs, for instance.

PIERRE: Are you happy with your success? Do you ever feel you want to just quit the business? Do you ever get in a slump?

124

PHIL SPECTOR: Oh no, no, no. I don't think about the business that much. The only time I ever really felt that all of it didn't matter was one day I was arrested. That can happen to anyone because of the police. And that's another thing: the laws have got to change – police enforcement is very dated. They have a funny way of carrying out the law. When they arrest you, they say: "You're just another number," and that's when you realize that's all you *really* are – just another number.

PIERRE: The depersonalization of the human being?

PHIL SPECTOR: Oh that's what they do, the whole game.

PIERRE: Why were you arrested?

PHIL SPECTOR: I was arrested because of a policeman's inability to cope with seeing a limousine being occupied by a long-haired individual with a chauffeur. I think that was the whole basis.

PIERRE: You mean this limousine is coming along and there's a chauffeur in the front and you're in the back and the cop arrests you?

PHIL SPECTOR: Oh yeah! "Pull over, wise guy," you know and, "I want to search you!" "Well, you *can't* search me." "Well, I want to." I said: "Well, you've got a gun. I'm not going to argue with you." I told him it's the only reason. So they searched the car, searched everything. They arrest you and then you find out that it's really *their* world – that they have no authority to respond to. Their authority tells them it's okay to do that: *"Who cares about the Fourth Amendment? It was written in 1700 by a nut. It's old and dated. If he wants to do anything about it, there's nine men up there. Let him go to them."*

PIERRE: What *did* you do about this? Your rights were violated. Did you take action against them?

PHIL SPECTOR: Oh, yes. I am presently doing it. I made a deal with Melvin Belli: half and half.

PIERRE: To get back to the subject at hand – what do you say to adults who say: "You are corrupting youth; you are exploiting the teens with this dreadful music?"

PHIL SPECTOR: Oh, I turn them on.

PIERRE: But what's your answer? Do you bother with one?

PHIL SPECTOR: What do you say to somebody when they say: "Go and fight in Vietnam and die?" I don't know. I don't have answers to those questions. "Liquor's okay, but marijuana isn't." I don't know; I don't have the answers. "You're under arrest." What can you say? It's too hard to answer those questions because they don't make any sense. And I consider the source: it's obviously somebody who's frightened or threatened by me, or by something he lacks or doesn't lack. People who are frightened become very threatening. Lack of understanding bars all communication and you just can't relate or communicate with somebody who doesn't understand. If you don't understand them, and you only respond to people when you see somebody who looks the way you want them to look, you respond to him in a certain way. If you saw somebody repulsive, you'd respond the other way.

PIERRE: The kids you know say there's a lack of communication between their world and the adult world.

PHIL SPECTOR: Sure.

PIERRE: But communication works two ways. You have said: "They don't communicate with me, so why should I communicate with them?" Maybe the younger generation should now try communicating back.

PHIL SPECTOR: Well, it's always been a little bizarre to me that the child has to take care of the mother.

PIERRE: Maybe the mother needs it.

PHIL SPECTOR: I know. But the child has so much to worry about, I don't know if it can do it. I don't think that the child should feel guilty.

PIERRE: I wonder why there is so much insecurity now? In the Thirties, there was enormous financial insecurity; in the Forties, everyone was being killed in the war. It seems to me that there should be *less* insecurity in the Sixties; but there seems to be more among you people. Why?

PHIL SPECTOR: They've got more to live up to, I guess, or maybe they've got nothing to live up to. That's it – they have nothing to live up to. They should have more to live up to. They have nothing.

PORTRAIT

OF AN ANTI-HERO

"If you start out broke
and a nobody, what can
anybody ever do to you?"

Michael Caine, an owlishly handsome young Cockney, is a charter member of Britain's Swinging Set — the group of young anti-Establishment photographers, models, actors, and pop singers who have been dubbed The New Aristocracy. Members of the group include Terence Stamp, the actor who dates Jean Shrimpton; David Bailey, the photographer who discovered Jean Shrimpton; and John Barry, the composer who has less to do with Jean Shrimpton but who wrote the score for The Ipcress File, *the spy film that made Caine a star.*

Caine himself has referred to The New Aristocracy as The Cult of the Anti-Hero. Qualifications for membership include an impeccable working-class background ("something lovable, like Cockney, preferably") and immense good looks—but not the traditional British good looks associated with French windows and croquet lawns. One must have, again in Caine's words, "a lived-in face."

Caine fits this image easily, just as he fits the mood of the new

Britain: "cool," hedonistic, and utterly iconoclastic as far as the old values and the old relationships are concerned. Caine symbolizes a kind of upward mobility that is new to Britain – a crashing through class lines made possible by mass pop culture.

His own story is spectacular enough. He was born in 1933 on the Old Kent Road, the son of a Billingsgate fish porter and a charwoman. He has worked at perhaps a score of menial jobs, from making meat pies to mixing cement. But his ambition, since he left school at sixteen, has always been to act. He began to scramble for small theatrical parts some seven years ago, serving out a long, hard apprenticeship in minor roles (playing, usually, Cockney spivs) and eking out an existence, between engagements, washing dishes "in every restaurant in London." Television gave him his first real foothold: he appeared in 125 TV plays, achieving some critical attention but little public acclaim. Then he moved into films. The Ipcress File was his third; in it, significantly, he played the kind of anti-hero so much admired by young Britain. It made him a name star and allowed him to live in the style to which he had always aspired.

I was anxious to meet Michael Caine in London, shortly after The Ipcress File was released, but I was not prepared to like him. Frankly, the Fleet Street news clippings made him sound like a bit of a creep. One should learn never to trust Fleet Street. I found him refreshingly frank, thoroughly likeable, and – though he would detest the word – a little ingenuous. I began by asking him what his father thought when he learned his son wanted to be, of all things, an actor.

◯

MICHAEL CAINE: Yes, he was a little shocked because, being a Billingsgate fish-market porter – you can get a rough idea of the type of man he was – he was a very tough sort of guy, and suddenly he has this son who says: "I want to be an actor," and from then on he sort of used to give me askance glances. He used to worry about just what was happening to me.

PIERRE: What was his ambition for you?

MICHAEL CAINE: His ambition for me was to follow him into the market, or at least to do something that he considered honourable and masculine: like be a City of London policeman, because

128

they're taller than ordinary policemen, or be a soldier, but not just an ordinary soldier – to go into the Guards because, you know, they're taller. I'm over six feet tall, and he was very proud of this.

PIERRE: Did he live to see you become rich and famous?

MICHAEL CAINE: No, he didn't. This is one of the great regrets of my life, actually. He died eight years ago, and at the time he died I think I'd been out of work six months and was borrowing money off him.

PIERRE: But your mother did.

MICHAEL CAINE: Yes, she's still alive.

PIERRE: Now, you went from that kind of a background to a background in which you make as much as £ 1,000 a week. Tell me this: rich people keep saying money is *not* the key to happiness. Are they right or wrong?

MICHAEL CAINE: I think they're right in *saying* it because they're keeping everybody else sort of wondering. But, of course, they're wrong, and they know they're wrong. I used to say to people: "I'd like to be rich!" They'd look shocked, as though I was some kind of vulgar sort of person, and they'd say: "Well, money won't make you happy, you know." And I'd say: "I realize that, but the point is that I *am* very happy, except for the fact that I'm broke; so then if I *do* get money, then I'll be happy." And they'd say: "Well, you won't." Everybody said to me, for instance, when I was at school: "You'll hate it when you leave school, you know." I said: "I hate school. I *want* to leave it!" They said: "You'll hate it." Well, I've loved every moment since I left school, and I've never believed any of these things where people who have been somewhere before me say: "Well, you're going to hate it when you get there." I go and find out for myself, and I usually find them wrong.

PIERRE: Do you spend all the money you make or do you save?

MICHAEL CAINE: Haven't saved yet.

PIERRE: You haven't?

MICHAEL CAINE: No. Like, first, I had to find a house 'cause I shared a flat with another actor, Terence Stamp. We did this for economic reasons. Directly they went, we decided to get a flat each. I had to get a house, and I had to furnish it. I mean I moved in with an electric razor and a teaspoon, you know. And I had no clothes as far as anything to change into. I had to have a complete wardrobe.

PIERRE: Now you've said that you believe in acting like a movie star. How does a movie star act? How do you act now that's different from the way you did when you were a rising and struggling actor?

MICHAEL CAINE: I've just got to think about that question. I can't remember saying it, actually, but I do agree with it. I've always thought – when I've seen in the papers that someone says, "I've won £150,000 on the football pool, but I'm still going to go to work and be ordinary and live in a council house," and all that sort of thing – well, I think that's nonsense. And take people who are in show business: for a start, if you're an actor, you're sort of outside of the laws and things – you can't get insurance on your car; nobody will give you hire-purchase unless you're famous enough for them to know that you can continue to pay. At one time, you weren't sort of accepted into people's homes, and you still aren't accepted into people's homes unless you're famous. And so what I actually mean by behaving like a movie star is that the rules aren't valid for me when I was not well-known and didn't have any money; so now I don't have to go with all the social bit that everybody abides by. I go my own way. So long as I don't hurt anybody or upset anybody, I don't mind.

PIERRE: You were quoted awhile ago as saying that your dream was to have the most beautiful house in the world, full of the most beautiful paintings in the world and the most beautiful girls in the world. Have you made it yet?

MICHAEL CAINE: No.

PIERRE: What's missing? Girls, paintings, or the house?

MICHAEL CAINE: Well, I've gotta sorta qualify that a bit. The most beautiful house in the world would cost a fortune. I don't suppose I'll ever make that much money. I would bring it down a little. I don't think I said the most beautiful *girls* in the world, just the most beautiful girl in the world. And even so, I'm having a few rough edges knocked off at the moment.

PIERRE: What do you mean "rough edges knocked off?"

MICHAEL CAINE: Well, I was at first very impressed by everybody who was very beautiful, but I've found, you know, that all that glitters is not gold.

PIERRE: You once said: "I can't go out with an ugly girl."

MICHAEL CAINE: I don't want to go out with the bride of Frankenstein purely because it would scare me, you know, if we met in the dark.

PIERRE: But do you choose girls only for their looks? Surely there's something else to a girl?

130

MICHAEL CAINE: Oh, there's a lot more to a girl. I choose girls . . . [pause] I don't *choose* girls. You make me sound like some sort of maharajah!

PIERRE: It's you who said it.

MICHAEL CAINE: I've let myself in for this. Yeah, I know.

PIERRE: It's you who said that you and Terence Stamp had started the trend back to women again. Now what did you mean by that?

MICHAEL CAINE: I'll tell you what I meant by that: I was doing an interview, you see, and the woman said to me: "Would you call yourself one of the hell-raisers?" So I said no. And she looked very disappointed. She thought: "What am I going to write about him? He's not a hell-raiser." She said: "Well, what do you do?" So I said: "I go out with girls." So she said: "Well, isn't that being a hell-raiser?" I said: "No. 'Hell-raiser' is a euphemism for a drunk, isn't it? A hell-raiser is a guy who can't hold his drink and goes in somewhere and smashes the place up. I don't. I go into everywhere very quietly and I'm very polite and I'm very nice to everybody. I don't embarrass anybody. I walk away with a girl I want." And this is my way of doing things. This is hell-raising on the quiet scale, but I'm not interested in who sees it. I'm interested in the end result, you see. And so . . . yeah, I was just going to tell you what I said, but I can't say that to you – not on television. Anyway that's what I meant by starting the trend towards girls. And another time someone said to me: "Do you go out with a lot of girls?" And I said yes.

PIERRE: A girl a week, you said.

MICHAEL CAINE: Something like that. Because now and again you *do*, if you haven't got a regular girl friend. So I said yes, and everybody sort of wrote letters as though I was some kind of sex maniac, or something. You know, in England everybody *does* go out with lots of girls, but nobody talks about it, and I sort of mentioned the fact. In England, if you mention it, they sort of look at you and they say: "Why isn't he married, then, and living a moral life!" And then I did eight articles on moral degeneracy or something after that, you know.

PIERRE: You also said that you could have any girl you wanted.

MICHAEL CAINE: Oh, I don't think I said that.

PIERRE: Well, maybe the papers have it wrong. I've been doing some research.

MICHAEL CAINE: Yeah, you obviously have.

PIERRE: Well, look: you're a good-looking, virile, famous, wealthy guy. Surely you can do pretty well with girls.

MICHAEL CAINE: Oh, you can do pretty well with girls. I mean, little men of sixty who are millionaires do pretty well with girls.

PIERRE: Are you doing better now than you did when you were a struggling and starving actor?

MICHAEL CAINE: No, and I'll tell you why: it's this awful reputation I've gotten. They say, "Well, I'm not going to be on *your* list!"

PIERRE: Hoist by your own petard.

MICHAEL CAINE: I walk around for three weeks without a girl friend, and I finally fall in love with somebody, and I say: "Would you come out with me?" She says: "No, I'm not going to be one of *those* girls." I say: "One of *what* girls? I haven't been out with a girl for three weeks!" And they all burst out laughing 'cause they think I was with five girls yesterday. In any case, I work very hard. You get tired around ten-thirty, you know.

PIERRE: How do you feel about yourself and about what is called the image and about success? Have you got an image in mind for yourself? Have you worked at this?

MICHAEL CAINE: No. The only image I would want I haven't got. I want to be one of the best actors around. I'm not even ambitious enough to want to be the *best* actor. Success? I'm very happy with it. I'm not one of those people who says: "It's a drag and all that sort of thing." It's great! It's marvellous! I love every moment of it because I spent thirteen years trying to achieve it.

PIERRE: How has it changed you?

MICHAEL CAINE: Very much for the better. I'm less miserable, less worried; I pick up tabs at dinner. I'm very much more pleasant now.

PIERRE: You like yourself better?

MICHAEL CAINE: I do. I'm not saying I like myself in a conceited way, but I think I've improved and I'm much happier, so that makes people who are close to me much happier, I should think.

PIERRE: You did a whole lot of menial jobs before you got into acting. What were some of them?

MICHAEL CAINE: I used to work in a laundry as a labourer. I've worked as a labourer in a tea warehouse. I've worked on pneumatic drills on the road. I've been a night porter at a hotel. I've washed up in most of the restaurants I eat in. What else? I've made jewel boxes. And I've been a soldier, which is the most menial of all the tasks. I've done a lot of things, but I never, ever did them with a spirit of adventure. I did them just in the spirit of getting the rent.

PIERRE: Now that you have money and have no real worries, for the moment at least, what's the best thing about it? Is it the girls? Is it the ability to pick up cheques? Is it having a pad of your own?

MICHAEL CAINE: No. No.

PIERRE: Or is it something else?

MICHAEL CAINE: It's . . . the best thing of all about it is the security for myself and for my family. I don't come from a very wealthy background and, without being maudlin about it, saying: "I've done this for my dear old mother!" still I'm able to do everything that needs doing.

PIERRE: You persuaded her to stop working finally?

MICHAEL CAINE: Oh yes, she's stopped working. Now I'm going to move her into a house when I can find one where she wants to live. The thing about it is this: if I go to my mother's house, as I often do on a Sunday for lunch, and I see something that's making her uncomfortable, I don't think: "One of these days I'm going to change that." I get on the phone Monday morning, and it's changed immediately. Because my mother for a start is sixty-five, you know, and she obviously hasn't got another sixty-five years to live. She's had a very hard life and, therefore, I try to make things as good as possible for her as quickly as I can. The greatest pleasure is the immediacy of things.

PIERRE: How does she fit into the new circle of friends that you must have made in the acting world?

MICHAEL CAINE: She fits in very well because she's quite a character, you know, and she's very adaptable. I don't want to give a sort of a wrong impression. I'm not a sort of mother's boy that takes my mother everywhere. But at the same time, you know, I do like her. And I look after her and that's that.

PIERRE: I want to change the subject and ask you about the breaks in the business. Yours came when you made a picture called "Zulu," right?

MICHAEL CAINE: Yes. The thing is I played a very upper-crust, very aristocratic lieutenant.

PIERRE: The point being you didn't use a Cockney accent.

MICHAEL CAINE: Yes. For many, many years I'd been typed as a Cockney on television and in what little theatre I've done in the West End. When I went up for "Zulu," I went up to play the Cockney part but it was already cast, and they gave me this other role, after a screen test. Which is really what changed everything for me, as far as breaks go because everybody had said: "He's a very good Cockney actor, that boy, you know, and if you ever get a Cockney part, you ought to use him, not too big, but use him."

But once I played in "Zulu," I just became known as an actor with a limitless field within my own physical limitations.

PIERRE: But this is really where it all changed?

MICHAEL CAINE: This is where it changed for me, because I was very well known on television but only by insiders. When people see you on television, they never watch the credit titles, so they don't say: "Ah, that's Michael Caine!" They come to you and say: "Ah! you're *him*, aren't you? You're the – you know the one I mean." Movie producers watch television and they say: "He's a very good actor, but will he come across on the screen?" Because these two don't go hand in hand. Just because you come across on a television screen doesn't mean that you're going to come across on a movie screen. So they have to see a film of you, especially American producers. You can walk into their office and do the most fantastic interview, and at the end of it they'll say: "Well, have you got two minutes of film we can see on you?" And you say: "Well, I have a television play which they'll run for you." They'll say: "No, have you got any *film*?"

PIERRE: Do you think there's anything in this? Do people come across differently on film?

MICHAEL CAINE: Yes, I believe so. I've watched a lot of television and I've been in a lot of television and what makes somebody a movie star is not necessarily what makes somebody a television star. For one thing, you have to appeal to a much lesser audience – usually an audience of your own nationality, for a start, and you have to appeal to three people at a time in their own natural surroundings, which is their living room.

PIERRE: Before the big break, what was the lowest period of your life?

MICHAEL CAINE: When my father died.

PIERRE: You once wrote that, after your marriage broke up, you went to Paris and that your life was in ruins.

MICHAEL CAINE: Yes.

PIERRE: What did you mean by that?

MICHAEL CAINE: My father died and my marriage broke up at exactly the same time. I was also out of work, had been out of work for a long time, very broke, had been broke and looked like being broke and out of work for a long time. In that sort of situation you get panic-stricken and confused, to put it mildly, I suppose. A psychiatrist would have called it a nervous breakdown, but I didn't go to anybody. There was a little life-insurance policy for twenty-five pounds on my father, and my mother could see that I was in a bit of a state, so she just said: "Well, take the twenty-five pounds and go away."

PIERRE: So you went to Paris. What did you do?

MICHAEL CAINE: In Paris, I slept in the air terminal on the chairs where you wait to catch a plane. The guy on the sandwich bar – the only guy who was up all night there – was an American student, and he never used to throw me out. He knew me and I talked to him, and he used to give me a ham sandwich and a cup of coffee in the morning. I sort of eked out the twenty-five pounds over a couple of months.

PIERRE: That's all you did, just lived in the air terminal?

MICHAEL CAINE: Yes.

PIERRE: You lived in the air terminal for two months?

MICHAEL CAINE: Yeah. I slept in there as though I was going to go on an airplane. I used to sleep on the benches.

PIERRE: Did you never change your clothes or get a bath?

MICHAEL CAINE: Yes. I'd buy the cheapest possible underwear and socks and stuff, and I could have a sort of a wash-down in the middle of the night in the air terminal toilet.

PIERRE: This was a low period. People who've had no money in the past and then get it are sometimes still panic-stricken about insecurity. Do you have any feeling now of financial insecurity? Do you think you're set now for life?

MICHAEL CAINE: No, I don't for one moment think I'm set for life.

PIERRE: Does it worry you?

MICHAEL CAINE: Yes, from time to time it worries me. I'm not panic-stricken because my own feeling is that even if I go back to where I came from I can still work in a tea warehouse. I'm still strong enough.

PIERRE: And?

MICHAEL CAINE: And . . . these few years are extra, you know. Because, by rights, I shouldn't be here and I am; and that's the way I look at it. The thing is, if you start out broke and a nobody, what can anybody ever do to you?

THE FACE ON THE COVER

"I think it's rather good
that the public loses interest . . .
I think that's healthy."

*Jean Shrimpton, who is perhaps the most famous cover girl of all
time, is also part of Britain's New Aristocracy. She belongs in the
same category of the instantly famous as Mary Quant, the "in"
dress designer, Vidal Sassoon, the "in" hairdresser, and the Rolling Stones, that "in" singing group that has managed to make the
Beatles look almost square. (Mick Jagger, in fact, dates Jean
Shrimpton's sister.)*

*Yet, in a sense, Jean Shrimpton is less a member of the swing-
ing set than she is a creature of it. She is less talent than she is
raw material, to be moulded, groomed, prettified, arranged, photographed, and displayed on the cover of a fashionable magazine
or the arm of a fashionable man. She is not driven by the fierce
desire to Make It Big, which motivates the activists. She drifts
almost casually down the pathway to easy success like a leaf
caught in the breeze. Nor is she attracted by the equally fierce
compulsion to Live It Up. She views the Swinging Life almost
vicariously, through the eyes of a mentor. Until recently, at least,*

137

her own opinions and tastes simply mirrored those of the "in" crowd.

Until the age of seventeen, she was a gawky farm girl – "tall, thin, and toothy," to use her own phrase – with a convent-school background (tennis and grass hockey), and a farm upbringing (horses). When I met her in London in February, 1966, she was twenty-two, and her face was perhaps the best-known in all England, next to the Queen's. Yet it occurred to me that she might easily walk down the street unobserved; for this was not quite the girl I'd grown to know from the newsmagazine covers and the Vogue layouts.

She is still gawky in real life and a little toothy – a skinny girl in a short skirt, with a fabulously careless hair-do. The sophistication that oozes from the David Bailey photographs was not here: what emerged was a painfully shy creature, hesitant about her very first appearance on television, yet somehow determined to tell as much about her real self and her own feelings as she was able to put into words. I remember her saying, just before we began: "Half an hour is an awfully long time to talk, isn't it?" But it wasn't, really. I started out by asking her about her book on modelling, which, in pocket form, was on all the newstands. What did she think of it? I wanted to know; and had she really written it herself?

▢

JEAN SHRIMPTON: No, I didn't, and I think it's terrible.

PIERRE: Why do you think it's terrible?

JEAN SHRIMPTON: Well, I did it rather a long time ago, and I admit I was with a different agency and I was very naïve. The suggestion was brought up that I should write a book, you know, and that I would make money, and my agent said to me: "That's a very good idea, sign here." About six months later they appointed a ghost writer for me. I knew nothing about ghost writing, so I left it entirely up to her. Then I left for New York and the proofs were sent to me there, and I read them and I was horrified, you know, because I thought the book was a load of common rubbish. I said, "I'm not fussy, but I'm sorry I can't put my name on this," and I sent the proofs back. They were rewritten and came back again, and there wasn't really very much change because I think the ghost writer was just not capable of writing differently. If she'd done it a hundred times, it wouldn't have improved. So I was stuck and I made what alterations I could, which were completely disregarded anyway, and gave in. I've forgotten about it as best I can.

PIERRE: The ghost writer: did she talk to you about it? Did she extract information from you, or did she just make it all up?

JEAN SHRIMPTON: No. I spent like one day with her, which is ridiculous. I mean I have only myself to blame.

PIERRE: Yes?

JEAN SHRIMPTON: I mean it was because I was very ignorant at the time. I'd be much more careful now. And it was . . . well, it was started off about three years ago, and you learn an awful lot in three years.

PIERRE: I bet *you've* learned a lot in three years.

JEAN SHRIMPTON: I think I have.

PIERRE: You know, I read a quote from one of the first men to photograph you. He said of you: "She was the most gawky, awkward thing I've ever seen." Do you still feel gawky and awkward sometimes, or have you got over that?

JEAN SHRIMPTON: No, I don't think I have got over it completely. I think I'll always be gawky.

PIERRE: But this doesn't show in your photographs.

JEAN SHRIMPTON: No, no. Photographs are very different from real life.

PIERRE: There must be a lot, then, to the business of being a photographer.

JEAN SHRIMPTON: Yes. I think there's a lot more to a photographer than meets the eye, you know. A fashion photographer must have a flair for clothes; he must see the feeling of the clothes — whether they're young, they're sophisticated, whether they're geometric or soft. And lighting plays a very important part.

PIERRE: I would think also your mood would play an important part.

JEAN SHRIMPTON: Yes. You know almost the moment you walk in the door how you're going to work with someone. You can tell whether they're going to be in control or whether you are. *They* should be in control. I don't know . . . you just sort of *know*.

PIERRE: The photographer who really made you famous was David Bailey. You said of him: "I owe everything I am as a model to David Bailey." What did he do in the studio that made you successful?

JEAN SHRIMPTON: I think when I said this — which was probably two or three years ago – I think I *did* owe an awful lot to him. I don't think you can owe everything, because if there's nothing there you can't work on nothing. But when I met him I was eighteen. I'd come straight from the country. I was very naïve and very easily influenced. I think he did have an influence on my life in the right way: he influenced the way I dressed and looked, and he said: "Don't try and copy other models, you've got scraggy hair and long legs and I like them and I'm going to use you for that reason." And we spent a lot of time together, but I feel he couldn't have done it if I were nothing, and since then I think I've gone on on my own, but he was a great influence and a great help to me.

PIERRE: What did he tell you to do? Did he tell you exactly how to sit – how to look? How much of this is you, and how much the photographer?

JEAN SHRIMPTON: It's so hard actually to explain, because it's never the same two times running. You get to the studio and he'll probably put you into a pose. If you feel something different, you do it. If he likes it, he says *yes*; and if he doesn't, he says *no*. You can't really describe it or break it up, you know. It just *happens*.

PIERRE: I read once that Richard Avedon photographed you – but that it was a very tiring session. When he took the last three or four pictures of you, he didn't realize that you were sound asleep with your eyes open. Can you sleep with your eyes open?

JEAN SHRIMPTON: I think that was a slight exaggeration. I think most things are a slight exaggeration. It was true that I was very tired. I'd been working eighteen hours non-stop, and I think I was just about asleep, but I don't think I was actually asleep.

PIERRE: He claimed he got his best pictures of you this way. Do you agree with that?

JEAN SHRIMPTON: No.

PIERRE: You said that when you first began this business, Miss Shrimpton, you were very naïve and that you've learned a lot. Could you tell me something about what you have learned, apart from wearing clothes?

JEAN SHRIMPTON: Well, I was naïve because I'd lived in the country, and I'd had a very untouched, very simple life which I think is marvellous, you know, because it makes you very basic and very stable. But coming to London as a model: well, first of all I travelled, and you *must* learn by travel. I mean, you see this and you see that and you find out and you ask why and wherefore, etc. I met a lot of people, all of whom were of superior intelligence to me, and obviously, you know, you pick things up. Then after awhile, I thought – well, I was too easily influenced, I hadn't got a mind of my own. This is really why I went to New York on my own and stood on my own feet for a change.

PIERRE: Did you feel at a certain point, as many models feel, that you were a puppet in the hands of others, that you were being manipulated and pushed and pulled?

JEAN SHRIMPTON: Yes. I feel that very strongly at the moment. I've had a lot from modelling: I've had travel, I've had experience, I make a good living, and I'm my own boss, which is very important to me. If I don't want to go to work at nine o'clock, I don't. But I've had enough, really now, because it's not creative. You are a puppet, making up every morning and wearing clothes, which I find rather boring, to be quite honest.

PIERRE: Do you sort of feel that you're just a clothes horse and nothing more? That you're just a rack for other people's designs?

JEAN SHRIMPTON: People think that. It doesn't worry me, because I know I'm not. It's a funny business. You can only do it for so long, you know. I think the novelty's worn off.

PIERRE: It's been said that David Bailey was a Svengali in your life – that he really over-directed you. Do you feel that now?

JEAN SHRIMPTON: He was a great influence and the reason, you know, that I did suddenly feel that every thought in my head, perhaps, had been put there by him and a few other people. Mostly by him. That was why I had to break away. I had to establish myself as a person. I suddenly realized that though what I said wasn't wrong – perhaps perfectly intelligent – it wasn't really what *I* thought; it was what somebody else thought.

PIERRE: People were telling you what to read ... and where to go ... and what to say?

JEAN SHRIMPTON: Yes. And you know, I talked about photographers because *he'd* mentioned them, because *he* thought they were great, and without really looking at the pictures and deciding for myself. Or even anything; paintings, furniture, everything. Books? Yes.

PIERRE: The time comes when you really have to make up your own mind.

JEAN SHRIMPTON: Oh, yes. You know, you can't go through life like that.

PIERRE: How did you get into this business? Was there a lucky break, or was it just hard work or what?

JEAN SHRIMPTON: Well I was at school and had done the G.C. Level as we call it here. I didn't really want to go to university, I wanted to leave school, and I wanted to be independent – my own independence has always been of importance to me – I didn't really know what to do. I did a secretary course for a year, but I can't do anything with my hands. I couldn't type, and I didn't really think I wanted to be a secretary. And while I was there, a film director stopped me on the street and said I should do films or be a model.

PIERRE: You mean you were stopped on the *street*?

JEAN SHRIMPTON: Yes I was, actually.

PIERRE: That's like the legendary Hollywood beginning.

JEAN SHRIMPTON: That actually did happen. We used to go for lunch in Hyde Park, and coming back one day with a couple of other girls from lunch, this man sort of rushed up. We'd disappeared. We were down in the basement, and he called over the railings, "Hey, Miss!" Of course, you know what girls are like – always giggling. Then he said: "You know, you should be a model," and so I thought: "Oh, well, perhaps I'll try that."

PIERRE: And you went to what? A model school?

JEAN SHRIMPTON: Yes. I went to the Lucy Clayton Model School.

PIERRE: I know that your career was really launched with the fourteen pages in the British *Vogue* by David Bailey. But how did this happen? How did he meet you?

JEAN SHRIMPTON: I'd been around for about six months, I think, and you do the rounds and you have a composite sheet with terrible photographs, which is really pathetic. But that's how you get started. And he just happened to see me one day, you know, and decided he wanted to use me. I was very awful, but he saw something. I wasn't really very enthusiastic about my job. I was a bit slap-happy. I used to come up from the country every day with sandwiches and shoes all in one bag and traipse around. It wasn't very important to me, and I think that's half why I've been successful. It isn't that important. I've never tried to be successful. It doesn't worry me. It just came.

PIERRE: Is it against your character to do what you're doing?

JEAN SHRIMPTON: A tiny bit. Clothes are not of that great interest to me. I go into a shop to buy something, and the first thing I put on, if it doesn't fit, I'm out.

PIERRE: You don't spend hours in shops as some women do?

JEAN SHRIMPTON: No, I get bored. I'm not madly interested in fashion.

PIERRE: When you go out on your own, and you don't have to care about your appearance, do you bother about it?

JEAN SHRIMPTON: No. Not very often. Not enough.

PIERRE: You wear any old thing? What about your habitual wear? What would you wear if you could get away with it?

JEAN SHRIMPTON: Oh, I wear what I like. I mean I'm not afraid of whether I can get away with it.

PIERRE: I see.

JEAN SHRIMPTON: I wear trousers most of the time. Just trousers and skirts and sweaters because I *must* be comfortable. If I want to sit on the floor, I want to sit on the floor. I don't want to think: "This suit's white and it's going to get dirty."

PIERRE: So are you bored now?

JEAN SHRIMPTON: A little. I, you know, want to do something different. It's very hard to know where to go. I don't think I'm drawn terribly to the limelight; I mean it's had a lot of advantages.

PIERRE: You must have had film offers.

JEAN SHRIMPTON: Yes, I have. And though I haven't felt the urge to do films, I feel now that if a marvellous director came to me and was very keen to put me in a film – that he could really manage me and could make me do as he wanted to, and it was a really well-known director, not a commercial director – then I would certainly consider it. But I don't want to be a James Bond girl or something like that, you know. It's not me.

PIERRE: I'm sure you could have been in a film long ago if you had wanted to.

JEAN SHRIMPTON: Yes, I think so.

PIERRE: At least walk-on parts. You turned them down?

JEAN SHRIMPTON: Well it's so unsatisfying. I think it's a bit humiliating. That's awful to say that, but I don't want to know about a walk-on. I know I can do a walk-on – that's just my appearance. I'm not saying I can act; I'm sure I *can't*. But I hope I have more to myself than just my appearance.

PIERRE: Your career has a very short life. It's based entirely on your youth, isn't it?

JEAN SHRIMPTON: Yes.

PIERRE: It's based on a very fickle public, who will build you up one day but, the moment that you begin to lose your looks, will forget about you. Have you thought about this much?

JEAN SHRIMPTON: Yes, you have to think about it. You ride the crest of the waves, come to the top, and face downfall. It doesn't worry me unduly. I'm aware of it. I hope that I'll be able to cope with it. It isn't terribly important to me, I think. You mustn't take yourself seriously. If you realize you're just a model, you're really very unimportant. You don't do anything creative. It doesn't matter if you die tomorrow. If you realize that, and you're very basic about things, you're all right. As long as you've got other interests, as long as you've got friends and you're self-sufficient to a certain extent.

PIERRE: How about the public? I suppose this is the most fickle public in history. It makes and breaks stars almost overnight in the whole pop or mass field of which you are a part as a model.

JEAN SHRIMPTON: Yes. I think the fact that it makes and breaks pop stars overnight isn't bad. I don't think pop stars or models are important enough to deserve a long run. I think it's rather good that the public loses interest and wants something new. I think that's healthy. And though I'm mad about pop music, I don't think it deserves to run that long; it doesn't have that much validity.

PIERRE: Is that true of models?

JEAN SHRIMPTON: Yes.

PIERRE: How long is the life of a model now, tell me? How long is your career going to be?

JEAN SHRIMPTON: I don't know. I think if you become well-known, it's probably shorter, because you're more exposed. Girls who do a lot of commercial work, who aren't known, go on for years. Some go on for ten years. I've been doing it for five. I think I could still work for a few years, but I'm not sure that I want to.

PIERRE: How many hours a week would you work?

JEAN SHRIMPTON: I don't work an awful lot now. I charge more money and work less. It suits me fine.

PIERRE: How do you spend your spare time? What do you do?

JEAN SHRIMPTON: I'm quite lazy, you know, I don't get up very early. Riding is about my only sport. I love animals – sounds a bit soppy, but I do.

PIERRE: Well, you were raised on a farm.

JEAN SHRIMPTON: Yes, and I'm interested in films, just to watch. I see a lot of films. But I have a very close circle of friends. I prefer to be with people I know well – to have dinner. I don't like parties or night clubs or anything. I don't like crowds.

PIERRE: Do you feel fulfilled at the moment?

JEAN SHRIMPTON: No.

PIERRE: You don't?

JEAN SHRIMPTON: I'm a woman. I won't feel fulfilled until I've had children.

PIERRE: There's no prospect of marriage in your life at all?

JEAN SHRIMPTON: No. I like the idea of marriage. I want to get married and have children; it is quite important for me. I think that the general attitude towards marriage today tends to be rather flippant. When I get married, I want to get married with the idea that I'm going to stay married. Therefore I'm in no hurry. There's plenty of time.

PIERRE: Are you saying that some people in this country think of marriage as a transitory thing?

JEAN SHRIMPTON: I think a lot of girls get married knowing that they can get divorced, and I think they get married without giving it a lot of thought and consideration. A lot of people get married, in my mind, much too young. I thought that at twenty-one I was mature, but even two years later I feel that I know much more. I think people do get married without thinking about it a lot.

PIERRE: Besides marriage, what else are you looking for?

JEAN SHRIMPTON: I don't know. I'm not very ambitious, I don't think I know really what I'm looking for.

PIERRE: Does this bother you that you don't know?

JEAN SHRIMPTON: Well, it's simple. I have no talent. I mean I can't draw, I can't write, and if I do something, I've got to do it well or I'd rather not do it at all. I don't think I have any talent for anything artistic; I'm not sure what I can do.

PIERRE: You move now with an artistic crowd. Does that make you feel you should have a talent?

JEAN SHRIMPTON: No. I don't feel I should have a talent; I just feel it would be nice to have it.

PIERRE: I suppose when you're at the top, too, Miss Shrimpton, everybody is waiting for you to slip. Do you have this feeling? That you're teetering on the brink?

JEAN SHRIMPTON: I don't think it's terribly vicious. I think if you're at the top of anything in the publicized life – like modelling or films – that when you get to the top you have to fight to stay there. But I think . . . I'm sure it's the same in business, you know. I think if you get to the top in anything, people are waiting for you to come down. You either ride the crest of the wave or you go to the top and you come down, you know.

PIERRE: Of course. You didn't claw your way up, did you? It sort of happened.

JEAN SHRIMPTON: Yes, that's true. I didn't really think about being successful. It was never planned, and I never sort of courted publicity. It did just happen in my case. I had no choice.

PIERRE: Would it upset you if it all ended tomorrow?

JEAN SHRIMPTON: I don't think it would upset me a lot. I'm not saying it wouldn't affect me at all, I'm sure it would. I might think I'd like to be out of it. But when it happened I might not like it.

WIDOW TO A LEGEND

"I thought I was marrying
the Foreign Editor
of the *Sunday Times*."

*She had no idea, of course, back in 1952, that she was marrying
into the great cult of the Sixties. James Bond had not yet been
invented, and her new husband – her third – was a journalist and
an ex-Naval Intelligence man of impeccable background (Eton
and Sandhurst) who collected rare first editions, enjoyed spear-
fishing, cards, and golf, and had a place in Jamaica where he spent
two months of every year.*

*But the marriage had come only after a period of shattering
personal complexity for both of them. Her first husband, Lord
O'Neill, was killed in action in 1944. Her second, Lord Rother-
mere, the press baron, divorced her in 1952, naming Fleming as
co-respondent. They were married at once, he for the very first
time. Marriage, Ian Fleming was to write later, "is a very painful
thing at the age of forty-four, so to take my mind off the whole
business, I sat down and wrote a novel." Its title:* Casino Royale.
Unknown to either of them, the seeds of the cult were germinating.

Of the Anne Fleming of those days, it has been written that "she provokes extreme reactions, like a wasp provokes panic. Her friends adore her. Others, intimidated by what they consider to be her ruthless vitality, are more reserved in their response." Among those who adored her were: Lady Diana Duff Cooper, Somerset Maugham, Cecil Beaton, Noel Coward, Cyril Connolly, Evelyn Waugh, and Sir Frederick Ashton. Her legendary literary dinner parties – *"gastronomic sessions combined with intellectual punishment"* – were scarcely part of Ian Fleming's world. He shunned them, preferring bridge at the Portland Club. The diners, in their turn, paid him and his work little heed.

It was a little more than a year after Fleming's death (queues for Goldfinger encircling Leicester Square) that on visiting London, in November, 1965, I thought of inviting the author's widow to talk to me on television. She had been in seclusion, but I had heard that she was disturbed, if not a little embittered, over the red tape that had enmeshed his literary estate. She agreed to come down to the Westbury Hotel and appear before the cameras.

At fifty-six, I found her a still-handsome woman. She must once have been very striking indeed. It is possible to perceive the steel within her, but this does not mean she is not charming. Behind the wall of reserve, behind the very British tendency to hold herself in check, there emerges the driest of wits. She answered all my questions readily enough but, as the transcript shows, without a great deal of elaboration. I began, of course, by asking her opinion of James Bond.

○

MRS. FLEMING: I'm ashamed to say I never was a Bond addict.

PIERRE: You never were? Why not?

MRS. FLEMING: I thought he had very little sense of humour.

PIERRE: James Bond?

MRS. FLEMING: *Very* little sense of humour.

PIERRE: He's not the sort of person you would have invited to dinner had he been real?

MRS. FLEMING: I don't think more than once.

PIERRE: In spite of his known love for good food and fine wines? Things like that. Not much of a conversationalist?

MRS. FLEMING: I think I always get James Bond and Ian Fleming mixed up, and I think he did in the end, more and more with every book that he wrote.

148

PIERRE: Did he become a prisoner of his creation?

MRS. FLEMING: I think so. I remember consulting Cyril Connolly about that. I said: "Has any author invented a character that has got hypnotized by it and become like it?" And he said: "This has happened frequently. I'm very sorry for you."

PIERRE: In what way did your husband become a prisoner of his character?

MRS. FLEMING: Well, when he was getting ill, and I was imploring him to stop writing the book, I spoke to Somerset Maugham about it, and Maugham said: "He'll never be able to rest now because the public won't let him, and he won't really want not to satisfy his public."

PIERRE: He'd had one serious heart attack, hadn't he, before his death?

MRS. FLEMING: He had a very serious one six years ago.

PIERRE: But this didn't stop him?

MRS. FLEMING: It didn't stop him writing. But he should have stopped playing golf and he should have stopped drinking, but he wouldn't stop either.

PIERRE: Did he know that his years were numbered, at this point?

MRS. FLEMING: If he'd been sensible they needn't have been.

PIERRE: Then he must really have enjoyed writing the Bond books, or he wouldn't have kept on.

MRS. FLEMING: I think he enjoyed it enormously. He enjoyed all the research he did in the months before he went to Jamaica and settled down to write, and then he used to get through the book, the plot, and come home and correct it for the next six months.

PIERRE: Were you much involved with these books yourself? Did he talk to you when he was writing them?

MRS. FLEMING: Well, *he started* by talking to me about them, but he stopped because, I remember – I think it's the book where two thousand sharks are eating someone – I said: "I think it would be much more exciting if there was only *one* shark; it's worse." This was supposed to be the wrong kind of criticism. But I understand, from talking to other writers' wives, that it's far better not to discuss books at home.

PIERRE: You've been asked this question, I'm sure. In what ways did Ian Fleming resemble James Bond? For instance, was he the gourmet that James Bond was supposed to be?

MRS. FLEMING: Well, he was very fond of scrambled eggs, probably you know from reading the books. I don't think he liked very elaborate meals; I think he liked rather simple things extremely well-cooked. He was very fussy that his boiled eggs should always be just three and a half minutes. That was Bond.

PIERRE: Was he fussy about wines?

MRS. FLEMING: No. He liked any kind of red wine. He called it "infuriator." That's what they call cheap red wine in the Navy. I don't think he minded very much what sort of red wine it was.

PIERRE: Did he invent that cocktail that James Bond drank, with vodka shaken up, not stirred?

MRS. FLEMING: As far as I know this he invented completely.

PIERRE: I wonder if this wasn't a bit of the Walter Mitty in Ian Fleming? If this wasn't a projection of his dreams?

MRS. FLEMING: I am sure it was. I think he very much enjoyed being in the Naval Intelligence during the war. What he did there he wouldn't have dreamt of telling me. Nor was it possible to find out because John Pearson, who's writing Ian's life, is finding it quite impossible to get anyone in Naval Intelligence to tell him anything at all. But I think this was a projection of that, and a projection of a way of life which he thought was ceasing to exist. He didn't care for a sedentary existence. He liked travelling and he liked adventure.

PIERRE: How did the Bond idea come about? I would be interested to know, for instance, if you knew he was going to write spy thrillers before he actually sat down and wrote the first one – *Casino Royale*.

MRS. FLEMING: I hadn't the remotest idea. *I* thought I was marrying the Foreign Editor of the *Sunday Times*.

PIERRE: Did anybody know?

MRS. FLEMING: He told about five of my best friends and three of his that he intended to write the greatest spy story in the world. But he never mentioned it to me.

PIERRE: He was right, wasn't he?

MRS. FLEMING: He was right.

PIERRE: He wrote once, himself, towards the end of his life, that "the gimmickry grew like bindweed." This was all the business of the guns, the cars, and the very special products that surround James Bond. Were you aware of this?

MRS. FLEMING: Well, he got very excited by this. He took enormous trouble over the book jackets, which I think are extremely good.

PIERRE: Yes, they are. I remember half-way through the series he changed guns because, apparently, the gun that Bond was using originally wasn't a very good gun. Were you involved in this?

MRS. FLEMING: I'm ashamed to say I'm so uninterested in ballistics

150

that a lot of this used to pass me by. But there *were* unending conversations about guns, certainly.

PIERRE: At what point did you actually read the Bond books? Or have you read them all?

MRS. FLEMING: I have. But I get them a bit mixed up in my mind sometimes. But I have read them all. I read them, usually in Jamaica, when they were first in manuscript.

PIERRE: What were his working habits?

MRS. FLEMING: Well, six weeks in Jamaica to two months when he used to get it all down on paper. In the next six months, he used to obviously go over it, all over it all over again, elaborately; and it was shown to William Plomer, that charming writer, who used to read for him in Cape's. William, I think, used to take out some of the more exaggerated effects.

PIERRE: Oh they toned him down a bit, did they?

MRS. FLEMING: Sometimes, yes.

PIERRE: There was a legend around, I don't know whether it's true or not, that the reason Bond was made into a gourmet was that he was eating so many scrambled eggs that somebody said: "Look, this isn't proper for a secret agent. In fact, it would identify him too easily, a man who always eats scrambled eggs. Vary the menu." Have you heard that story?

MRS. FLEMING: I think I have. I think it must have been William.

PIERRE: The same man?

MRS. FLEMING: I think so, yes.

PIERRE: How long would he write during a day? What were his work habits?

MRS. FLEMING: Well, in Jamaica it fitted in very well, because one can't sit in the sun all day and do nothing – at least neither of us could. So he would have breakfast about eight – having swum before breakfast – and then he would type for three hours. Then he would reread that in the evening.

PIERRE: Not a bad existence.

MRS. FLEMING: He found it perfect.

PIERRE: Why would you say, then, that this contributed to his heart attack?

MRS. FLEMING: Well, because after his heart attack we had a steep staircase down to the beach there, very steep, about forty steps, which he should never have walked up and down. And he got pains whenever he went underwater swimming. And he should have given up all these things and golf, and he wouldn't give them up at all.

151

PIERRE: There's a great deal of golf and skin-diving in his books. These were a part of your husband's life.

MRS. FLEMING: Yes, that's it.

PIERRE: Your husband was also a gambler. In *Casino Royale*, Bond was very expert in gambling.

MRS. FLEMING: I never thought he was a real gambler in the serious sense of the word. He was Scottish, you know, and fairly careful. If he did gamble, he was rather good and usually won, but not for the enormous stakes you'd expect James Bond to play for.

PIERRE: But talking of gambling and talking of money, let's talk about the estate. This is surely one of the largest literary estates in history – with the motion picture rights and everything else.

MRS. FLEMING: I think it is. From time to time Ian said if we left England we would be very, very, very rich, indeed, and I said: "I can't bear leaving England so we won't." And he didn't want to. Of course, Somerset Maugham's estate was huge because he left England and went to France. But we stayed here, and then at a given moment the taxation was going to be so tremendous he sold the book royalties.

PIERRE: He sold all his royalties in the future?

MRS. FLEMING: All the book royalties forever and ever, keeping forty-nine per cent of the shares – a minority share, so that the estate gets a tax dividend whenever they choose to declare it, which isn't a fortune, really. Taxation being what it is.

PIERRE: Do you personally get much money out of the Bond estate?

MRS. FLEMING: Well, it will probably take another three or four years to settle at the present rate. I've no idea. But there's not very much at the moment.

PIERRE: Are you bitter about this? I've heard that you were.

MRS. FLEMING: I think if it's there I might as well have some of it.

PIERRE: And you can't get at it?

MRS. FLEMING: Not at the moment.

PIERRE: Why does it take so long?

MRS. FLEMING: Estate Office, estate duty. I think they're trying to work out estate duties on any films that may be made in the future, which seems to me rather hard.

PIERRE: You mean they've really got to guess? They don't know what this estate is worth? It depends on how successful the films are?

MRS. FLEMING: The films are taken up one after the other. The film people would stop taking them up if they stop being a success. At the moment they are so successful that this is very improbable.

PIERRE: Do you own the rights yourself, or does the estate own the rights to the Bond books?

MRS. FLEMING: Well, the books and the films are quite separate. The films go straight to the estate and the royalties go to a man called Jock Campbell, the chairman of an enormous concern called Booker Brothers.

PIERRE: They bought the rights from your husband?

MRS. FLEMING: Yes.

PIERRE: But there's forty-nine per cent of that left. Is that willed to you?

MRS. FLEMING: Forty-nine per cent of the shares go to the estate. Left all in a trust.

PIERRE: Have you any say over what happens?

MRS. FLEMING: I'm always trying to have more say than I ought to have now I've pulled myself together. I didn't take much interest to begin with. Then I started fighting about it.

PIERRE: I read the other day that Kingsley Amis, who's a great Bond expert, has been asked to continue your husband's character, James Bond, in a new series of books. How do you feel about that?

MRS. FLEMING: Well, I was very angry because I know Kingsley fairly well. I thought he might have rung me up and asked me what I thought about it. And I also thought Sir Jock Campbell, whom I know, might also have rung me up and said: "What do *you* feel?" Whereas in fact they were pretty well ahead signing up when I heard about it.

PIERRE: You tried to stop it?

MRS. FLEMING: And with some aid, it's been stopped at the moment.

PIERRE: Is this your doing or somebody else's?

MRS. FLEMING: I was rather helped by uninvoked aid.

PIERRE: Why don't you want the Bond character to continue?

MRS. FLEMING: It's emotional at the moment, naturally. I feel rather emotional about it. I'm sure it couldn't come off.

PIERRE: It's never come off in the past. Sherlock Holmes . . . Fu Manchu really couldn't have been continued.

MRS. FLEMING: No, well John Pearson, who's writing Ian's life and had all the letters from his office, found a very funny letter from Ian to Mrs. Sax Rohmer who had written to Ian asking if he'd continue Dr. Fu Manchu. I have never seen this letter, but I understand that Ian wrote a very funny reply – saying that he did not think this could ever be done.

PIERRE: Mrs. Fleming, somebody wrote that the violence in the

James Bond books was part of the strange decadence that affects Britain today. Would you agree with that?

MRS. FLEMING: Oh, I do hope you're not right. It's a very difficult question, isn't it?

PIERRE: Yes.

MRS. FLEMING: Isn't there a great deal of violence in America?

PIERRE: Yes, there is. Maybe it's part of the strange decadence that affects the world, if indeed the world is faced by decadence.

MRS. FLEMING: I don't know if it's *decadence*. It's a tremendous period of change . . . readjustment . . . newly educated people. I mean, vast masses of people are now educated. Look at Africa.

PIERRE: Tell me, would you have liked your husband to have written books other than the spy thrillers?

MRS. FLEMING: Yes. He wanted to write the life of a woman whose name I can't remember. She shoved out all the brothels in Paris. She was a French cabinet minister. He wanted to write her life, but he then got so occupied.

PIERRE: He once said, in the last interview with him, that if he had enough concentration, he could have written a book comparable to *War and Peace*. Is this possible?

MRS. FLEMING: I'm very surprised to hear that he said it. No, I'm sure he couldn't.

PIERRE: But do you think he had a sneaking feeling that he should write something else than spy books – or was he satisfied with this?

MRS. FLEMING: Well, he was very full of humility about it, at the beginning; and he was tremendously pleased and very excited when the first book was accepted. He didn't expect it to be.

PIERRE: And, indeed, it didn't do very well at the beginning.

MRS. FLEMING: I don't think it did. I don't think it sold very many. I don't remember how many. He was overwhelmed by this rolling-stone success.

PIERRE: When did that happen? When were you aware suddenly that there was a kind of a mania going on about James Bond?

MRS. FLEMING: When you live with some growing legend, you're never conscious of a particular moment. As far as the sales of Pan Books were concerned, it was after the first film. I think the director of the first film, Terence Young, was brilliant in that he managed to get 'U' certificates so that everybody could take their children, and he took out this hero-masochism a lot and made it a joke.

PIERRE: Did your husband take himself seriously?

MRS. FLEMING: He didn't take Bond seriously, no, he didn't.

154

PIERRE: He didn't even like him, he said once.

MRS. FLEMING: I think he probably grew to think of him as a sort of Frankenstein's monster at the end.

PIERRE: You have a reputation for holding literary salons. In fact, I think that this is part and parcel of your life, isn't it? You have a great many literary friends.

MRS. FLEMING: I enjoy literary friends, yes – very much.

PIERRE: Malcolm Muggeridge is one, isn't he?

MRS. FLEMING: I haven't seen Malcolm for a long time. I bitterly resent what he wrote about Ian. I don't know if you happened to see it. It was quite awful. I have not seen Malcolm since then.

PIERRE: I was wondering what your other friends thought of Bond?

MRS. FLEMING: Well, Malcolm was really Ian's friend – well, both our friend, but particularly Ian's – so I thought it was not a very kind way to behave. I think he resents all success.

PIERRE: When you had these literary salons, did your husband attend?

MRS. FLEMING: Not often; but then a literary friend of mine called Peter Quennell, who's written a good deal about Byron, you know, says it's rather boring to be at a dinner party where everybody's works are discussed except your own. Then there was a moment about three or four years ago when the highbrows got interested in Ian, which pleased Ian. He got reviews from a lot of them. Then, of course, Cyril Connolly wrote that parody which was brilliant.

PIERRE: What did he think of the Bond parodies?

MRS. FLEMING: He enjoyed them very much.

PIERRE: But Bond was not a subject of literary discussion at your salon?

MRS. FLEMING: Not, I'm afraid, until he became a success. I now think that phenomenal success interests everybody, whether they are highbrows or lowbrows.

PIERRE: It is interesting that the highbrows did not take over Bond until he became part of the social fabric. I suppose it became fashionable to pay attention to him then.

MRS. FLEMING: He became a figure one could no longer deny.

PIERRE: Are you astonished by the whole Bond business? There are Bond sweat shirts out, Bond magazines, guns . . . all sorts of different things.

MRS. FLEMING: Well, the lady who did my hair early this morning asked if I'd seen the James Bond car. I haven't.

PIERRE: You don't get involved much, then, in this sort of thing?

MRS. FLEMING: Well, I'm just intending to write to the merchandising people. I'd like them to send some of them free, perhaps, to give as Christmas presents.

PIERRE: Who owns the merchandising rights?

MRS. FLEMING: I believe one-third goes to the film people, one-third to Jock Campbell's company, and one-third I believe to Ian's estate.

PIERRE: So in the end you may benefit from this?

MRS. FLEMING: I think so.

PIERRE: When it's all settled.

MRS. FLEMING: I'm just about to write and ask if I couldn't be told about it.

PIERRE: It would be nice to know, wouldn't it?

MRS. FLEMING: *Wouldn't* it!

PIERRE: Don't you feel out of things?

MRS. FLEMING: Well, I was too unhappy for a long time to care; but now I've got frightfully aggressive about it.

PIERRE: How does all this affect your thirteen-year-old son?

MRS. FLEMING: I try to keep him out of it, because I think all father images shouldn't overshadow a child's life. I think he'd better make his own life. He's terribly interested in Egyptology and antiquities at the moment.

PIERRE: Are the Ian Fleming books in his school library?

MRS. FLEMING: He was asked about that. He was asked to write why they weren't when he was ten. I was a little surprised. He was offered ten pounds to write fifty words. He said: "I can say it in three and I don't want ten pounds. They're too sexy."

PIERRE: Since the Westbury Hotel, from where we're broadcasting, is on Bond Street, it occurs to me to ask if it has any connection at all with James Bond; or if your husband was at all interested in the fact that there was a street named after his character?

MRS. FLEMING: Suddenly he was, after Bond became such a success. He played golf with a man who works in the College of Heralds office, so he found out all about the name. It was called after some family that apparently live in Somerset. I believe there was an original Bond who was a well-known clubman. Ian then got very interested and found out what the family motto was: "The World Is Not Enough." He was longing to adopt it for himself. It wouldn't have been a bad motto for him really.

THE QUEEN OF
THE FAN MAGAZINES

"A lot of stars lead pretty
dull, placid lives, and you've
got to give them glamour."

*The Hollywood fan magazines are a concomitant of the Teen
Revolution. Once designed for middleaged housewives, they are
now directly tuned to subteen girls. To the casual reader, they all
seem to have been written by the same person, and this, it
develops, isn't as far-fetched as it seems. Entire issues of entire
magazines have been written by a cheerfully cynical woman of
twenty-nine named Dixie Dean Trainer. Mrs. Trainer (formerly
Dixie Dean Harris) has to her credit, under a variety of bylines,
such tales as* "I LOVE YOU! CONNIE CRIES WITH JOY ON HER
WEDDING NIGHT" . . . "WHY DOCTORS WON'T LET ROCK HUDSON
MARRY" . . . "RICHARD BURTON'S WEDDING NIGHT CONFESSIONS."
*If these titles promise more titillation than they deliver, it is of
little moment, since the turnover in readership is enormous anyway: the nymphets have scarcely grown into the fan magazines
before they have grown out of them again.*

*Mrs. Trainer is a freelance writer with a special gift: she can
take a few stray facts, spice them with a lively imagination, and*

produce a magazine article. She writes for the fan magazines, the confession magazines, the confidential magazines, and (under a masculine byline) for the men's magazines. She writes for money, and the way she tells it, she'll write almost anything. She started as a teenager with a high-school gossip column, and after graduating cum laude *from college, she served as a press agent, photographer, and travel agent — a brief but useful career which has allowed her to lard her pieces with knowing references to far-off lands. In 1961, she joined Country Wide Publications and began turning out entire issues of movie magazines under as many as seven different pseudonyms for one hundred dollars a week.*

Now she's a freelancer (married to a securities analyst) and a remarkably frank one, as my staff discovered when they tracked her down in New York in September, 1965, and persuaded her to appear on my program. I began by asking if it was true that she wrote about many Hollywood stars, described how she had been invited to their homes, quoted them on various subjects, but never actually saw or spoke to them.

◻

MRS. TRAINER: Yes, I'm afraid so.

PIERRE: Tell me, what percentage of the stars that you write about do you actually meet?

MRS. TRAINER: Well, I guess altogether I've met less than ten per cent of the stars I've written about.

PIERRE: I've got some magazines here. You have written seven or eight features in the same magazine. How do you do that?

MRS. TRAINER: Well, you use the sources that are available to you — under the public domain so to speak — from other newspapers, other articles, and so on. In a way, it is kind of like a regular academic technique. You go out and get all the stuff available and you put it together and you have another story. It is almost like you're writing a real biography.

PIERRE: Yes, but you write stories in which you say, for instance, that you went to the subject's home, when in fact you didn't go near it.

MRS. TRAINER: Well, you have to start somehow.

PIERRE: There are stories here in which you have quoted long discussions that have taken place on people's honeymoons. Did you take along a tape recorder or something?

158

MRS. TRAINER: No. That's sort of artistic dialogue. I do interior dialogues too. You know – sort of the subconscious mind thinking.

PIERRE: You make that up? Like what Debbie was thinking: "What am I going to do now?"

MRS. TRAINER: Yes . . . now that Harry Karl has lost his shoe empire . . . that sort of thing.

PIERRE: And yet people may not have thought these things at all?

MRS. TRAINER: Oh, I'm sure it never crossed their minds.

PIERRE: You're very frank. Aren't you afraid, by telling me all of this on television, you'll be out of a job tomorrow?

MRS. TRAINER: Well, I may be as far as the movie magazines are concerned, but I write for other publications as well so. . . .

PIERRE: You just don't give a hoot?

MRS. TRAINER: Oh, I think it's fun.

PIERRE: I've heard that once, on the strength of a two-line gossip item, you were able to write a twenty-five hundred word exclusive interview with Bobby Rydell. Is that true?

MRS. TRAINER: Oh, yes. It was sort of interesting, the way it started out. It was going to be an interview, and I sold the idea to a movie magazine, but he was going to be out of town or something.

PIERRE: But that didn't stop you?

MRS. TRAINER: Oh, no. It was a set-back sort of thing, but that really didn't stop me. I got together with a press agent and I used the two-line gossip item from the press story, and then she gave me a biography and promised to send me some more stuff which she never did. Then she gave me some quotes about things Bobby Rydell was supposed to have said, and what the girls said about him and so on. So since the interview part was really necessary to this story, I had to do *something*. Well, when I was walking home, I walked by the Tavern-on-the-Green, which is in the middle of Central Park; it's really very nice. So I put that in and described how I met Bobby.

PIERRE: At the Tavern-on-the-Green?

MRS. TRAINER: Oh, yes, and how he lit my cigarettes and put me at ease, and how he was just great, and how I figured if I ever met him I knew I çould go out with him. How he was just marvellous.

PIERRE: Isn't this what they call "should-have-been" stories?

MRS. TRAINER: Yeah, they're the ones that should have happened, but didn't happen. At least they *could* have happened. There is usually some reason for them.

PIERRE: Let's look at some of them. Here's one you wrote: "LIZ BREAKS HER MARRIAGE VOWS . . . AND YET BURTON MUST TAKE

HER BACK." I read this piece with bated breath, but I couldn't find out where she had broken her marriage vows.

MRS. TRAINER: Oh, yes, she promised that she and Richard would never, ever be separated when they got married. And then they had to be separated on account of there was some death in the family; so she had to go to the funeral.

PIERRE: *This* was the marriage vow she broke?

MRS. TRAINER: Oh, yes.

PIERRE: Have you ever met Miss Taylor?

MRS. TRAINER: Oh, no.

PIERRE: But that doesn't stop you from writing about her?

MRS. TRAINER: Oh, no. There is plenty in the public domain about her. That is no problem.

PIERRE: Now here is one that you wrote called "THE STORY BEHIND THE SECRET MARRIAGE OF TROY DONAHUE AND SUZANNE PLECHETTE. EXTRA! WILL HE CHEAT AGAIN?" Now I read this. But I find there was no secret marriage at all. They just went to Mexico together.

MRS. TRAINER: Yes, but they were *going* to get married; and if I recall that story, they were quite on the verge of it, and they sat under sort of a banyan tree and discussed it.

PIERRE: That's what you have them doing: " 'I don't want to do it, if it will turn out badly. The fault isn't yours, it's mine, quite frankly. When I do get married I want to be a good 'husband.'" That's Troy talking I guess. " 'I want my marriage to be a truly successful one. I know I couldn't be a good husband right now. It would be absolutely impossible.' He reached over to take her hand gently."

MRS. TRAINER: Doesn't that sound beautiful, though?

PIERRE: You're very proud of your work, aren't you?

MRS. TRAINER: Well, I think it's funny.

PIERRE: Were you hiding in the banyan tree at the time?

MRS. TRAINER: Yeah! I was right up there – right up on top.

PIERRE: You were in your office all the time making it all up?

MRS. TRAINER: That's more like the truth.

PIERRE: You do this all of the time? There seem to be a half a dozen stories here by you in this one issue of *Movie*–TV *Secrets.* "THE SECRET MARRIAGE OF TROY AND SUZANNE," "RICHARD BURTON'S WEDDING NIGHT CONFESSION," "AN OPEN LETTER TO NATALIE WOOD," "GARY CAN'T FORGET CONNIE'S MEN," "JUNE ALLYSON'S QUESTION," and so on. How long does it take you to put these together?

160

MRS. TRAINER: Well, it depends on how much pressure you're under. If you're really under pressure, you can turn them out in a morning.

PIERRE: A whole article?

MRS. TRAINER: Oh, in a morning or less. You know: two or three hours. You get a little dizzy after you do this all day long without rest. I got to the point that I was just having nightmares about all these people. You know, Rock and Doris, Steve and Natalie, were just tramping through my dreams. I thought I'd quit writing full time because I found out, after three or four weeks, that a lot of people didn't really *care* about Troy and Suzanne. Like, I really cared. You know, I knew everything about them. Real crazy.

PIERRE: So you're back in the real world, eh?

MRS. TRAINER: Yeah, I don't know if I like it so well, but I'm back.

PIERRE: Tell me this now. I would be very angry if someone wrote that kind of stuff about me . . . put words in my mouth . . . thoughts in my head. Don't these stars get angry? Don't they sue? Don't they say: "You can't do this?" Don't they get upset?

MRS. TRAINER: Well, I'll tell you, that's very peculiar. You would think that's right, logically. But you know, it's topsy-turvy in Hollywood. It doesn't work that way at all. Really, you can write the most fantastic, incredible, far-out things – a story that has nothing to do with the truth – and nobody pays any attention. Absolutely none! But if you write a story that begins to get a little dangerously *close* to the truth, that's when the law suits begin to pour in, and they get all madly upset. I can give you a very good example of that: I think it was perhaps the most famous one, too. I think it was when they were filming "Cleopatra" and all the movie magazines were running stories about Liz Taylor running around with Richard Burton. Eddie Fisher, who was then her husband, got so upset he couldn't stand it, and he clapped law suits on every magazine you could possibly imagine. And I think the total amount of the suits ran up to about a total of two million dollars. Well, we all know what happened. And that was sort of the end of the law suits. Now, if we had said she was running around with Roddy MacDowall, nobody would have cared.

PIERRE: Do you get a kick out of doing this?

MRS. TRAINER: Yeah, they're fun. It's not terribly hard, and it's interesting. You know, you have to laugh when you hand in a title like "TONY CURTIS'S CHILD BRIDE."

PIERRE: Yes, let's get to that. Here is the cover of *True Movie*, and

161

it says: "A SHOCKING STORY OF CHRISTINE, TONY CURTIS'S CHILD BRIDE," and here is a photograph of this terrible man Tony Curtis with a child of five years old.

MRS. TRAINER: Read the small print.

PIERRE: Oh, it says "Tony with Daughter Kelly." Doesn't Tony Curtis get mad about this?

MRS. TRAINER: Well, he might have gotten a little mad over that one.

PIERRE: "She's twenty years younger than he is. She's young enough to be his daughter. She's too innocent to know the dangers. Forced to grow up over night, she . . . . Story continues on page 14." What *is* the secret of Tony Curtis's child bride? Just that she is younger than he is?

MRS. TRAINER: Yeah, that is pretty much it. She will have to grow up and –

PIERRE: What do you mean "dangers"? Is Tony Curtis dangerous?

MRS. TRAINER: Oh, I don't think he's going to knock her on the head, if *that's* what you mean. But he will have to adjust his life.

PIERRE: How does the editor of *True Movie* magazine – a respectable man, I'm sure, who takes a dry martini before going home to his wife, and is president of the local Kiwanis Club – how does he justify putting out this junk?

MRS. TRAINER: Well, that's rather a tricky question. In one way, you justify it simply in terms of economics. After all, they *are* in the business of selling magazines. It is a very crafty way of putting it, but it happens to be true.

PIERRE: I suspect, however, that some of them attempt to rationalize a little more than that.

MRS. TRAINER: Well, yeah. I'll tell you one story that has to do with Elvis Presley. This is how sometimes they rationalize it. This is a friend of mine, and I guess like all editors he finally got bitten with the idea that he could do a little educating. He'd been reading all the stories in the newspapers about the alarming increase of teenage marriages – you know, kids fourteen, sixteen, running off and getting married, and so on. So he decided to do something about it. He realized that after all *he* was reading these alarming stories, but the kids weren't. He wanted to get the message across to the children who were getting married. So he hoked up this story that was a cover story, and it said: "THE GIRL WHO TOLD ELVIS SHE WAS PREGNANT." The implication was that Elvis was the father, but he wasn't. The whole bit was that Elvis had gone on a personal appearance tour, and he was sitting in his dressing room and the attendant brought in this girl because she had fallen down in line from the heat and so on.

PIERRE: And kindly Elvis helped her out?

MRS. TRAINER: Yes. Then she sat down and burst into tears because she was married and she was going to have a baby and she was only fifteen. And they got into this whole business about the dangers and the pitfalls about the problems of teenage marriages through this dialogue. Strictly funny dialogue between Elvis and the girl.

PIERRE: But look at the ads: "Scanty panties, the barest necessities. . . . How to firm up your natural bosom. . . . Thirty ways to win a man. . . . Sassy stories. . . . Bedside fun. . . . Kiss and cry no more. . . ." Somebody said that these books are written by would-be nymphets for nymphets and pre-nymphets. Is that right? Who reads them?

MRS. TRAINER: Well, girls between thirteen and fifteen.

PIERRE: What do you think these books are doing to them?

MRS. TRAINER: I hope they entertain them. I really don't think most of the kids even believe it. Well, practically none, really.

PIERRE: But how about the so-called "true-confession" magazines, which you also write for?

MRS. TRAINER: They're even worse than the movie magazines.

PIERRE: In the old days, *True Story* insisted on an affidavit from the writer, saying that every confession was true.

MRS. TRAINER: I think they still do that. "True-to-the-best-of-my-knowledge" sort of thing.

PIERRE: *Are* they true to the best of your knowledge?

MRS. TRAINER: Oh, no, Good Heavens, no! The funny thing is that the readers *believe* that they are quite true.

PIERRE: They do?

MRS. TRAINER: Oh, yes. You'll get in just stacks and stacks of mail if you run a story like "My Baby is Dying of Something and What Should I Do?" You get mail from all over the country just telling you what you should do. It's just extraordinary.

PIERRE: What is your formula? Sin, suffer, and repent?

MRS. TRAINER: Oh, yes.

PIERRE: Evil is always punished?

MRS. TRAINER: Definitely.

PIERRE: Tell us the formula for a confession story as you write it.

MRS. TRAINER: Well, the narrator is usually a girl, because most of the readers are women, and they identify more quickly with a girl.

PIERRE: And terrible things happen to her?

MRS. TRAINER: Oh, yeah; the worse the better. For the teenagers, there are about four: the story about the girl who runs away from home and gets into terrible trouble; or the girl that stays at home and gets into terrible trouble; or the girl who runs off and marries her boyfriend and gets into terrible trouble; or the girl who goes all the way and gets into terrible trouble. It's always terrible trouble.

PIERRE: And then she finds God or a good man and she repents?

MRS. TRAINER: Well, either. Spiritual or inspirational is what it is called.

PIERRE: What do you think of your own readers? Do you like them or do you despise them?

MRS. TRAINER: Oh, I kind of like them, I think. They may be a little silly if they're going to buy all of this stuff, but I *do* try to entertain them and give them as much as their money calls for.

PIERRE: Apart from professional reading, what do you read for fun?

MRS. TRAINER: I read *The New Republic* and *The Reporter*.

PIERRE: How much money do you make?

MRS. TRAINER: In a good day, if I work at it, I can make a hundred dollars.

PIERRE: Do you like most of the movie stars you write about?

MRS. TRAINER: You mean do I like them *personally*?

PIERRE: Yes.

MRS. TRAINER: Oh, no. Some of them I hate. I think they're terrible phonies.

PIERRE: Who do you hate?

MRS. TRAINER: I hate Doris Day.

PIERRE: Why do you hate Doris Day?

MRS. TRAINER: Well, you know, she is such a phoney, really. It's kind of sad to say that, but you know, she comes on like she's twenty-six and she hasn't been anywhere and she doesn't know anything and, really, she is forty-one and she still runs around blowing bubble gum, for heaven's sakes, and drinking malts, and you know the facts of her life are quite different. She started out singing on the road with bands at one-night stands at the age of sixteen. She was married at seventeen, had a son at eighteen, and was divorced at nineteen. And if she's an innocent, little girl who is so wet behind the ears, then I'm Al Capp, for heaven's sakes.

PIERRE: Do you write fan-magazine articles about Doris Day?

MRS. TRAINER: Not as much anymore. I had a one-woman campaign going for a while trying to discredit her, but I just ran into a blank wall. I was a voice in the wilderness.

PIERRE: When you write these pieces and make up all these stories, do you ever pick up some other magazine and realize that some other writer has stolen all of these fantasies?

MRS. TRAINER: Oh, yes. Once I did an "interview" with Dick Chamberlain, you know, Doctor Kildare, and it was a great interview. He was very witty and very funny, and he came out with all these very quotable quotes and so on. But a friend of mine had actually made them all up. She made up the answers as well as the questions. A couple of months after the magazine hit the stands, she picked up one of her competitor's magazines, and there was a story on Dick Chamberlain, and there were those quotes of hers throughout it.

PIERRE: I'd guess Dick Chamberlain never looked better.

MRS. TRAINER: He looked great.

PIERRE: Is this one of the problems? That a lot of stars lead pretty dull, placid lives, and you have to give them some glamour?

MRS. TRAINER: Oh, yes. The ones that do weekly television series – that's *all* they do. Take Chamberlain, for instance. What does he do? He gets up in the morning and goes to the studio and works all day and then he comes home at night and goes to bed.

PIERRE: That's not the Dick Chamberlain we know and love in the movie magazines.

MRS. TRAINER: We make up all these marvellous stories – about him having all these great romances with all these lovely girls, and his fans love it and everybody loves it.

PIERRE: He should have it so good?

MRS. TRAINER: He should have it so good.

THE YOUNG TURK
AND THE OLD GUARD

"The public likes to see a
nice, stable, quiet man."

*I first met Robert Macaulay in 1944, when we were classmates at
the Royal Military Staff College studying Army Intelligence. My
original impression was of a young man with wit, a quick, supple
mind, and a great deal of energy and ambition. I haven't changed
that original assessment. In the intervening years, Macaulay has
zoomed through an entire political career – one which normally
ought to have occupied a lifetime. He is only forty-three; but he
has it all behind him.*

*Consider his record: At twenty-eight, a member of the Ontario
Legislature; at thirty-five, a cabinet minister; at forty, an aspirant
for the leadership of his party. And Macaulay was no ordinary
cabinet minister: at one point, while still the youngest member of
the inner circle, he held three cabinet posts. And he wrote books
in his spare time.*

*If there ever was a politician for the Sixties, it was Bob
Macaulay, a man who set a whirlwind pace, suffered few fools,
combined pragmatism with idealism, spoke brilliantly, was not*

afraid to say what he thought, and acted crisply and decisively. He came from a political family: his father was a cabinet minister before him, and young Bob was out canvassing from the age of fourteen and speaking from the age of sixteen. But this was no ward-heeler. His mind stretched far beyond the borders of his constituency. He collected modern art and he wrote a book about rare porcelain. He taught himself speed reading and gobbled up information. When he became Minister of Energy Resources he delved into the mysteries of nuclear fission and wrote a book about that for laymen. A Conservative by birth, he was an idealist by bent. For fourteen years he ran a free legal-aid clinic for his constituents (he once helped get a wrongly convicted man out of jail), and he pushed for higher old-age pensions and two-week vacations with pay.

"There is no substitute for hard work," he used to say. "I know people think I'm overly ambitious. Frankly, I don't understand this. I think any man without ambition is a vegetable."

When Leslie Frost stepped down as Premier of Ontario, Robert Macaulay was the first cabinet minister to throw his hat in the ring. He fought a hard, energetic whirlwind campaign, and if this were one of those political novels, we would have him besting the Old Guard and emerging victorious, the youngest premier in Ontario's history. But in real life, Macaulay didn't have a chance from the beginning – or so the political experts said later. The party organization had decided in advance to support a "safer" candidate in the person of John Robarts, an uncontroversial and uncomplicated man who now heads the Ontario Government.

Shortly after the leadership race, Macaulay suffered a mild heart attack and gave up his cabinet posts on doctor's orders. In May, 1964, he also resigned the house seat which he had held for fourteen years and entered private business and a law practice.

Why did Macaulay lose out? Possibly because of the very characteristics detailed above. The Old Guard was not yet ready for a transfer of power and, though John Robarts is a contemporary of Macaulay's, he is clearly an Old Guard man in his policies, attitudes, pronouncements, and actions.

Why did Macaulay quit – aside from health reasons? He had said, privately, that he was "cheesed off" – not a very felicitous phrase for a politician to use, perhaps, but one that was characteristic enough. When he appeared on my program, early in 1966, to talk publicly for the first time about his political career, I began by asking him why.

168

ROBERT MACAULAY: I think that sounds a little harsher, Pierre, than I felt it to be. "Cheesed off" is, perhaps, not a very nice phrase; but it's a phrase that I use – meaning that I had sort of done all in the job that I had been asked to do, that I felt I could creatively do. I was running out of steam; I needed to recharge my batteries. I'm the kind of feller who every so often has to change what he's doing to get a challenge out of it and to keep going in a creative way. That's what I felt.

PIERRE: And the official reason given for your leaving was the old one of health. You had a mild heart attack, but I suspect that if you had won the leadership race and been premier of Ontario, a heart attack wouldn't have stopped you from going on. Is that right?

ROBERT MACAULAY: Well, it might not have. I would have felt obligated to have gone on – I'm quite sure of that. But, meantime, John Robarts had been selected and was doing a good job, and there were lots of other people in the House. Therefore I felt, after nearly thirteen or fourteen years as a member, I had made what contribution I could and perhaps now I could lead a little of my own life.

PIERRE: Did you feel tired?

ROBERT MACAULAY: I was very tired, as a matter of fact, because I had travelled a great deal around the world as a minister. I guess I had perhaps put too much into what I did. I was very tired at this time.

PIERRE: You felt frustrated, too?

ROBERT MACAULAY: Well, people use this word "frustration." I mean, does it mean that you're not getting your own way?

PIERRE: Yes.

ROBERT MACAULAY: Well, sometimes – naturally. Since I was in charge of three departments, I was likely getting my way more than anybody else. We started the Trade Crusade, and it was quite a successful thing at the time; and this required a tremendous amount of energy. I finally got to the stage where I felt I was sort of running out of steam. Secondly, I was getting a little crabby and cross. People would come to me and say: "Oh, you're absolutely wrong on this policy," and I started to believe *they* must be wrong and I was right. So I thought, when a politician really believes all his own press releases, that perhaps he ought to try another venture in life.

PIERRE: You were the boy wonder. Did you worry about getting an over-inflated sense of your own importance?

ROBERT MACAULAY: Well, I did. I worried about that at the very beginning, as a matter of fact. It worried me more at the end. And I think this was one of the real reasons that I got out of politics. I had the chance to do a great many things, and I started believing, I think, too much in my own invincibility or my own infallibility. I started when I was twenty-eight, and that was quite a disadvantage.

PIERRE: Too young?

ROBERT MACAULAY: Oh, much too young. Much too young.

PIERRE: Smart aleck.

ROBERT MACAULAY: Yes; right. This may be a characteristic that I show in any event. I had been brought up in politics. I knew I was going to become a member and I wanted to become a cabinet minister. I had ideas that I wanted to bring with me into the Government. I had had these for many, many years, so the day I stepped in I didn't just *then* start to acquire convictions; I had had them for a long time.

PIERRE: What did the other, older boys think of you?

ROBERT MACAULAY: They were always very nice to me. But I think there's inevitably going to be a feeling. A fellow who's been there for a great many years and suffered through all kinds of adversities of his own and all kinds of frustrations, seeing a fellow of twenty-eight arrive and look, perhaps, as if he might advance up the ladder – this can cause some problems. I felt it did.

PIERRE: It must be kind of a lonely job, isn't it? Especially when you become a cabinet minister, though not as lonely as being premier or prime minister.

ROBERT MACAULAY: No, I would think being premier of this province or the prime minister of Canada is perhaps the loneliest job there is in the country. I don't think most people realize that you must keep your own counsel. You really can't tell anybody anything. You can't even intimate, sort of, what you're doing. This must make it a very lonely job. In a more restricted way, this is true as a cabinet minister within your own areas because – because there are all kinds of things that you can say or do that can have a very serious influence on companies that are affected by the decision and on the stock market.

PIERRE: So you had a lot of secrets?

ROBERT MACAULAY: Well, some.

PIERRE: And I suppose that everybody would come to you with their problems, but there was really nobody *you* could go to?

ROBERT MACAULAY: Except my wife. I think, perhaps, this is one of

170

the hardest parts of having a family in politics. The person I turned to in almost every case was my wife; and I think after twelve or fourteen years, you start to get a little sick of it. And I think now Joy is happy to be living a joint life rather than living, as she did, *my* life.

PIERRE: She was different from the other politicians' wives in that she didn't go to the teas . . . the political meetings. You kept her pretty well out of that side of it, didn't you?

ROBERT MACAULAY: Well, I didn't really keep her out of it. I would have been happy to have her go if she'd wanted to go. But we had a young family, and that was more important to her than to be involved in the social side of politics.

PIERRE: Isn't this a liability for a politician?

ROBERT MACAULAY: Yes, it is. But it wasn't one of which I ever complained, because I always felt that a man, when he goes into politics, should be the person who should be the one who carries the election or the responsibility or whatever it may be. It shouldn't have to be the wife.

PIERRE: But this isn't the way politics works in this country. Women are supposed to get out and help.

ROBERT MACAULAY: Now, all right, I understand that! This is just another small reason why I'm now in business and not in politics.

PIERRE: Your wife is a good-looking girl; she dresses well; and she stayed away from it all. Was there much jealousy?

ROBERT MACAULAY: My wife's very pretty. People did express, from time to time, that if she really had my interests at heart, she would attend more social functions politically. But I would never convey this message to her because, frankly, I was more interested in a happy home than I was in having somebody at a meeting.

PIERRE: This kind of a job – when you're holding three cabinet positions – must be tough on your family life.

ROBERT MACAULAY: Well, it was to me. You see, the last two years I think I travelled about fifty thousand miles, and you can't do that. I was in Japan, Israel, Greece, England, Paris, France – all over the world really – trying to sell Canadian goods. I don't know that I sold them effectively, but this was a new era when we started this Trade Crusade. It may be old hat now, to see ministers all over the place. But in those days, I tell you, the first time I went to Israel, there were all kinds of eyebrows raised – even within the Government. What did I think I could possibly do there? Well, we're now selling many millions of dollars worth of tobacco to

171

them, just as a result of those trips. I don't say I did it; but you have to get out.

PIERRE: Which meant that you weren't home.

ROBERT MACAULAY: I wasn't home.

PIERRE: Even when you were in Toronto, you must have been away a good deal.

ROBERT MACAULAY: I had I think three deputy ministers and nine secretaries, and I had a lot of work to do in my office; I was trained by my father and others to speak from a very early age; I was invited to speak a great deal, and you're expected and you must do a certain amount of it.

PIERRE: Going back to the business of politicians' wives, Bob; is a bachelor or a divorcé at a disadvantage in politics in this country because he has no wife?

ROBERT MACAULAY: Do you know, honestly, I would think that a bachelor had a *great* advantage over a married man; but the concept of politics is completely the reverse. The public likes to see a nice, stable, quiet man and to see what he's produced – his wife, his family, and the children all in a nice little row . . . everything ship-shape. Even if they themselves don't behave that way, *he* should. But, on the other hand, a bachelor has a tremendous advantage. First of all, he doesn't have to introduce his wife to all kinds of people whose names he's forgotten, which I always found was very difficult. Then, secondly, he can be – and I'm just analyzing what I saw – a bit of a flirt. And if you get away with it, this can be a great advantage.

PIERRE: Is a divorce a liability still in politics?

ROBERT MACAULAY: I would think it was some liability; but not nearly as much as it used to be.

PIERRE: Suppose that a politician ran for office and let it be known, not flamboyantly, but let it be known that he didn't attend church and didn't intend to attend church – that he had no religious beliefs. Would this be a real liability to him?

ROBERT MACAULAY: Why: are *you* seeking a nomination somewhere?

PIERRE: No.

ROBERT MACAULAY: I don't think it would do one any good, and I can't for the life of me think why a person would go out of his way to say: "Now, look, I don't go to church and I don't this, that, and something else." The public, as a whole, look on politicians in quite a different way than they might look on other things. It's a sort of "do as I say and not as I do" philosophy.

172

PIERRE: Can a politician in this country afford to be slightly flamboyant or eccentric?

ROBERT MACAULAY: I don't think so. I think that this is fine for American politics. I think it is becoming more so here. I don't think it is part of the Canadian way of political life. Now mind, it is more difficult in a large city riding even to *exist*: John Robarts used often to talk about this. He represented the riding of London. One newspaper, one television station, one radio station. He was the only member; so whenever he had a cold, it could well be carried in the paper. I could have stood on the City Hall steps upside down with nothing on, and it couldn't conceivably have competed with other stories that were available that day in Toronto.

PIERRE: But you often made the news doing such eccentric things as riding a bicycle.

ROBERT MACAULAY: Well, all right, I rode a bicycle because I wanted the exercise, and I had to travel so much in planes and trains and sit in meetings that I thought it was a very good thing. But I ran over one sewer at the corner of Avenue Road and Bloor three times, and went right over the handlebars, and it became too dangerous. I also thought there were several people lying in wait for me, and it would be just as well, perhaps, if I either changed my route or gave up the bicycle.

PIERRE: I was told that you would really like to have driven a Rolls Royce to work but figured you couldn't do it as a politician.

ROBERT MACAULAY: I always wanted to have a Rolls Royce, even if I couldn't afford it. A second-hand one and very old.

PIERRE: As a cabinet minister, could you have driven one?

ROBERT MACAULAY: Oh, *no*.

PIERRE: Why?

ROBERT MACAULAY: Well, because it would have been thought by others around me as either an honest display of money that I must obviously have married, inherited, or stolen or, alternatively, as a flamboyant gesture that would reflect very badly on my colleagues. I think they're quite right. These are not the characteristics you would expect of a politician in Canada.

PIERRE: Bob, you're an intellectual, you have some artistic interests, some people would call you "arty." You've a sardonic and ironic wit. Are these assets or liabilities?

ROBERT MACAULAY: First of all, I'd have to deny I possess any of them. A sardonic wit?

PIERRE: You can be sardonic, you can be blunt, you can be outspoken.

ROBERT MACAULAY: Well, this *is* a disadvantage to a politician. But let's face it, Pierre, you have brown eyes, and you can't do a thing about it. It's like looking at your daughter, with whom you may have become a little impatient, and saying: "Look, I'm sick of this. Tomorrow afternoon you'll be fourteen." Well, she's just not going to *be* fourteen. Now I happen to have the characteristics I've inherited from my family. With what I had, I tried to do the best I could. I think to be overly expressive, to seem to be at all aggressive, is except in an emergency *not* considered to be a desirable qualification or characteristic of a politician in Canada. I can't remember what the other things you said I possess were. Oh, I think you said I was "arty." I really don't know exactly what that means.

PIERRE: Well, some people would call you "arty."

ROBERT MACAULAY: I'm interested in Canadian art and I'm on the Art Gallery directorship and –

PIERRE: You collect paintings.

ROBERT MACAULAY: Yes, and I'm interested in supporting Canadian artists and this kind of thing. And I read books.

PIERRE: More than that. I went into your office once in Queen's Park. It looked as much like a politician's office as the Taj Mahal looks like my place.

ROBERT MACAULAY: Well, I remember the first time Mr. Frost came into my office. He asked me when the artist was going to come back and finish the painting that was hanging over the mantel. It happened to be by Borduas, one of the finest painters this country has ever produced. Of course, Leslie Frost had the attitude that unless a painting contained at least one birchbark canoe and several coonskin caps it just ain't art. If that makes me "arty," because I don't happen to subscribe to that philosophy, well, then, I'm arty.

PIERRE: Were your colleagues suspicious of you? Did they think you're arty?

ROBERT MACAULAY: Oh no. I don't think so. I think your questions suggest that they were spending a lot of their day thinking about my office and my characteristics.

PIERRE: I had some of that feeling.

ROBERT MACAULAY: I wouldn't make a comment about that. Whatever they may have said that I haven't or have heard is up to them. I remember Jimmie Auld, who is the Minister of Tourism

174

now – I think that's what he calls himself – referring to one painting. He asked me to tell my seven-year-old daughter how much he had enjoyed the painting. Actually, that painting happened to be by Riopelle, the second greatest, or perhaps the greatest, painter that Canada has produced. Now, on the other hand, Jimmie's interest in various other forms of art would be far more sophisticated than mine.

PIERRE: Do you move with politicians anymore?

ROBERT MACAULAY: No.

PIERRE: Do you see them socially?

ROBERT MACAULAY: I should say no; I don't at all.

PIERRE: Are any of your close friends politicians?

ROBERT MACAULAY: Yes, some. For instance I go and have lunch from time to time with the premier. We don't talk about politics. I really grew up with him in a way. We came into the House together and we shared an apartment for a few years before I was married, when he was living here, and his family was in London. I see a few of them from time to time; but not often. I always felt that if you're not cooking in the kitchen then get out. When I withdrew, I went back into business, into the practice of law which I am enjoying very much. I want to practise law and I want to do business, and the parts that I am involved in don't require me to come into contact with the Government.

PIERRE: Did you find a lot of the time that your social contacts with politicians bored you?

ROBERT MACAULAY: I don't think so. I'm not easily bored. I'm a person who's very restless. I find, for instance, sitting still here very hard on my system, because part of my way of expressing myself is with my body and movement.

PIERRE: Did you feel a sense of great disappointment when you lost in the leadership, Bob?

ROBERT MACAULAY: Yes, I think I did.

PIERRE: You expected to win, didn't you?

ROBERT MACAULAY: No, I didn't. No, I didn't. I *hoped* to win. I hoped to win because there were some things I really wanted to do. The Trade Crusade, for instance, was one of them. But I had an opportunity of doing this in any event.

PIERRE: Did you feel the fix was in?

ROBERT MACAULAY: No.

PIERRE: I thought it was. I thought the thing was preordained – cut and dried.

ROBERT MACAULAY: I think the party organization decided that John

Robarts was the man they wanted to support. He was – he is – a less flamboyant man and therefore they considered that, perhaps, from a political point of view he was more "stable." I hate the word, frankly, because I think of the most stable thing in the world as a rock.

PIERRE: Well, what you're saying is that the party organization thought *you* were too flamboyant, too outspoken, too courageous, and too colourful.

ROBERT MACAULAY: Oh, I haven't said any such thing. All right *you've* said it; so let's leave it there. I accepted their decision. We had a very good run. Look, there's never been a man from Toronto has ever won the thing, and there were two of us both from Toronto, Kelso Roberts and myself. On the first ballot, John and Kelso Roberts and Jim Allen and I each had about 340 votes, and I got them all outside of the city. So from one point of view I was very pleased. From another, I was very disappointed, and my wife, who has no great political leanings at all – if anything, she leans *away* from politics – was very disappointed too. You know, you get torn up into an emotional storm and suddenly, when it's all over, you get very disappointed. I got over that because there was too much to do.

PIERRE: Is there any conceivable situation that would get you back into politics?

ROBERT MACAULAY: I think so; but not at the moment.

PIERRE: What conceivable situation?

ROBERT MACAULAY: The passage of time; maybe seven or eight years. The need, if I could serve somebody or some cause in the national field. I would never enter again into provincial politics. Not for any special reason. But I was there. When I was there I gave it everything I'd got. I made a decision to leave. And this would be it.

THE UNLOVED MOTHER

"I've never really had anything
that I could call my own."

The dialogue that follows is self-explanatory and needs very little elaboration. The New Morality has not yet been able to cope with the old problem of pregnancy among the unmarried: indeed, all the available evidence indicates that it is increasing, especially among teenagers. One of these is Jane Freeman, an attractive girl of nineteen, who readily agreed to appear on my program without any disguise except a change of name. Like so many of her generation, she told her story and discussed her problem without emotion or embarrassment; perhaps that is why the effect on the screen was so deeply moving. In spite of her age and background, she is a girl of considerable dignity and poise; and, perhaps because of her experience, a girl of considerable insight. I began by asking an obvious question: How did she feel when she discovered she was unmarried and pregnant?

JANE FREEMAN: Well, I was happy that I was going to have something that was mine. But yet I was all mixed up. I didn't know what to do.

PIERRE: But you were in love?

JANE FREEMAN: I thought I was.

PIERRE: You had every intention of getting married?

JANE FREEMAN: Yes, I did. But he didn't.

PIERRE: How did you feel about that at the time?

JANE FREEMAN: Well, I thought that after the baby was born he would change his mind and everything would be just sweet as roses for us.

PIERRE: Everything wasn't as sweet as roses really.

JANE FREEMAN: No.

PIERRE: In that respect, though, perhaps it's fortunate for you that you didn't marry him.

JANE FREEMAN: Well, I think so.

PIERRE: We'll go to that area in a moment, but let's find out first from you, Jane, what you decided to do originally about the baby. Did you consider having the baby adopted?

JANE FREEMAN: Oh yes, the baby's father and I both went to the Children's Aid and proceeded to go through adoption and filled out papers.

PIERRE: Was this before the child was born?

JANE FREEMAN: Yes.

PIERRE: So you had no real contact with the child except she was inside you?

JANE FREEMAN: That's right.

PIERRE: How did you feel at that time about losing your baby?

JANE FREEMAN: Well, it's something that's there and you can't . . . I would rather have cut off my right leg or something than lose her.

PIERRE: Even at that point?

JANE FREEMAN: Yes.

PIERRE: Before you saw the baby, you didn't want to adopt her out?

JANE FREEMAN: No. But I felt that for her sake it would have been better.

PIERRE: What did they tell you at the Children's Aid? Did they advise adoption? Did they advise you to keep the baby – or what?

JANE FREEMAN: No. They just pointed out the views on keeping her and giving her up, and that it would have been better for her if she had been adopted. She would have had a proper home and proper parents. But they don't try to encourage you one way or the other.

178

PIERRE: Did they point out any advantages in you keeping her?

JANE FREEMAN: No, not really. They just told me that it would be hard, and since I wasn't married not to depend on getting married after the baby was born.

PIERRE: You still thought you were going to get married. And then you signed some papers. But, of course, you couldn't put your baby out for adoption until the baby was actually a person, could you? Actually born.

JANE FREEMAN: No.

PIERRE: Then what made you decide *not* to go through with the adoption?

JANE FREEMAN: Well, I don't know really. I suppose as it gets closer to the time you can feel that child and you realize it's really yours and nobody can take it away from you. It's something that *no* one can take away from you. When she was born and when I saw her — well, she wasn't the most beautiful thing, but she was still mine and that was all.

PIERRE: This made a difference when you held her for the first time?

JANE FREEMAN: Oh, yes.

PIERRE: And then it became impossible to give her away?

JANE FREEMAN: Oh, I just couldn't do it. I couldn't.

PIERRE: What did you tell the Children's Aid?

JANE FREEMAN: I just told them that I changed my mind and they said, well, if I changed my mind again they would still be there.

PIERRE: Now at what point did you decide that you really didn't want to get married?

JANE FREEMAN: Well, I lived with the baby's father from the time I was about three months pregnant until last March. The baby was seven months old then, and things just were going the wrong instead of the right way. We had nothing, the baby had nothing, and I thought that I should try and give her something.

PIERRE: What was the father's attitude towards the baby?

JANE FREEMAN: Well, I don't think it really hit him that he had a dependant until I did leave. And when I left, it sort of hit him with a bang, you know.

PIERRE: Then did he want to marry you at this time?

JANE FREEMAN: Yes. *Now* he wants to marry me. But I don't.

PIERRE: So although you could get married to the father of your child now and, as some people would say, "make the marriage respectable," you are intent not to. Would you explain that? A lot of people, you see, think that they should get married at all costs. You obviously don't think this.

179

JANE FREEMAN: No. You cannot marry someone for the sake of the child. Sure, the child has the right to have a father as well as a mother; but I don't love this man. I was infatuated with him at the time — I must have been. I must have had *some* feeling. But I can't marry him. I don't love him. I see him and I just, you know, don't want to be near him. I know he loves his child; but he has never really given her anything that a father would give a child.

PIERRE: Strange, isn't it, how feelings that intense can suddenly change?

JANE FREEMAN: Yes. Puppy love.

PIERRE: Well of course you were only seventeen, weren't you?

JANE FREEMAN: Yes.

PIERRE: I suppose that's what's facing thousands and thousands of teenagers across the country.

JANE FREEMAN: Well, they should stop and think before they do anything. I didn't think.

PIERRE: Well, now you've had great difficulty, I would think. You're a single woman with a child; you must have had difficulty getting a job. You haven't got a job, in fact.

JANE FREEMAN: No. Well, I've worked in a few restaurants and attended night school, but I had to quit because I just can't find a baby-sitter to baby-sit while I'm going to school at night.

PIERRE: You were getting job-training for what?

JANE FREEMAN: Clerk typist.

PIERRE: Now you can't even get that because of the child. Have you ever regretted the decision not to adopt the baby out?

JANE FREEMAN: No, no.

PIERRE: How would you feel now if you lost your baby? Suppose the Children's Aid came and said: "You're not a fit mother. We're going to take the baby away." How would you feel?

JANE FREEMAN: I don't know . . . I don't know. I think I'd go jump in the nearest lake or something. Life just wouldn't be worth living without her.

PIERRE: So, to you at this moment, the baby is the most important thing in your life?

JANE FREEMAN: She's the *only* thing in my life.

PIERRE: You said it was nice to have something that was yours. Is this because you've never had anything really that's yours until the time you had this baby?

JANE FREEMAN: I've never really had anything that I could call my own.

180

PIERRE: Is that because you were yourself in a foster home at the age of five?

JANE FREEMAN: That's right.

PIERRE: And all of your life was spent in foster homes?

JANE FREEMAN: That's right.

PIERRE: How old were you when you were taken from your parents?

JANE FREEMAN: Five years old.

PIERRE: There were four of you children. Were you all taken by the Children's Aid?

JANE FREEMAN: Three were.

PIERRE: Can you remember any of this? I suspect this experience isn't one you forget easily, even though you were only five at the time.

JANE FREEMAN: No, it isn't. I remember the day I went into the Children's Aid. I remember my mother dressing me and what she put on me and so forth. I remember like . . . like it was yesterday.

PIERRE: This was just before your fifth birthday, wasn't it?

JANE FREEMAN: It was the day before.

PIERRE: What kind of a birthday did you have?

JANE FREEMAN: I don't remember.

PIERRE: You don't remember *that* day?

JANE FREEMAN: No. I don't remember.

PIERRE: How did you feel as a child leaving your parents? Did you feel anything?

JANE FREEMAN: Well, I don't think it really hit me. I was with my sister, and she was two years older than I. I guess you could say my sister was more my mother in a sense.

PIERRE: Your seven-year-old sister was a mother to you?

JANE FREEMAN: In a way I felt that she was. I guess I must have, you know.

PIERRE: And then you didn't see your parents again and you didn't see your brothers for how many years? Twelve . . . thirteen?

JANE FREEMAN: Something like that.

PIERRE: Is this what you mean when you say that until you had a baby of your own you had nothing of your own — because you had no real anchor?

JANE FREEMAN: I had nothing to hold on to. My sister and I were in the same foster home for a number of years, but then we were separated and ever since then it just seemed that people just kept taking things away from me and not giving anything. And that I had to fight for what I got, and after I got it it was just taken away again. So what was the use of fighting if you didn't get anything?

PIERRE: I think I'd like to explore further this experience you had in various foster homes. That first foster home, which you went into at the age of five – you were in that seven years. How did you like it?

JANE FREEMAN: Well, it was all right.

PIERRE: Did you have the feeling that the people there were your mother and father?

JANE FREEMAN: Yes, I did.

PIERRE: Were there other children too?

JANE FREEMAN: No. Just my sister and I.

PIERRE: Why is it that they didn't adopt you?

JANE FREEMAN: Well, I don't really know. I think that they wanted to but for some reason they didn't. I don't know why.

PIERRE: Why did you leave that foster home?

JANE FREEMAN: I don't really know that either.

PIERRE: You were just taken?

JANE FREEMAN: Well, my sister moved to go to a different high school. And after that she went into nursing and then, the following year, I went into high school too. I left about six months to a year after she did. I think it was mainly because of the schooling, I don't really know.

PIERRE: Do you ever have any communication with these people?

JANE FREEMAN: No.

PIERRE: You've never seen them since?

JANE FREEMAN: No.

PIERRE: So that you led a family life for seven years and then it's just cut off. There's nothing there to cling to? There's no anchor?

JANE FREEMAN: There's nothing, really, I want to cling to.

PIERRE: You couldn't have thought of them very warmly, then, if you don't want to see them again.

JANE FREEMAN: Oh, I did while I was living with them. But you find out things as you, you know, leave people. You find out things afterwards. I think I feel a little bitter towards them now.

PIERRE: Do you feel it's a rejection – that you were allowed to go so easily?

JANE FREEMAN: Well, there are things that can't be discussed, but I do have my reasons.

PIERRE: All right. The fact is that you were moved. And from there where did you go?

JANE FREEMAN: To a receiving home for unadoptable children.

PIERRE: Why were you unadoptable?

JANE FREEMAN: Well, I was thirteen.

PIERRE: And then you went to this succession of foster homes over the next two years?

JANE FREEMAN: Yes. From the receiving home to a foster home and then back to the receiving home. There were nine different moves.

PIERRE: You made nine moves?

JANE FREEMAN: Nine moves.

PIERRE: Some of those families treated you very well, others didn't treat you so well, I gather from what we've found out.

JANE FREEMAN: Yes.

PIERRE: In one family the man beat his wife, is that not true?

JANE FREEMAN: That's true.

PIERRE: Not a very good atmosphere for a child, is it?

JANE FREEMAN: No. They had three children of their own. I was a little older than they were, but for their own children it was even worse.

PIERRE: Were you always treated differently from the other children in the household in these cases?

JANE FREEMAN: Well, in that case I think I was. I was more of a built-in baby-sitter at that place – a maid and so forth. But in most of the other homes I was in I was treated like one of the family.

PIERRE: Why did you keep moving? Was this because you were hard to get along with? Or did they take you for a certain time? Or what?

JANE FREEMAN: No. I've never been hard to get along with, but I think it's pretty hard to take a teenager and then just place her in a home. I know that the Children's Aid do their best to find parents suitable, but still things develop and, you know, it's pretty difficult to find the perfect parent for anyone.

PIERRE: Did you feel at sea in this period? You must have felt that you had no real home of your own, didn't you?

JANE FREEMAN: Well, after a while it seems like a habit. After two or three foster homes, you just don't try any more because, you know, you figure: "What's the use? I'll be out some day." You just don't bother trying any more. You say: "Well, I'll be eighteen soon, and I'll be out and that'll be it."

PIERRE: So it becomes only a way-point in your life, not a permanent stopping place?

JANE FREEMAN: Yes. You feel like a vagabond, you know, drifting from home to home.

183

PIERRE: Do you ever see any of these people now? You've had a couple of nice experiences, I know.

JANE FREEMAN: Well, I could go back and see them if I wanted to; but it's too far to go.

PIERRE: You have no real desire to see them?

JANE FREEMAN: No. I mean, if I saw them I wouldn't ignore them, but I have no desire to go back to them.

PIERRE: Now you didn't wait till you were eighteen to leave. You came to the big city when you were what age?

JANE FREEMAN: About sixteen.

PIERRE: Were you anxious to get out on your own at this point?

JANE FREEMAN: Yes. I thought: "Maybe now that I can I'll find my own home. I don't need anyone's help," sort of, you know.

PIERRE: You came from a smaller town. How did you find Toronto?

JANE FREEMAN: I moved to Toronto through the Children's Aid to go to Hairdressing School. I was living in a boarding house where there were several other girls from the Hairdressing School, and it was, oh, it was just wonderful at first, you know. At sixteen.

PIERRE: Freedom?

JANE FREEMAN: Sixteen! Big Toronto! All by myself, you know? But that wears off in a few months.

PIERRE: And then you get lonely?

JANE FREEMAN: I found the people in Toronto are not very friendly.

PIERRE: Not having seen your parents since the age of five, you sought them out?

JANE FREEMAN: Well, I had seen my mother and, apparently, I had seen my father, too. But I didn't recognize him, or I didn't know who he was. When my sister and I were living on this farm, they used to come and visit. Then, for some reason, they stopped. I think because we were made permanent wards of the Children's Aid Society, they weren't allowed to see us anymore, I don't know. But I didn't want to find my parents. I thought that if I did, then I'd have to go home and live with them, and I wouldn't be able to finish my course. And that's exactly what did happen. I put it off for about a month, and then I just couldn't stand it any longer, knowing they were living in the same city and. . . . There was a telephone in front of me, I just had to see them. I had to at least see what my father looked like, you know.

PIERRE: Are you fairly close to your parents now?

JANE FREEMAN: Yes.

PIERRE: How did they feel when you were pregnant and had a baby?

JANE FREEMAN: Well, when I told my parents I was pregnant, it hurt them, but they never interfered at all. It was my own decision to make. They came in to see me in the hospital, and they never said, you know, give her away, or keep her. They told me that if I wanted to keep her, there was room for me and the baby at home, if I wanted to come home. But if I wanted to go and live with the baby's father, that was my own business. But I do wish they had told me – get home, you know.

PIERRE: Get home?

JANE FREEMAN: With the baby. I would have been a lot better off.

PIERRE: Do you care what people think?

JANE FREEMAN: Well to a certain extent I do. I mean, well what do you mean?

PIERRE: Well you must have had people look down their noses at you because they knew you had a child.

JANE FREEMAN: Oh, yes. They say: "My goodness, she's nothing but a little so-and-so," you know.

PIERRE: Do you care about that?

JANE FREEMAN: Not really.

PIERRE: Has it caused you trouble getting jobs?

JANE FREEMAN: In some places it has, yes.

PIERRE: Has it caused you trouble getting a place to stay?

JANE FREEMAN: Well, I had an apartment just a few months ago, my girl friend and I and the baby. The landlord didn't think too highly of it. He thought it was kind of strange if I had a boy friend come in after school. I finished school at eleven. If he came in for a cup of coffee or something, he always complained to me that his neighbours didn't like it. He didn't mind, he said, but his neighbours didn't like it. So, I never tried too much after that. Well, I looked in a few places, but they just don't take children.

PIERRE: Especially without fathers, I guess?

JANE FREEMAN: Yes.

PIERRE: Do you think you're ready for marriage yet?

JANE FREEMAN: No, no. I'm not looking for a father. She has one, and I know I can go to him if I want to, but I don't want to, and if I were ready to get married, I'd marry him. But I'm not ready to get married. I'm much too young to get married, I think. But I still have a responsibility, and I'll take care of that the best I can. But getting married, that's a long way off.

PIERRE: What kind of a husband are you looking for in the end, or do you know? He'll have to be a special kind of man, because he'll have to accept a baby that's not his.

JANE FREEMAN: Well, there are lots of those around. You'd be surprised, really. That was one problem that I thought of quite deeply when I decided to keep the baby. Would anyone want me?

PIERRE: You've had offers?

JANE FREEMAN: Oh, yes, I've had offers. I was wondering: would anybody go out with a girl that has a baby, you know? But then I got to the point that I didn't care. If I do go out with a boy now, the first night I go out with him, I tell him, I have a baby. If he's not broad-minded enough to see things like this, if he goes away, if I never see him again, well then, he's not worth it. I mean, it could very well happen to him.

JEAN
TEMPLETON

EPILEPTIC

"Dandruff can cause you
a lot more trouble."

The first producer of The Pierre Berton Show *was Ross McLean.
Towards the end of our first year, he and I decided we'd do a
program about epilepsy, a subject few used to discuss in public
until the New Frankness. With some difficulty, we persuaded two
epileptics to appear on the program, identify themselves, and talk
openly about the public attitude to their illness. We learned a bit
about epilepsy that afternoon; but within the the next two years
Ross, especially, was to learn a good deal more.*

*He had just married a pretty, red-headed comedienne named
Jean Templeton who was making a name for herself as a writer
and performer of off-beat revue material. As a matter of fact,
they were married in the middle of one of our marathon taping
sessions in New York City, and I was best man. I guess it would
be about a year after that program on epilepsy that a bizarre
incident occurred in the same studio at* CFTO-TV *where my own
show was then being produced.*

Jean was appearing as a guest panelist on To Tell The Truth, *and the show was actually underway when she herself experienced, without warning, and in full view of the cameras, the audience, and her fellow performers, what turned out to be an epileptic seizure. Her eyes rolled back, she foamed at the mouth, she fell to the floor and kicked about.*

It was some time before her ailment was correctly diagnosed. There was a fear, at first, that she might have a brain tumour. When she finally discovered what was wrong with her, she made no effort to hide it from anybody; nor did she stop performing. Indeed, she launched a revue of her own at the Dell Theatre Restaurant in Toronto in which she appeared nightly.

Once, I remember, Jean turned up on the stage with a broken nose. She made light of it, but the truth was that she had experienced another seizure during which she banged her face on the floor. It failed to daunt her. When I asked her if she would return to the same TV studio where that original dramatic incident had occurred, and talk about it, she cheerfully assented with the proviso that I wouldn't make it lugubrious. We began by discussing the fact that, until very recently, epilepsy wasn't a subject that had been talked about much in public or even in private. Why was that? I asked.

▭

JEAN TEMPLETON: I think there are several reasons. First of all, some of us don't talk about it easily because we don't talk about our appendectomies either. We have some sense of the fact that it's a boring story. But I think the thing that makes it difficult for me to talk about it is that, out of this experience, I learned something: that it's kind of a shattering thing to find people feeling sorry for you when you don't feel sorry for yourself. Now you know that there's no *reason* for anyone to feel sorry for you, but there's a kind of moment there where you're a little bit shattered and you wonder if you have the right picture of yourself.

PIERRE: I know that you treat it about the way you'd treat a broken leg, but that's not the way the general public treats it, is it?

JEAN TEMPLETON: You know, dandruff can cause you a lot more trouble.

PIERRE: Tell me a bit about what happened when you had your first seizure at the television studio. What do you remember of that?

JEAN TEMPLETON: I don't remember anything, fortunately. I fell over. Part of my trouble has been that I've never seen an epileptic seizure that I know about. I've had fairly lurid descriptions of what happens from other people – more or less lurid, depending on how tactful the other people are. But I know I fell and I fractured – what do you call those little round bones in your back? Vertebrae? And it was after that the testing started and so on.

PIERRE: Was there a doctor in the house?

JEAN TEMPLETON: There was one in the audience.

PIERRE: And your first memory, I suppose, would be of the doctor leaning over you?

JEAN TEMPLETON: Yes, and he kept asking me about medication, and he assumed I guess that I knew that I was an epileptic – and I didn't. He was trying to get me to say my name. When you're coming out of a seizure, you can be very foggy. That's why sometimes epileptics are taken off to police stations and booked as drunks. Your speech can get very sloppy, and your muscles really aren't working again yet properly, and you're just in kind of a fog which is very much like being drunk, really. You don't know where you are or who these people are all around you.

PIERRE: And only then did the doctor begin to realize that you didn't know what was wrong with you and that they had to find out?

JEAN TEMPLETON: Yes.

PIERRE: But you'd had a seizure before this and didn't know it was epilepsy, right?

JEAN TEMPLETON: That was before our daughter was born.

PIERRE: Were you pregnant?

JEAN TEMPLETON: Yes. Sometimes when people have toxemia in pregnancy they have convulsions, and usually when that happens the birth is induced – very quickly. So that's what happened: our daughter was born about five weeks early and had to be kept in a little glass box which was a very frustrating time in my life. It was thought then that it was just a result of the pregnancy, or related to the pregnancy.

PIERRE: But it turned out that though it may have been triggered by the pregnancy, it was actually something that you were going to have to live with for a while. What kind of emotions went through you when you were finally told you were an epileptic?

JEAN TEMPLETON: I was terribly relieved. I said, "Is *that* all?"

PIERRE: You thought it was something worse?

JEAN TEMPLETON: I knew it could be. I began to get kind of nervous when I was told the tests were going to start; I thought I could sense a kind of evasiveness.

PIERRE: People whispering around behind your back?

JEAN TEMPLETON: No, nothing that deliberate, really, but you can tell when doctors are being a little bit cautious with you, either because they don't know yet or because they don't know what your emotional response will be. So I found one doctor who did know me better, and I said: "What is this?" He said: "Do you want to know what the worst possibilities are?" And I said yes, and he said: "You could have a tumour," and then he explained that only about ten per cent of brain tumours are malignant. He said: "You could have an aneurism, you could have some form of meningitis, etc . . ."

PIERRE: No wonder you were relieved. Tell me, Jean, a lot of epileptics get warnings of a seizure. Does this happen to you?

JEAN TEMPLETON: It never has, and I don't know whether it's because I haven't had enough seizures to recognize something or not. But I've always been very much concentrated on whatever I was doing and very interested in it, and suddenly . . . it's a very nice way to snap out because there is no warning. It's not unpleasant at all and not painful.

PIERRE: How many seizures have you had?

JEAN TEMPLETON: Oh dear. I can't count them, Pierre. Say, maybe ten, maybe fifteen.

PIERRE: Now you're on some kind of pills. How do they tell which kind of pill to give you?

JEAN TEMPLETON: There is some experimenting done because there is a variety of these drugs. They're all anti-convulsants.

PIERRE: Like tranquilizers?

JEAN TEMPLETON: No, they're not like tranquilizers. I discovered that one day, because I ran out of pills and I was too lazy to go to the drugstore and get more, so I took tranquilizers instead, thinking they were the same thing, and they didn't work. But some of them are used as tranquilizers. For instance, phenobarb is used as a sedative. I took that first and found it just dreadful because I love tranquilizers but *I* want to decide when I'm going to be tranquil and I was very tranquil all the time. After a while I would aim for a door and sort of hit the side of it, and I would watch television, and there would be three or four of the same person. I didn't realize that this was the cumulative effect of the drug. I thought it was the epilepsy that was doing this to me.

PIERRE: So how many pills do you take a day now?

JEAN TEMPLETON: Five. And there's no sleepiness at all.

PIERRE: It's pretty expensive, isn't it?

JEAN TEMPLETON: Yes, it is. I often wonder how it is for people to whom five, ten, or fifteen dollars a month can make a real difference. There are lots of people in that position.

PIERRE: Is there any kind of medical scheme now that covers pills?

JEAN TEMPLETON: No.

PIERRE: So until such a medical scheme comes in, you'll be stuck with a fair medical bill?

JEAN TEMPLETON: Yes.

PIERRE: What were the reactions of your friends when they found out that you were an epileptic? Did they avoid the subject? Were they embarrassed?

JEAN TEMPLETON: Well, most close friends, like you, reacted as you did. They were relieved it wasn't anything serious. Other people said rather funny things. Somebody said: "I guess that's why you're like that." I said: "Like *what*?" and they said: "Well, you know, how you get lost in the Dominion Store." You know, I *do* every Saturday. I can never remember where the butter is. I told this to the doctor, and he said: "This is a physical problem or I wouldn't be treating it, and you can tell your friends that you'll still be vague and confused." Other people said: "Oh, I won't tell anyone, don't worry!"

PIERRE: That's an odd reaction.

JEAN TEMPLETON: That was the first time I realized there is a problem this way; people think of it as being something rather secretive and embarrassing. That's when I evolved the dirty-diaper theory.

PIERRE: What's the dirty-diaper theory?

JEAN TEMPLETON: Well, I learned in the past few years that the first time you change a dirty diaper it's a pretty depressing routine, right? And the second time and the third time, too. But when you've changed four thousand two hundred and sixty-three dirty diapers, it doesn't mean anything anymore. Now a lot of epileptics, particularly the people who have an aura or a warning, will go home. Some of them have time to do this – at least time to hide themselves so that no one will see the seizure. They are inclined to keep themselves private while it's happening, and parents are inclined to be this way with their children. And I suddenly thought if everybody had seen lots and lots of epileptic seizures, they wouldn't mean very much, and so there would be no need for embarrassment or discomfort.

PIERRE: No. Because actually, contrary to popular opinion, it's not a terribly dangerous thing, is it? But as an actress, weren't you afraid you'd have a seizure in public – on the stage when you were performing in your revue at the Dell?

JEAN TEMPLETON: Yes, I was terribly afraid, and as a result it wasn't a very good show. I didn't perform very well because this was on my mind all the time. I think probably that's why I did it because it was one minor worry I had at the very beginning, you know: "Do I have to find another way to earn my living?" Also partly because of what had happened on the TV show. So I was trying to find out if I could get through a performance every night without this happening. I didn't really know. And each night, when I was finished, about the only thought I had was: "Well, it didn't happen." Then one night it occurred to me that, if it had, it might have been more entertaining than the prepared material.

PIERRE: Are you over that feeling now?

JEAN TEMPLETON: Oh, very much over it. I don't think of it anymore.

PIERRE: But you still can't drive a car can you?

JEAN TEMPLETON: You have to be seizure-free for two years.

PIERRE: Your seizures are getting further apart?

JEAN TEMPLETON: That's right.

PIERRE: And that's a good sign?

JEAN TEMPLETON: Oh, a very good sign, because the interesting thing about the phenomenon is that you stand the greatest chance of having a seizure just after you've had one.

PIERRE: They run in streaks, do they?

JEAN TEMPLETON: They generate themselves, yes, and if you can go for a long period without one, your brain sort of forgets how to do it, which is a silly, simple way of explaining it.

PIERRE: Thanks to these new pills, you're looking towards the day when you won't really be an epileptic at all?

JEAN TEMPLETON: Yes. Some people can even stop the drugs eventually, after they've been without a seizure for several years.

PIERRE: Meanwhile, do you worry about carrying your two-year-old? Do you worry that you might fall down with her?

JEAN TEMPLETON: That's the only thing I still worry about. I think this must be a tremendous problem for some people, because I want to have more children. One thing that I did was teach her to go up and down stairs by herself. That's about the only thing I tried to teach her deliberately. When we're alone I don't carry her on the stairs ever. But I can arrange to have someone in the house if I'm going to be alone for long periods, and this is why I feel I'm fortunate this way. I'm sure there are a lot of women who can't, and I'm sure this must upset them all the time.

PIERRE: Are you worried about another pregnancy? Because it was really a pregnancy apparently that triggered this. What about getting pregnant again? Might it bring it all back again and increase the number of seizures?

JEAN TEMPLETON: Yes, it might.

PIERRE: But you're still going ahead.

JEAN TEMPLETON: I would like to. Either that or adopt a child.

PIERRE: Can an epileptic adopt a child?

JEAN TEMPLETON: This is a real problem. It's difficult. The only thing I know is that a P.R. for the Toronto Children's Aid told one of the researchers on *This Hour Has Seven Days* that they couldn't remember ever having given a child to parents with epilepsy, particularly an epileptic mother. When they were asked why, they said that having a mother who is disabled places too great an emotional strain on a child. So they wouldn't consider it for that person.

PIERRE: This must have infuriated you to be called disabled.

JEAN TEMPLETON: Yes, and "handicapped" was another word that was used. It's kind of curious because I think, my goodness, lots of people can't see very well, and they wear glasses, and lots of us have holes in our teeth, even *with* Crest toothpaste. It's kind of upsetting to think that somebody will label you that way.

PIERRE: A lot of epileptics, of course, feel discriminated against. Maybe for a certain kind of sensitive person this would produce in them the kind of feeling that Negroes have in our society. Before coming on the program, you used the phrase "professional epileptics," which I thought very interesting.

JEAN TEMPLETON: Oh, I was referring to people who allow this particular thing to become the centre of their lives. Sometimes they can't help it. The people who sort of clutch on to it, you know: "This is *my* illness." They treasure it.

PIERRE: Of course, you're in a pretty good position. You're a house-wife. You've got a working husband. You can do your job, as you've shown. But a man who is in the construction business and has to climb high buildings can't do that, can he?

JEAN TEMPLETON: Right, he can't. The people who really suffer the most, I think, are high-school dropouts who have no skilled trade.

PIERRE: Of course, they suffer anyway in this society.

JEAN TEMPLETON: Yes, but they suffer even more when they can't, for instance, work with machinery. For these people, there should be some kind of program retraining them so they can equip themselves for other jobs. There's nothing like that now because the epilepsy information service in this city exists on $8,000 a year.

PIERRE: You know, you're lucky in another way, too. This didn't hit you till you were a mature woman. Obviously, you've taken it in your stride. How about a little kid that's got to go to school?

JEAN TEMPLETON: This is something that worries me, too, because a year in the life of an adult, when that adult is a little foggy, perhaps from drugs or something, is not so much. But for a child in school, perhaps not being able to see the blackboard, being confused, it might mean losing a year. That's a pretty shattering experience, particularly if their parents don't approach it in the right way. There are still people, unfortunately, who keep their children home from school for a whole week after they've had a seizure, which is nonsense. But you can sympathize with them because I think most of us are inclined to protect our kids, even if they don't have anything wrong with them. I suppose it must be kind of frightening to watch your child have a convulsion, particularly if you've never had one yourself.

PIERRE: What should you do? Suppose you and I were walking along the street, or sitting in my living room, and suddenly you have an epileptic seizure. What do I do?

JEAN TEMPLETON: What do you do? I'll tell you what: please hold my nose.

PIERRE: That's all?

JEAN TEMPLETON: I think so. I think that the main thing is to make sure that the person isn't going to fall and bang against something and break a bone or get bruised.

PIERRE: So I should just let you roll about?

JEAN TEMPLETON: Yes. And as long as people aren't in a position where they're going to have trouble breathing, they're going to come out of it no matter what you do. So you may as well sit down and watch and enjoy it.

PIERRE: How long do these things last?

JEAN TEMPLETON: I think a matter of a few seconds. I honestly don't know because I've never been awake when it was happening. But it can be anything from a few seconds, for instance, in the case of a *petit mal* seizure, where there is no convulsion.

PIERRE: *Petit mal* is a little one. You have *grand mal,* that's big.

JEAN TEMPLETON: Yês, and it can be from a few seconds up to a few minutes.

PIERRE: And then you said afterwards you felt a little drunk. For how long does that last?

JEAN TEMPLETON: Oh, maybe a couple of hours. It gets progressively better.

PIERRE: Then are there any after-effects?

JEAN TEMPLETON: No.

PIERRE: How did your husband react the first time he saw you having a seizure?

JEAN TEMPLETON: That's an interesting question. I think in the beginning – and the same thing applies here as with parents and children – that he felt too sorry for me. He was inclined to be very protective. That was nice in the beginning, but we really both gradually had to get to the point where we realized this wasn't something that he should get upset about.

PIERRE: Do you belong to any of the epileptic clubs that are formed?

JEAN TEMPLETON: *No!*

PIERRE: Why do you say it so strenuously?

JEAN TEMPLETON: Well, I think it's so funny for all the people who have epilepsy to meet one night a week and do something together. Like I think: "Why shouldn't all the people with athlete's foot get together on the third Thursday of the month for a dance?" I once talked to a couple of friends. One had diabetes and the other one was also an epileptic. We thought the ideal solution would be to form a club of people with all different diseases or ailments, and we should get together on Saturday nights and trade drugs for kicks.

PIERRE: What you're saying, Jean, is that you are not a joiner.

JEAN TEMPLETON: It's more than that. I'm very much against these clubs, most particularly for youngsters, because I think they have the effect of making them feel like a separate group rather than part of the whole world. I think that's a very bad thing. I guess it's fine, as a temporary measure, for teenagers to go to the epileptic dance, if they want to. But they should also be going to the dances at school with all the other kids.

PIERRE: In other words, if apartheid is bad because of colour, it's also bad because of what ails you?

JEAN TEMPLETON: Right.

MEMBER OF
A MURDER JURY

"It's a bit like
a high-level charade."

I've known Matt Saunders for more than fifteen years, and every time I run into him I am reminded that he is a remarkable man. He is a strange mixture: part hard-headed businessman, part left-wing idealist. He has held a variety of jobs, from business manager of a theatre company to real-estate salesman. At the moment, he's a school-teacher.

In private, Matt Saunders can be both abrasive and charming. He loves a verbal battle, and he argues with the gloves off, always eloquently, always heatedly. His voice has an organ-like quality that surmounts the babble around him. Since he is always in orbit, one is instantly aware of his presence, even at a large gathering.

When I ran into Saunders at a Unitarian Church culture festival one day, and learned that he had served, not long before, on a murder-trial jury, I was intrigued. For Saunders, a confirmed foe of capital punishment, had helped to send a man to the gallows.

197

More than that, this man, Ron Turpin, was probably the last man to hang in Canada – such is the effect on the federal cabinet of changing attitudes to capital punishment.

Turpin's trial in Toronto was a matter of intense public interest – as was his death. He had been dubbed "a man born without a chance." A child of the Hungry Thirties, the product of a broken marriage, a long-time ward of the Children's Aid Society, a graduate of half a dozen foster homes, Turpin was in reform school at the age of eleven. From then, until 1960, he was in and out of prison – a small-time hood who stole cars, forged cheques, broke into stores. Quiet, dapper, and polite, he was not known as a bully but had the reputation of being a generous spender and a big tipper – a little guy, in short, with big ideas.

The crime for which Turpin was hanged occurred at 2.00 A.M. on February 12, 1962, when a Toronto police constable, Fred Nash, stopped an old model truck for investigation. A gun battle ensued, which left Nash dying on the sidewalk with three bullets in his body and Turpin vainly attempting to escape with three bullets in his. He survived to stand trial and walk to his death, nine months later, while a group of student pickets carried placards bearing some of the slogans of the Sixties: "State Killing is Capital Murder . . . Revenge Does Not Deter."

Matt Saunders, with his own trenchant views on the subject, might easily have been one of those pickets. So, after he had agreed to appear with me and talk about jury duty and what it had done to him – and for him – I began by asking him how he could remain on a murder-trial jury holding the views he did.

◻

MATTHEW SAUNDERS: Well, I only learned this afterwards, but evidently some of the most famous jurists, trial judges in the United Kingdom, themselves have sentenced many a convicted criminal to be hanged, and they also did not believe in capital punishment.

PIERRE: In the end you voted for this man's conviction. How did you feel about it, from a conscience point of view?

MATTHEW SAUNDERS: Well, it was easy for me to rationalize because, right from the first day, the bench told us that we were not to be concerned about the sentence; that our duty and our role was to determine the guilt or innocence of the accused under the charge.

PIERRE: But why did you go on the jury at all?

MATTHEW SAUNDERS: I was summoned as a citizen.

PIERRE: But you could have stood up and said: "Your Honour, I don't believe in capital punishment," and they would have instantly excused you.

MATTHEW SAUNDERS: It all happened so quickly. . . .

PIERRE: You just didn't think of that?

MATTHEW SAUNDERS: Well, I did, but before I knew it, I was sitting in the box. Also, I was extremely anxious to participate in a murder trial. At the last moment, I decided that if the jury was left to be filled by people who believed in capital punishment, that probably wasn't the right thing to do.

PIERRE: Now this must have been quite an experience for you. It lasted seventeen days, during which you were locked up with the jury; you didn't see your wife, you didn't see your friends, you weren't allowed to discuss the trial, you couldn't read newspaper reports or see television reports of it. It must have left a lasting impression on you. Did it in a sense change you? Did it change your life?

MATTHEW SAUNDERS: Yes, it did. It did.

PIERRE: In what way?

MATTHEW SAUNDERS: In a number of ways. In the first instance, it opened up to me an area of human life and an intimate knowledge of one side of our life that I think the average citizen, even a well-informed one (and I pride myself on being reasonably well-informed), really doesn't have a clue about – and, to make matters worse, he really has a good deal of misinformation about.

PIERRE: You were surprised, I gather, by the whole business of a murder trial – how it worked? You had never seen this before except on television? You didn't know what happened to a jury?

MATTHEW SAUNDERS: It's a bit like a high-level charade. It's almost like a game.

PIERRE: What do you mean, a game? A man's life is at stake here.

MATTHEW SAUNDERS: Yes, a man's life is at stake. Most of the other people are playing roles which are well-defined and clearly laid down. But he's almost another one of the spectators.

PIERRE: He's almost not involved in his own trial?

MATTHEW SAUNDERS: Correct. Turpin was a very wise and witty man. I think he knew from the start what the outcome was going to be. I think to some degree he actually enjoyed the trial just as I did.

PIERRE: Now tell me a bit, before we get into the business of the character of Turpin, what jury duty was like for you. You were really incommunicado, weren't you?

MATTHEW SAUNDERS: Yes, completely. In our jurisdiction, here, the sheriff of York County and his employees, the sheriff's officers, take these duties enormously seriously. There is no deviation from absolute incommunicado status for the jurors.

PIERRE: Where did you stay?

MATTHEW SAUNDERS: The Lord Simcoe Hotel.

PIERRE: And were you walked into it and walked out of it by guards?

MATTHEW SAUNDERS: Just like prisoners.

PIERRE: It was rather like being in jail?

MATTHEW SAUNDERS: Well, no, it wasn't. It was rather pleasant. It was like being in the army again. Apart from the fact that you quickly got used to this being walked around — taken to lunch in a well-known restaurant on Yonge Street. I frequently saw people whom I knew there because my place of business at that time was only two blocks away.

PIERRE: You couldn't say hello to them?

MATTHEW SAUNDERS: I could only nod.

PIERRE: And you're not generally allowed to read newspapers or see television in these jury trials?

MATTHEW SAUNDERS: No. The existing regulations for juries are framed to meet the average conditions of a murder jury which is locked up. In most cases, the average trial lasts less than four or five days.

PIERRE: But I gather you finally complained and got newspapers with the stories of the trial cut out?

MATTHEW SAUNDERS: No, the word "finally" is not accurate. The moment I raised the matter with the judge, I got action. Perhaps you know that the jury is really his instrument. He is in sole charge. Right from the outset he invites the jurors to level with him on all matters. He wants them to be happy so that they can properly fulfill their role, and after several days, when it became apparent that we were going to be there a very long time, I asked in writing whether or not this no-newspaper thing could not be mitigated — why we couldn't read the *New York Times*, for instance.

PIERRE: It wouldn't be covering a Canadian trial.

MATTHEW SAUNDERS: Exactly. The judge, who was a very reasonable man (he's since gone on to a very high position on the Ontario bench), immediately assented. He'd never been asked before evidently.

200

PIERRE: You were also cooped up for long periods of time in the jury room, when they were arguing points of law which the jury weren't allowed to see. What was that like?

MATTHEW SAUNDERS: Very unpleasant. It's a very small room. It contains little more than a large table and twelve or thirteen chairs, a wash basin, and an open lavatory.

PIERRE: Not much to do either?

MATTHEW SAUNDERS: No.

PIERRE: Did you talk about the case with each other? You're not supposed to, are you?

MATTHEW SAUNDERS: You're not supposed to. We did for a little while at the beginning – but throughout the trial, no. All of us soon got to see that the judge was, in fact, wise – that talking about the case until the entire trial is finished is really wrong. Like a charade, the last piece has to be in place before you can properly judge what's happening.

PIERRE: This must have been a considerable sacrifice for some of the jurors. They only got seven dollars a day. They didn't get paid, some of them, by their employers. They couldn't see their wives or friends.

MATTHEW SAUNDERS: Some of them were self-employed, and they were extremely hard-pressed. In a few cases, it may have given them an economic blow from which they haven't yet recovered.

PIERRE: If a person died, you couldn't go to the funeral?

MATTHEW SAUNDERS: No.

PIERRE: Did this happen, by any chance?

MATTHEW SAUNDERS: Well, in one case one of the jurors had a very seriously ill child, and he could only learn about it through the sheriff's officer. He couldn't learn about it, even directly, from his own wife. In my own case, it wasn't nearly as serious, but my mother who wasn't living in Toronto – she lived in Winnipeg at the time – was making one of her very infrequent visits to Toronto, which had been scheduled before I knew I was going to be locked up in the jury. She was at my home for seven days.

PIERRE: And you never saw her?

MATTHEW SAUNDERS: I never did see her.

PIERRE: Is this why you asked the judge at the end of the trial if he'd give you all a letter excusing you from ever serving on a jury again?

MATTHEW SAUNDERS: Yes, and he gave me one. I don't know whether he gave the other jurors one because I've not seen a single member of the jury since.

PIERRE: You were thrown together for seventeen days, and then you went your way, and you've never seen each other again?

MATTHEW SAUNDERS: As a matter of fact, the last several days, when we knew the trial was going to finish, we spoke about possibly having a reunion at some time in the future – you know, as you did in the army or at school. But nobody has taken any initiative in that regard. Curiously enough, I go to a lot of publicly frequented places in this city, but I have never run into one of my fellow jurors in Toronto since.

PIERRE: Now, the interesting thing about this was that you really didn't know much about the murder. When they asked you if you had formed any preconceived ideas, you hadn't. You didn't even know who the murderer was, really, did you?

MATTHEW SAUNDERS: They didn't ask that. All the defence lawyer asked was: had I ever heard of the Fred Nash benevolent fund? I could in all truth answer that I had never heard of such a fund.

PIERRE: He was the constable who was shot by Turpin?

MATTHEW SAUNDERS: Yes.

PIERRE: What attitude developed towards the accused among the members of the jury? What did they feel about him?

MATTHEW SAUNDERS: I think as the trial progressed most of the jury became quite sympathetic to Ron Turpin, because he had a warm personality and he always conducted himself with great dignity.

PIERRE: They thought he was guilty, did they?

MATTHEW SAUNDERS: Oh yes.

PIERRE: How about you, how did you feel?

MATTHEW SAUNDERS: As I became aware of the nature of the charge and as the trial proceeded, we all became aware of the nature of the law. I also knew that he was guilty as charged.

PIERRE: But you conceived the idea of trying to get the jury to go for a recommendation of clemency, a rider to the guilty verdict. Tell us exactly what you did to do that?

MATTHEW SAUNDERS: Well, after we had been given, on the last day of the trial, a very lengthy and detailed instruction from the bench, where he went over many of the points of law, we then retired and were locked in for our final discussions. Here again it's a bit like a board meeting. We had earlier elected one of the more senior people – a man who had had considerable experience with the law (he was then a retired stock broker) – as our foreman. He literally acts as chairman, and he asked if there was anything that anybody wanted to discuss. By this time, we had for the last several

202

days, contrary to the instructions, done considerable discussion amongst ourselves. We had lots of time to do it every evening and in the morning on our way to and fro from the court. It was well known how the initial count was going to go. Well, in any event, I thought I'd delay the first vote to the extent of raising several points of law on which none of us was clear. We discussed this for a while to the point where we realized collectively that we had to ask for further instruction.

PIERRE: Now, just to speed things up, Matt, you felt that if you got a majority to vote for clemency, they would be able to attach that rider to the verdict. But that was wrong, wasn't it?

MATTHEW SAUNDERS: Yes. I didn't find this out until that last afternoon.

PIERRE: You were holding out. You were voting not guilty – but all your fellow jurors were voting guilty.

MATTHEW SAUNDERS: The first vote was eleven to one. A secret vote.

PIERRE: Did they get angry with you?

MATTHEW SAUNDERS: Not at all.

PIERRE: Not at any point?

MATTHEW SAUNDERS: No, they understood my position very well.

PIERRE: It wasn't because you believed Turpin to be innocent, really, but that you felt that a recommendation for mercy was necessary?

MATTHEW SAUNDERS: Yes; and also to prolong our discussions in the jury room. I always felt I had six or seven votes. And I knew – or at least I believed – that a majority would permit the jury to say: We find this man guilty but we recommend mercy or clemency.

PIERRE: But you found out later that you had to have a unanimous vote for clemency.

MATTHEW SAUNDERS: I found out later in the jury room. I can't remember exactly whether we were so instructed or whether it was by a note that we sent to the judge that a recommendation for clemency, like every other act of a jury, must be unanimous.

PIERRE: Do you really think that would have done any good, if you'd had that rider on? Does it mean anything really? Or is it just a sop to the jury's conscience?

MATTHEW SAUNDERS: At the time I thought it was very important, but I now realize that it's just a sop to the jury's conscience because, as you know, Pierre, not two weeks after the double hanging of Turpin and Lucas here in Toronto, one of the most grisly murders was committed in the city of Montreal by the so-called Santa Claus murderer. He, of course, had no recommendation for mercy at the end of his trial and, as you know, his sentence has been commuted.

PIERRE: Now you didn't attend the sentencing, did you?

MATTHEW SAUNDERS: No, I stood in the hall. I couldn't stand it.

PIERRE: Why?

MATTHEW SAUNDERS: Oh, I knew what was going to happen. The sentence follows directly from the verdict. It was hard enough to be called individually as we were and have to look at Turpin and say: "You are guilty" – although I realized, as he did, that he was not surprised.

PIERRE: Tell me how you felt about Turpin, and what you thought about his background. You learned a lot about him during the course of this trial. He became somebody that you really knew, didn't he?

MATTHEW SAUNDERS: Very well.

PIERRE: Tell us about him.

MATTHEW SAUNDERS: Well, I personally felt that we had here more than the classic case of a loser. Because, unlike so many losers, Ron Turpin came from the dominant group of our society: he was an Anglo-Saxon. He was born in our capital city, Ottawa. Yet he had spent most of his life – twenty-eight years of it – in the care of professional people who are supposed to save human lives, especially if a person is endowed with at least average intelligence. But it soon became apparent, as we learned about Mr. Turpin's life, that he was doomed. Whether or not he was doomed to the gallows, he was doomed. Anybody who becomes a ward at the tender age of four, in the city of Ottawa – well – the chances of him emerging are poor. Turpin fought hard to overcome this impediment of doom that he was carrying with him. He really fought right up until that morning when he had the misfortune to get involved in a gun battle in which one of the participants was fatally wounded.

PIERRE: What you're saying, really, is that not only was Turpin guilty but perhaps society was also guilty, because after twenty-eight years of trying we weren't able to cure him.

MATTHEW SAUNDERS: We were all guilty. And our guilt was compounded by the fact that the snowy night in December, when Ron Turpin was hanged – together with a Negro of American birth on a double gibbet (and I've never really been able to find out why this hanging was arranged in this way), only a very small handful of Unitarians in Toronto were sufficiently aroused to stand and mount a silent vigil outside of the Don Jail.

204

PIERRE: Do you think that Turpin could have been reformed and made into a useful citizen, had more care been taken with him?

MATTHEW SAUNDERS: Well, this is a matter of opinion. But my opinion is that we lost a better-than-average potential citizen when Ron Turpin was hanged.

PIERRE: Tell us about the defence. What kind of a defence did he have?

MATTHEW SAUNDERS: Brilliant. I thought it was brilliant and I, of course, say that only as a layman. He did what I'm sure no lawyer should do. He became very personally involved with both Turpin and Lucas whom he had also defended.

PIERRE: He spent a lot of his own money?

MATTHEW SAUNDERS: He absolutely abandoned his practice. The Crown does not help the defence at all. He was a legal-defence lawyer, and he personally conducted the defence. He had to hire photographers. He had to hire investigators. In a long trial of this sort, the amount of exhibits that have to be prepared are enormous.

PIERRE: Do you think, going back to Turpin, that in the times when he was out of jail and he was trying to go straight that he was ever given a chance to do that?

MATTHEW SAUNDERS: No, I'm afraid not. Take the time he returned from his most recent confinement in Kingston. I believe it was a sentence of two years less one day for common burglary (and this was all that Turpin had ever been criminally convicted of: burglary). He checked into one of our best hotels. He checked in because he legitimately wanted to go straight. In fact, he did establish himself in a completely legitimate occupation – he became a highly successful renter and leaser of furnished apartments in Bloorville, and received large commissions from some of the best trust companies in the country.

PIERRE: What happened when he checked into the hotel?

MATTHEW SAUNDERS: Within five hours he was invited to leave.

PIERRE: By the hotel at the request of the police?

MATTHEW SAUNDERS: So I understand, yes.

PIERRE: Yes, this sometimes happens.

MATTHEW SAUNDERS: He was driven, then, back into the close companionship of people who don't live normal, average lives, although I think the amount of serious crime that surrounded Turpin was negligible, because the most serious charge that he was ever wanted for, before murder, was being suspected of carrying a weapon.

PIERRE: Well, you know, a lot of people are going to say, Matt, this is all very well, but at this point in history Turpin had a heavy record, he had killed a police constable – perhaps the worst crime you can commit. What else could you do but hang him?

MATTHEW SAUNDERS: I think even a criminal has the right, perhaps a misguided right, to defend himself when he's engaged in a gun battle. Two men were lying on opposite sides of the Danforth, which is a wide roadway, and they were both excellent marksmen.

PIERRE: But you didn't acquit him for self-defence. You didn't believe that he shot in self-defence, or you would have acquitted him, really, wouldn't you?

MATTHEW SAUNDERS: Self-defence is not a legal ground for acquittal when a person who is judged legally sane does not deny having held a gun from which was issued a bullet which happens to kill a policeman.

PIERRE: I didn't know that.

MATTHEW SAUNDERS: No, I didn't either.

PIERRE: You mean to say that even if the policeman had fired first, he couldn't fire back?

MATTHEW SAUNDERS: This was the issue of the case.

PIERRE: It was?

MATTHEW SAUNDERS: And, incidentally, Constable Fred Nash never uttered a sound to any human ear again after he was shot.

PIERRE: Matt, has this experience prompted you to do anything positive since then on the subject of capital punishment and the law? Are you going to write a book or anything like that?

MATTHEW SAUNDERS: Yes, I plan to write a history of Ronald Turpin, murderer.

PIERRE: Have you been digging into Turpin's upbringing and background?

MATTHEW SAUNDERS: Yes.

PIERRE: So you're then even more confirmed in your belief that society is as guilty as he was of the murder of Constable Nash?

MATTHEW SAUNDERS: We're all guilty, and I hope perhaps my book will at least show us that in the future we may be less guilty.

206

MOM AND APPLE PIE

"Lee didn't have a formal education,
but he had the know-how."

*In October, 1964, Mrs. Marguerite Oswald came to Toronto for a
television appearance on the controversial CBC program* This
Hour Has Seven Days. *It did not seem to me that her appearance
was very effective because she was asked to discuss a subject on
which she was not an expert and had no first-hand knowledge:
the assassination of John Kennedy and her son's role in that crime.
She said she had circumstantial evidence, including documents,
which suggested there were people in the United States State Department "who wanted Mr. Kennedy out of the way," but these
remarks remained vague and unsubstantiated. She hinted that witnesses who might have appeared before the Warren Commission
and might have cleared her boy were not called; but she did not
name them or say what their evidence was. Accordingly, when
she phoned me at home the following day and offered to appear
on my program, I was disinclined to go over old and infertile
ground.*

But then it occurred to me that, though Mrs. Oswald was in

207

*no sense an expert on the assassination, she was an expert on the
assassin. On the subject of his family background and upbringing,
she did have first-hand knowledge. She had repeatedly indicated
to the Warren Commission that Lee Harvey Oswald had enjoyed
a normal upbringing and that his background was that of a typical
American boy. How normal? I wondered. How typical? I invited
Mrs. Oswald to appear on the program to discuss this subject and
this subject only. She agreed.*

*On first acquaintance, Marguerite Oswald is a disarming per-
son. Walking into the television make-up room, she might have
stepped directly out of one of those Florists' Telegraph Delivery
ads that appear around Mother's Day. She projects the kind of
image one generally associates with apple pie – a plump, homey-
looking matron in a black wool suit and a black velvet hat, quiet-
spoken, pleasant, just a little sad. Make no mistake about it – this
was Mom herself, and it was as Mom that I interviewed her. I
began by establishing the fact that Lee Harvey Oswald was born
without a father.*

□

MRS. OSWALD: Yes, that is correct. Lee was born two months after
the death of his father.

PIERRE: So in his early years, before you were married again, he was
literally fatherless?

MRS. OSWALD: Yes, he was.

PIERRE: How did this affect him, not having a father? This would
make you have to work a little harder at being a parent, I guess.

MRS. OSWALD: Yes, I was the one parent, the only parent of three
boys; but you must understand Lee had two brothers, so he wasn't
actually raised by a woman alone. He had a brother who was
seven years old and another brother who was five, at the time that
he was born.

PIERRE: Your husband left you without very much money, and you
had to go out and work at this time. Is that correct?

MRS. OSWALD: That is correct. I stayed home approximately two
years with the children because I believe that a mother should be
with the children as much as possible and then, naturally, I had
to go out to work in order to support them.

PIERRE: What were you working at in those days?

MRS. OSWALD: Oh, I have always been in retail merchandise.

208

PIERRE: You were in real estate, too, I believe, were you not?

MRS. OSWALD: No, no, insurance.

PIERRE: I thought you were also selling, at least, your own house and property.

MRS. OSWALD: Well you might say, if you want to say real estate, but I had no agents or anything. I did it all on my own, in order to supplement my salary which was very, very small. I would buy a piece of property, near a school always, because I was told you could always resell, and we would live in it for a year or two, and maybe I'd make $1,500, and that $1,500, supplemented to the salary I was earning, helped the four of us to survive.

PIERRE: You therefore moved from neighbourhood to neighbourhood?

MRS. OSWALD: Well, not in any short length of time. Sometimes we would stay two years or three years, which really isn't a home which like, you know, you buy and stay in. But I think this was very good, because it did give us a sort of a decent living, where if I had to depend just on my salary for four, we would really have been poverty-stricken from the very beginning.

PIERRE: As it was, you didn't have a great deal of money.

MRS. OSWALD: No, and you must understand when my husband died that the Social Security Law was not in effect. He died in August, 1939, and it didn't become effective until January, 1940. So I had no support for myself and three children like the women have today.

PIERRE: So who looked after the boys when you went out to work?

MRS. OSWALD: Well, it was during the war years. Now we're coming to about 1942, you see, where it's awfully hard to get help. And many, many a job I had to leave in order to stay home and mind my children, because the maids wouldn't show up. I was a church member – I am Lutheran – so it was decided that we would place the two older boys in a Lutheran Church Home. Lee was not eligible. He had to be three years old in order to go to the church home.

PIERRE: The two older boys left leaving you with one child. Who looked after him?

MRS. OSWALD: Well . . . baby-sitters and people I had living in the home with me, just like the women today when – well – we have many women today who have husbands who go out and work and leave their children home with baby-sitters. But as I explained before now, we're getting into the war years where it was awfully, awfully hard to get help. My sister helped to take care of Lee when the maids wouldn't show up, and many a job I had to quit. This was a very sad thing. I needed the money in order for our support, yet I was obligated to quit a job in order to stay home and mind my child. Then when Lee was three years old, I put him in the Lutheran Church Home with his brothers.

PIERRE: How long was he in that home?

MRS. OSWALD: He was only there a year when I contemplated marriage. I remarried.

PIERRE: So when you remarried he had a stepfather?

MRS. OSWALD: Yes.

PIERRE: Would you say that he was close to that stepfather?

MRS. OSWALD: No, I really wouldn't say so. He was an electrical engineer, and we travelled, and Lee and I travelled with him. And, of course, I was the mother of the boy, and this was the stepfather, and the three of us were together, but travelling and living in hotels. Lee was more with me because the father was working and in conference, and so on, and so forth. But he did have a father, if you want to put it this way. Now he had a father.

PIERRE: Was this your second husband?

MRS. OSWALD: Yes.

PIERRE: And you've been married again since? You've had three husbands. Would you say that he was a real father to Lee?

MRS. OSWALD: No. No, he wasn't a real father to Lee. This man that I married had a woman before he married me. And he also had the same woman while he was married to me. I left him. Of course, I didn't know about the woman when I left him the first time. I left him because I really wasn't his wife. I will say it this way: I didn't share in his bank account, his insurance, or anything. Actually, I was his second mistress. He had one that he even took along with him, that I didn't know about, of course, and he allowed me one hundred dollars a month. He made ten thousand dollars a year and had an expense account. In 1945, that was quite a bit of money. And out of the hundred dollars a month, when we didn't travel, this was money to run the house. I was supposed to account for every cent that I spent, which I wouldn't do because this is not my disposition, and so we fought back and forth because I wanted to be his wife. I think the wife should share in the husband's finances and insurance.

PIERRE: Were you able to confide in your son about this situation? Was he aware of it?

MRS. OSWALD: No, no. Lee was just five and six years old at the time. Then, finally, I did know about the woman, and I naturally

210

wouldn't live with him and expected to divorce him. But in the meantime, he filed charges against me, and he got the divorce from me, which was most unfair, because I had caught him in the woman's apartment with witnesses, and I thought: "Well now surely he can't get a divorce from me." The reason why I didn't divorce him immediately was that the other two boys were in a military school at my expense; I had sold my last piece of property, and it meant disrupting their lives. So I wanted to wait to divorce this man until the school term; but in the meantime, he filed charges against me and he did divorce me.

PIERRE: This breakup of your marriage would have occurred approximately at the time, then, that Lee began his first school year, wouldn't it?

MRS. OSWALD: Yes, yes, that's right, just about that time.

PIERRE: And as I understand it, he was in grade one three different times in three different schools. How did that come about?

MRS. OSWALD: Well, in all states your school system is different.

PIERRE: You were moving around at the time?

MRS. OSWALD: Well, I had left this husband as I told you. Then I went back to him. So I left Texas and went to Louisiana, and they thought he had never been to school when he was in the first grade; so they demoted him to kindergarten. Then, when I came back to my husband, we went back to Texas, then they put him in the second grade. It's just the difference in the school systems.

PIERRE: Well, did they demote him from the second grade again?

MRS. OSWALD: No, no. Just that twice.

PIERRE: How was he in school? Was he bright?

MRS. OSWALD: Yes. I have testified before the Commission and in 1959 I made this statement: Lee was the type child that needed special schooling because he was overly bright for schooling. There's some children that you can't teach anything to. They have wisdom. I would feel very self-conscious saying this now if I hadn't said it in 1959, but it's in print in 1959, when he was supposed to have defected to Russia. This was a boy who had wisdom.

PIERRE: How were his grades, Mrs. Oswald?

MRS. OSWALD: They were satisfactory. Just passing, which —

PIERRE: Just passing?

MRS. OSWALD: — which means satisfactory.

PIERRE: If they were just passing, that certainly doesn't indicate on the face of it that he was as bright as you say.

MRS. OSWALD: Well, because you have book learning, and you have wisdom. There's your difference, you see. He was further advanced than what they wanted to teach him. So that type child doesn't have a straight "A." Your straight "A," I think, comes from the children whom the teachers can teach. They can study and they make their straight "A's," and they have book learning. I might say this: the man we were speaking of, that I was married to, was an electrical engineer and a Harvard graduate; but he had book learning and that's all. He didn't know how to apply himself, and this is what I'm trying to say. Lee didn't have a formal education, but he had the know-how. There's quite a difference.

PIERRE: Would you describe your son as a loner in these formative years?

MRS. OSWALD: No, no, I wouldn't describe him as a loner. Many, many people since the assassination have remarked about the lonely look about the boy, and *Time* magazine has a picture of Lee when he was arrested, and it catches this lonely look, but he was not a loner.

PIERRE: But was he able to make close friends moving around as he was – as you were?

MRS. OSWALD: Well, actually, we didn't move around that much. The only places we were were from New Orleans to Fort Worth and from Fort Worth to Tovington for a short time, and Tovington back to Fort Worth and to New York.

PIERRE: Well, then, did he have any close buddies?

MRS. OSWALD: Yes, when we lived in Fort Worth, Texas. He went to school there up until the eighth grade, which is Junior High; all the children came to my house because this was a brand-new neighbourhood. I was not financially able to have the lawn sodded, and everyone else was having their grass growing, and the children were not allowed to play on the grass, so they all played in my yard and my grass and in my home.

PIERRE: In this period, when your son really didn't have very much money, did this have any effect on him?

MRS. OSWALD: You mean as he grew older? No, because Lee and I are very much alike, and we don't require money and don't think of money as a necessity. Now this might sound ridiculous, because we don't. I do know that money is a necessity, but I can live very, very cheaply. I do now. I live in a modest little home. I just pay thirty-five dollars a month rent. Yet every newsman and everybody who has been in the home has remarked what a lovely little place it is. Maybe three or four days before payday, if I was short on funds, which I was all the time, I knew how to manage: I would probably cook a big pot of soup, and we'd have substantial food, where maybe someone else would go out and spend that dollar-and-a-half for a few hamburgers.

PIERRE: It didn't bother him, then, that he had a bicycle at school when the other kids had cars?

MRS. OSWALD: Well, no, no. He asked me to buy him a bicycle; he was sixteen and a half years old when we had come back to New Orleans, and he was still at school and all the children had cars, as you said.

PIERRE: He was the only one with a bicycle?

MRS. OSWALD: That is correct.

PIERRE: I'm told that he was interested in many hobbies, such as astronomy and things like that.

MRS. OSWALD: Yes. From a little, bitty boy, he'd often climb the pillar of the porch and go up on the roof with his brother's binoculars and look at the stars, and I'd have to get his brothers to get him down off the roof. He loved animals, he knew everything there was about animals.

PIERRE: What did the other kids think about his stargazing?

MRS. OSWALD: Oh, well, this was the point that I tried to bring out before about his grades. Lee was quite advanced than his older schoolmates, even though he *did* have friends. He played chess and Monopoly; and these are things that require thinking. This is the type child I'm trying to picture.

PIERRE: Did the others tend to kid him because of the astronomy and the chess and things like that at school?

MRS. OSWALD: Yes. Because see their interest was different. The other children might want to run and play. Lee wanted to run and play and he did; and he liked comic books and he liked the radio programs. But most of all, he was interested in news and history, from a small child. I mean he did the other things. But what he liked was animals and news. In other words, if he was watching on television a Western story, and on another program news came on, he would turn that Western off and listen to the news. This was more interesting to him than ordinary, everyday things.

PIERRE: Was it a problem for him at the graduation ceremonies at the end of public school, because of his lack of clothes to wear?

MRS. OSWALD: No, but this was a problem for me as a mother because I felt very badly about it. Lee graduated from Junior High in June and in New Orleans, Louisiana, it is very humid and hot. All he had to wear at the graduation was a winter suit, which was

213

very, very heavy, and he was the only boy in all of the class that had on a winter suit. The other children had on summer suits. But I want you to know he didn't complain, and he went to his graduation exercises and the pictures were taken. Now I know many, many children would have balked at that and would have refused to have gone through with the exercises, but this didn't bother Lee.

PIERRE: I wonder how he felt *inside* at this time, Mrs. Oswald? Inside of himself.

MRS. OSWALD: Well, I think Lee was noticing things, and he wasn't saying anything. Because, in Moscow, he said: "I have always seen my mother as a worker, with always less than what we needed." So he was probably noticing these things, but he never complained.

PIERRE: He never let on outwardly, at least.

MRS. OSWALD: No, no.

PIERRE: Now you moved to New York and he entered high school there, correct?

MRS. OSWALD: Yes.

PIERRE: And he had trouble in high school?

MRS. OSWALD: Yes.

PIERRE: What happened?

MRS. OSWALD: Well, New York is New York, and that's a big city to everybody. So here is a thirteen-year-old boy going to New York with his mother, and the reason why we went: his second brother, Robert, joined the Marines, leaving Lee and me alone and his older brother, whose career is service, was living in New York married. I thought it would be better for Lee to be near family, so I moved to New York with him; after we were there a few days, he played hookey from school, and I call that quite normal. I don't say it's the right thing to do, but he's in a big city and he was in the Bronx Zoo, and they picked him up in the Bronx Zoo watching the animals. He was cautioned, and I was cautioned about him playing hookey and, of course, I thought Lee was going to school and he wasn't. He was riding the subway all day long and going to the Zoo and the Planetarium. This was something new. He had never played hookey before.

PIERRE: Well, they must have taken that fairly seriously at the high school, because he was remanded for psychiatric treatment, wasn't he?

MRS. OSWALD: Yes they did. In New York, they don't tolerate attendance away from school. In Texas, the children can stay home

214

months at a time, and they don't take this action. But in New York, they immediately took action, and because he was a child of one parent, then they thought that he might be better off in a home, than with the one parent who had to work.

PIERRE: But surely just playing hookey wouldn't lead them to give him psychiatric treatment, would it?

MRS. OSWALD: Yes, because it's this type of a home, surely. This would be normal procedure, and this home was a home for criminals also. They took this boy, who was a truant, and he was placed in this home where they had children who had knifed people and killed people and dope addicts. When I went to visit my son at the home, I was searched. I had brought candy bars and chewing gum and the usual things for a child, and the wrappers were taken off all the candy bars, and my pocketbook was searched. I asked why, and they said because many, many parents smuggle dope and cigarettes into their children. This was the type home that a truant boy was put into, which I wished I had the money or the education or whatever you want to say to correct these things that exist.

PIERRE: How long was he in the home, Mrs. Oswald?

MRS. OSWALD: Five weeks.

PIERRE: And then he was released on probation?

MRS. OSWALD: He was released to me by the judge, and the judge asked him if he would go to school, and he said yes, and he promised he would go to school. Then we were brought into a probation office, and the probation officer talked to him, and he said: "Yes, sir, I'll go back to school." He'd learned his lesson, and the probation officer said: "Well now, Lee, you're to report to me once a week." I said: "No, he will *not* report to you once a week, he has promised you that he will go back to school, let's give him that chance. If he doesn't go back to school, then I will allow my child to report to you once a week. He is not a criminal." So I made bitter friends with the probation officer, naturally.

PIERRE: Don't you think the probation officer may have been trying to help him?

MRS. OSWALD· Well, this isn't the point, though, the way I took it. Because if a child is going to report — we're talking about a thirteen-year-old child — if he's going to report weekly to a probation officer, that certainly in the rest of his life is against him. He wasn't a psychiatrist — I mean this was a probation officer. I believe to this day that I did right because, I said, "The boy has promised to go back to school to you and to the judge and to me, and let's give him this chance. If he doesn't go back to school, I will be the first to see that he reports to you." And Lee went back to school. He never had any truancy before or after this incident.

PIERRE: How long did he stay in high school?

MRS. OSWALD: He stayed in high school until his seventeenth birthday, and then he joined the Marines. That's the tenth grade in our home town.

PIERRE: He had a little less than two years of high school, then?

MRS. OSWALD: Yes.

PIERRE: How were his grades in high school?

MRS. OSWALD: Satisfactory, which means a passing mark.

PIERRE: He didn't distinguish himself as a scholar or student there, then?

MRS. OSWALD: No, no.

PIERRE: Again, this would be what you were talking about before?

MRS. OSWALD: Well, there are very few that go straight "A's." I mean satisfactory is the normal passing grade in the United States.

PIERRE: There's been a lot of discussion, as you know, in the public prints, about the fact that he didn't date girls at that time. Did he have a girl friend or not?

MRS. OSWALD: Yes. He had girl friends in school, and he used to be on the phone talking to girl friends; but there again, you see, you must understand things. We were poor people; we're living from mouth to mouth, payday to payday. This is a young boy, and I don't have the money to give him to date.

PIERRE: Did he go to dances at all – high-school dances?

MRS. OSWALD: Yes, if there was any school dances, he went to the dances, but I mean to date, well none of my children did for the same reason. The other two boys didn't date until quite later in years. It's because of your environment, let's say. Suppose I was a wealthy woman, had a lovely home, where I could have the children for parties, and my child would have the proper clothes and the money to spend on a date, he would have dated. But I was not in a position to give them money to date, and of course they depended upon me for that money. I had no money but what I earned. I had no Social Security or anything, and this is the part that the people must understand. You see, you have a difference in environment here. We have millions and millions of people in my circumstances.

PIERRE: Was he able to have a room of his own when he was a boy?

MRS. OSWALD: Yes, he had a room of his own. And now his older brother – and I haven't been able to contact him, and I felt very

216

bad about this – in the Warren Commission Report states that Lee had always slept with his mother, because when he joined the service, which was age seventeen, Lee was ten and sleeping with me.

PIERRE: At the age of ten?

MRS. OSWALD: You see, I told you I was married, and Lee had his own bed, of course, all the while. After I divorced this man, all I got from that divorce was fifteen hundred dollars, and I paid a thousand dollars down on a home. Well, I had to buy furniture. I bought used furniture, and one of the boys slept on an army cot, and the other in a twin bed and, because of circumstances, Lee slept with me; which was a short time because then his brother joined the service, and when he did Lee took his bed. But it just implies that all through his life he slept with his mother, which isn't the case, you see. It's quite a difference.

PIERRE: Now, when he joined the Marines, he also had some trouble with them. I believe there were two courts-martial there. Would you like to talk about that?

MRS. OSWALD: Oh, that's perfectly all right. I have talked to many, many men about this, and thank goodness the Warren Commission even gives him credit for this. He was supposed to have sassed a commissioned officer which we know thousands of men do all the time. We don't say it's the thing to do, but this wouldn't make him an assassin.

PIERRE: He was supposed to have illegal possession of a pistol, too.

MRS. OSWALD: Of a pistol. These two things. Otherwise he had an honourable discharge and a good-conduct medal.

PIERRE: Mrs. Oswald, the Warren Commission has portrayed your son as a lonely boy who did not have a normal home environment for his formative years. Would you like to comment on that?

MRS. OSWALD: Yes. It's a very sad thing. I have released sixteen letters that Lee wrote to me from Russia; "Dear Mother" and "Love and kisses" and a normal boy asking about his mother and writing about his family. *(she shows a card.)* This is a Mother's Day card sent to me in May of 1959, when Lee Harvey joined the service, rather went to Russia in October of 1959, a Mother's Day card, and this was sent to the Warren Commission and has exhibit number 266 on it, "To my mother on Mother's Day," and it's a beautiful card. So this refutes the Warren Commission's theory about the boy not loving his mother.